PENGUIN
SECRETS C

Osho defies categorization, reflecting everything from the individual
quest for meaning to the most urgent social and political issues
facing society today. His books are not written but are transcribed
from recordings of extemporaneous talks given over a period of
thirty-five years. Osho has been described by the *Sunday Times* in
London as one of the '1000 Makers of the 20th Century' and by
Sunday Mid-Day in India as one of the ten people—along with
Gandhi, Nehru and Buddha—who have changed the destiny of
India.

Osho has a stated aim of helping to create the conditions for the
birth of a new kind of human being, characterized as 'Zorba the
Buddha'—one whose feet are firmly on the ground, yet whose hands
can touch the stars. Running like a thread through all aspects of
Osho is a vision that encompasses both the timeless wisdom of the
East and the highest potential of Western science and technology.

He is synonymous with a revolutionary contribution to the science
of inner transformation and an approach to meditation which
specifically addresses the accelerated pace of contemporary life.
The unique Osho Active Meditations™ are designed to allow the
release of accumulated stress in the body and mind so that it is
easier to be still and experience the thought-free state of meditation.

OTHER BOOKS BY OSHO IN PENGUIN

- *Life's Mysteries: An Introduction to the Teaching of Osho*
- *The Inner Journey: Spontaneous Talks Given by Osho to Disciples and Friends at a Meditation Camp in Ajol, Gujarat, in India*
- *Osho: New Man for the New Millennium*
- *Little Book of Osho*
- *The Essence of Yoga*
- *The Science of Living*
- *The Book of Woman*
- *Little Book of Relationships*

OSHO

Secrets of Yoga

EDITED BY PREM CHINMAYA AND BODHITARU

PENGUIN BOOKS

PENGUIN BOOKS
Published by the Penguin Group
Penguin Books India Pvt Ltd, 11 Community Centre, Panchsheel Park, New Delhi
110 017, India
Penguin Group (USA) Inc., 375 Hudson Street, New York, New York 10014, USA
Penguin Group (Canada), 90 Eglinton Avenue East, Suite 700, Toronto, Ontario,
M4P 2Y3, Canada (a division of Pearson Penguin Canada Inc.)
Penguin Books Ltd, 80 Strand, London WC2R 0RL, England
Penguin Ireland, 25 St Stephen's Green, Dublin 2, Ireland (a division of Penguin
Books Ltd)
Penguin Group (Australia), 250 Camberwell Road, Camberwell, Victoria 3124,
Australia (a division of Pearson Australia Group Pty Ltd)
Penguin Group (NZ), cnr Airborne and Rosedale Road, Albany, Auckland 1310,
New Zealand (a division of Pearson New Zealand Ltd)
Penguin Group (South Africa) (Pty) Ltd, 24 Sturdee Avenue, Rosebank, Johannesburg
2196, South Africa

Penguin Books Ltd, Registered Offices: 80 Strand, London WC2R 0RL, England

First published as *Yoga: The Alpha and the Omega*, Vol. 8 by Osho International
Foundation
Published by Penguin Books India 2004

10 9 8 7 6 5

For sale in South Asia and Singapore only

Typeset in Sabon by Mantra Virtual Services, New Delhi
Printed at Baba Barkhanath Printers, New Delhi

Contents

Introduction

Osho is a drunkard.
Patanjali, as sober as a judge.

Patanjali is rational, totally scientific.

Osho is the irrational personified. He knows nothing of science, himself being a poet, a dancer, a comedienne.

Patanjali is painstakingly thorough, dazzlingly analytical, perfectly penetrating, minutely methodical.

Osho is a wild man, anarchist, genius of the absurd. He is a shit disturber! While Patanjali probes for ultimate truth, Osho enjoys being a perfect liar.

And so arises the big question: what do one of the foremost scientists of all time and one of the greatest gossips of all time have in common?

What they have in common is that both have transcended these very labels that we seek to put on them. They have gone beyond words, signs, illusions. They have gone completely beyond; they have disappeared into the divine. And, strangely enough, though they are gone, yet they are here. They play a game, and play it perfectly—for in their compassion, they wish to take us beyond.

Patanjali lived thousands of years ago. Osho is very much alive, a herenow master. In this series of books, Osho shows us the essence of Patanjali, that which is alive beyond time. And as he revives and reveals Patanjali's essence, so too his own light shines—and even our own potential luminous selves are conjured up out of the mist of our illusion. Patanjali is an alchemist. For the real alchemist, changing base metals into gold is just a façade, a cover. He is concerned with something immensely more valuable. He is uncovering, transmuting his own base metals into his golden, realized nature. The alchemist needs a cover because much of his work can be misused, and the alchemist himself can be persecuted by the narrow-minded masses.

Patanjali, the alchemist, has designed his message in such a way that if used wrongly, the 'black magician' will be thrown off course, misled. The masses will overlook it completely. Only the sincere seeker can find the keys contained within.

Osho is the modern day alchemist. He cannot be misled, for he already stands at the peak. And, he is such that he cannot be misused, either by the 'black magician' or by the idle tourist.

Here is a little anecdote Osho relates:

A madman of the way called at a shop and asked the businessman, 'What makes you sit there day in, day out?'
'In order to make profit.'
'What is profit?' asked the madman.
'It is the making of one into two,' said the businessman.
'This is no profit,' the madman said. 'Profit is when you can make two into one.'

Osho is the madman and his vision is diametrically opposite to us who are caught in the web of duality, the maya of desire. Our egos seek to divide, to separate, to alienate. In a thousand increasingly subtle ways we seek power, we seek to control others, nature, the process of the universe. The enlightened one has gone beyond the ego and knows the unity, the oneness of all things. The master points the way toward this oneness. What we must do is to make a one hundred degree turn; stop looking down into the valley and turn towards the highest peak.

Osho is an open secret, available to anyone with a real longing to know himself.

In this book, Osho makes himself available by reviving the essence of Patanjali. These sutras of Patanjali contain the keys to unlocking the self. Through making himself available, Osho makes the keys of Patanjali once more available. He gives us the keys in a modern form, removing the rust of time that has gathered on them. And, if the truth be seen, the sutras do not really contain the keys. As Osho states,

> The essential keys can be shared but cannot be talked about. Patanjali wrote these sutras so that he could share the essential keys with you, but those essential keys cannot be reduced to sutras. The sutras are just introductory, just a preface to the real thing.
>
> These discourses on the yoga sutras of Patanjali are just to bring that neglected thirst into the focus of your consciousness. This is not the real work; this is just introductory. The real work starts when you have recognized the thirst, accepted it, and you are ready to change, to mutate, to become new—when you are ready to dare to go on this immense journey, the journey into the unknown and the unknowable. It is just to create a thirst, a hunger.

In this book, we are blessed to have at our fingertips the words and silences of one who holds the keys, the true transmission. As you read on, make yourself available, open for this flavor. Allow your thirst to bubble up. Acknowledge your hunger and come to the feast.

One

Secrets of Death and Karma

By performing samyama on the two types of karma,
active and dormant, or upon omens and portents,
the exact time of death can be predicted.

By performing samyama on friendliness, or any other attribute,
great strength in that quality is obtained.

By performing samyama on the strength of an elephant,
the strength of an elephant is obtained.

By directing the light of the superphysical faculty,
knowledge is gained of the subtle, the hidden, and the distant.

By performing samyama on the sun,
knowledge of the solar system is gained.

I have heard a beautiful story. Once there was a great sculptor, a painter, a great artist. His art was so perfect that when he would make a statue of a man, it was very difficult to say who is the man and who is the statue; it was so lifelike, so alive, so similar. An astrologer told him that his death was approaching; he was going to die soon. Of course, he became very much afraid and frightened, and as every man wants to avoid death, he also wanted to avoid. He thought about it, meditated, and he found a clue. He made his own statues, eleven in number, and when Death knocked on his door and the Angel of Death entered, he stood hidden among his own eleven statues. He stopped his breathing.

The Angel of Death was puzzled, could not believe his own eyes. It had never happened; it was so irregular; God has never been known to create two people alike; he always creates the unique. He has never believed in any routine. He is not like an assembly line. He is absolutely against carbons; he creates only originals. What had happened? Twelve people in all—absolutely alike? Now, whom to take away? Only one has to be taken away. Death, the Angel of Death, could not decide. Puzzled, worried, nervous, he went back. He asked God, 'What have you done? There are twelve persons exactly alike, and I am supposed to bring only one. How should I choose?'

God laughed. He called the Angel of Death close to him, and he uttered in his ear the formula, the clue how to find the real from the unreal. He gave him a mantra and told him, 'Just go, and utter it in that room where that artist is hiding himself among his own statues.'

The Angel of Death asked, 'How is it going to work?'

God said, 'Don't be worried. Just go and try.'

The Angel of Death went, not yet believing it was going to work, but when God had said, he had to do it. He came in the room, looked around, and not addressing anybody in particular, he said, 'Sir, everything is perfect except one thing. You have done well, but you have missed one point. One error is there.'

The man completely forgot that he was hiding. He jumped; he said, 'What error?'

And Death laughed and said, 'You are caught. This is the only error: you cannot forget yourself. Come on, follow me.'

Death is of the ego. If the ego exists, death exists. The moment the ego disappears, death disappears. You are not going to die, remember; but if you think that you are, you are going to die. If you think that you are a being, you are going to die. This false entity of the ego is going to die, but if you think of yourself in terms of nonbeing, in terms of non-ego, then there is no death—already you have become deathless. You have always been deathless; now you have recognized the fact.

The artist was caught because he could not disappear into nonbeing.

Buddha says in his *Dhammapada*: If you can see death, death cannot see you. If you can die before death comes, death cannot come to you; and there is no need to make statues. That is not going to help. Deep down you have to destroy one statue, not to create eleven more. You have to destroy the image of the ego. There is no need to create more statues and more images. Religion, in a way, is destructive. In a way, it is negative. It annihilates you—annihilates you completely and utterly.

You come to me with some ideas to attain some fulfilment, and I am here to destroy you completely. You have your ideas; I have my own. You would like to be fulfilled—fulfilled in your ego—and I would like you to drop the ego, to dissolve, to disappear, because only then is there fulfilment. The ego knows only emptiness; it is always unfulfilled. By the very nature, by its very intrinsic nature, it cannot attain to fulfilment. When you are not, fulfilment is. Call it God, or give it a name Patanjali would like—*samadhi*—the attainment of the ultimate, but it comes when you disappear.

These sutras of Patanjali are scientific methods on how to dissolve, how to die, how to commit real suicide. I call it real, because if you kill your body that is unreal suicide. If you kill your *self*, that is authentic suicide.

And this is the paradox: that if you die, you attain to eternal life. If you cling to life, you will die a thousand and one times. You will go on being born and dying again and again and again. It is a wheel. If you cling, you move with the wheel.

Drop out of the wheel of life and death. How to drop out of it? It seems so impossible because you have never thought of yourself as a nonbeing, you have never thought of yourself as just space, pure space, with nobody there inside.

These are the sutras; each sutra has to be understood very deeply. A sutra is a very condensed thing. A sutra is like a seed. You have to accept it deep down in your heart; your heart has to become a soil for it. Then it sprouts, and then the meaning.

I can only persuade you to be open so that the seed can fall right in place within you, so that the seed can move into the deep darkness of your nonbeing. In that darkness of your nonbeing, it will start being alive. A sutra is a seed. Intellectually, it is very easy to understand it. Existentially, to attain to its meaning is arduous. But that's what Patanjali would like, that's what I would like.

So don't just be intellectuals here. Get in rapport with me; get in tune with me. Don't just listen to me—rather, be with me. Listening is secondary; being with me is primary, basic—just to be in my company. Allow yourself to be totally herenow with me, in my presence, because that death has happened to me. It can become infectious. I have committed that suicide. If you come close to me, if you are in tune with me even for a single moment, you will have a glimpse of death.

And Buddha is right when he says, 'If you can see death, death will not be able to see you,' because the moment you see death, you have transcended death. Then there is no death for you.

The first sutra:

> *By performing samyama on the two types of karma,*
> *active and dormant, or upon omens and portents,*
> *the exact time of death can be predicted.*

Many things. First, why be worried about the exact time of death? How is it going to help? What is the point of it? If you ask Western psychologists, they will almost call it abnormal morbidity. Why be concerned with death? Avoid. Go on believing that death is not going to happen—at least not to you. It always happens to somebody else. You have seen people die; you have never seen yourself die, so why be afraid? You may be the exception. But nobody is an exception; and death has already happened in your birth, so you cannot avoid it.

Now, the birth is beyond your power. You cannot do anything about it; it has already happened. It is already past; it is already done. You cannot undo it. Death is yet to happen: something is possible to be done about it.

The whole of Eastern religion depends on the vision of death, because that is the possibility that is going to happen. If you know it beforehand, tremendous is the possibility. Many doors open. Then you can die in your own way; then you can die with a signature of your own on your death. Then you can manage not to be born again—that is the whole meaning. It is not morbid. It is very, very scientific. When everybody is going to die, it is absolutely foolish not to think about death, not to meditate upon death, not to focus upon it, not to come to a deep understanding about it.

It is going to happen. If you know, much is possible.

Patanjali says that even the exact date, the hour, the minute, the second of death can be known beforehand. If you know exactly when death is coming, you can prepare. Death has to be received like a great guest. It is not the enemy. In fact, it is a God-given gift. It is a great opportunity to pass through. It can become a breakthrough: if you can die alert, conscious, aware, you will never be born again—and there will be no death anymore. If you miss, you will be born again. If you go on missing, you will be continuously born again and again, unless you learn the lesson of death.

Let me say it in this way: the whole of life is nothing but a learning about death, a preparation for death. That's why death comes in the end. It is the pinnacle, the crescendo, the very climax, the peak.

In the West particularly, contemporary psychologists have become aware that in a deep sex act, a certain peak can be attained, a climax, a great orgasm, which is tremendously fulfilling, exhilarating, ecstatic. You are cleansed; you come out of it rejuvenated, fresh, again young, again alive—all the dust gone, as if you have taken a great shower, an energy shower. But they have not yet come to know that the sex act is a very minor death; and one who can achieve deep orgasm is one who allows himself to die in love. It is a minor death, nothing to be compared with death. Death is the greatest orgasm there is.

The intensity of death is such that most people become unconscious. They cannot face it. The moment death comes, you are so afraid, so full of anxiety, to avoid, you become unconscious. Almost 99 per cent of people die unconsciously. They miss the opportunity.

To know death beforehand is just a method to help you prepare, so when death comes, you are perfectly alert and aware, waiting, ready to go with . . . ready to surrender, ready to embrace death. Once you have accepted death in awareness, there is no longer any birth for you—you have learned the lesson. Now there is no coming back to the school again. This life is just a school, a discipline—a discipline to learn death. It is not morbid.

The whole of religion is concerned with death, and if some religion is not concerned with death, then it is not religion at all. It may be sociology, an ethics, a morality, a politics, but it cannot be religion. Religion is the search for the deathless, but that deathless is possible only through the door of death.

The first sutra says, '*By performing samyama on the two types of karma, active and dormant, or upon omens and portents, the exact time of death can be predicted.*' The Eastern analysis of karma says that there are three types of karma. Let us understand them.

The first is called *sanchit*: sanchit means the total, the total of all your past lives. Whatsoever you have done, howsoever you have reacted to situations, whatsoever you have thought and desired, achieved, missed—the total—the total of your doings, thinking, feelings of all your lives is called sanchit. Sanchit: the word means the all, the accumulated all.

The second type of karma is known as *prarabdha*. The second type of karma is that part of sanchit which you have to fulfil in this life, which has to be worked out in this life. You have lived many lives; you have accumulated much. Now, a part of it will have the opportunity to be acted out, realized, suffered, passed through in this life—only a part of it, because this life has a limitation; seventy, eighty, or a hundred years. In a hundred years, you cannot live all the past karmas—the sanchit, the accumulated—only a part of it. That part is called prarabdha.

Then there is a third type of karma that is known as *kriyaman*; that is day-to-day karma. First, the accumulated whole, then a small portion of it for this life, then an even smaller portion of it for today or for this moment. Each moment there is an opportunity to do something or not to do something. Somebody insults you: you become angry. You react, you do something or, if you are aware, you simply watch, you don't become angry. You simply remain a witness. You don't do anything; you don't react. You remain cool and collected; you remain centred. The other has not been able to disturb you.

If you are disturbed by the other and you react, the kriyaman karma falls into the deep reservoir of the sanchit. Then you are accumulating again; then for future lives you are accumulating. If you don't react, a past karma is fulfilled—you must have insulted this man in some past life, now he has insulted you; the account is closed. Finished. A man who is aware, will feel happy that at least this part is finished. He has become a little freer.

Somebody came and insulted Buddha. Buddha remained quiet, he listened attentively and then he said, 'Thank you.' The man was very puzzled; he said, 'Have you gone mad? I am insulting you, hurting you, and you simply say thank you?' Buddha said, 'Yes, because I was waiting for you. I had insulted you in the past, and I was waiting—unless you had come, I would not be totally free. Now you are the last man; my accounts are closed.

Thank you for coming. You may have waited, you may not have come in this life and then I would have had to wait for you. And I don't say anything anymore, because enough is enough. I don't want to create another chain.'

Then the kriyaman karma, the day-to-day karma, does not fall into the reservoir, does not add to it; in fact, the reservoir is a little less than it was. The same is true about prarabdha—the whole life, *this* life. If in this life you go on reacting, you are creating the reservoir more and more. You will have to come again and again. You are creating too many chains; you will be in bondage.

Try to understand the Eastern concept of freedom. In the West, freedom has a connotation of political freedom. In India, we don't bother much about political freedom, because we say that unless one is spiritually free, it makes not much difference whether you are politically free or not. The fundamental thing is to be spiritually free.

The bondage is created by the karmas. Whatsoever you do in unawareness becomes a karma. Any action done in unawareness becomes a karma because any action done in unawareness is not an action at all; it is a reaction. When you do something in full awareness, it is not a reaction; it is an action, spontaneous, total. It leaves no trace. It is complete in itself; it is not incomplete. If it is incomplete, then some day or the other it will have to be completed. So if in this life you remain alert, then the prarabdha disappears and your reservoir becomes more and more empty. In a few lives, the reservoir becomes absolutely empty.

This sutra says, '*By performing samyama on the two types of karma . . .*' Patanjali means sanchit and prarabdha because the kriyaman is nothing but a part of prarabdha, so he divides into two.

What is samyama? That has to be understood. Samyama is the greatest synthesis of human consciousness, the synthesis of three: *dharana*, *dhyan*, samadhi.

Ordinarily, your mind is continuously jumping from one object to another. Not for a single moment are you in tune with one object. You go on jumping. Your mind goes on constantly moving; it is like a flux. This moment something is in the focus of the mind, next moment something else, next moment still something else. This is the ordinary state of mind.

The first step out of it is dharana. Dharana means concentration—fixing your whole consciousness on one object, not allowing the object to disappear, bringing again and again your consciousness on the object so that the unconscious habit of the mind of continuous flux can be dropped; because once the habit of continuous change can be dropped, you attain to an integrity, to a crystallization. When there are so many objects moving continuously, you remain so many. Understand it. You remain divided because your objects are divided.

For example, you love one woman today, another woman tomorrow, another woman on the third day. That will create a division in you. You cannot be one; you will become many. You will become a crowd; hence the Eastern insistence to create a love in which you can remain for a longer period, as long as possible. There have been experiments in the East in which a couple has remained together, a couple, for many lives. Again and again the same woman, the same man: that gives integrity. Too much change erodes your being, splits you. So if in the West schizophrenia is becoming almost a normal thing, it is not something to be wondered at. It is not strange; it is natural. Everything is changing.

I have heard that one film actress in Hollywood got married to her eleventh husband. She came home, introduced the new dad to the children. The children brought a register, and they said to the dad, 'Please sign it, because today you are here, tomorrow you may be gone, and we are accumulating the signatures, autographs, of all our dads.'

You go on changing houses; you go on changing everything. In America, the average limit of a person's job is three years—the job is also continuously changing. The house—the average limit of a person staying in one town is also three years. And the average limit of marriage is also three years. Somehow, three years seems to be very important. It seems that if you remain the fourth year with the same woman, there is fear that you may get settled. If you remain in the same job more than three years, there is fear that you may get settled. So people go on; they have become almost vagabonds. That creates divisions inside you.

In the East, we tried to give a job to a person as part of his life. A man was born in a Brahmin house: he remained a Brahmin. That was a great experiment to give stability. A man was born in a shoemaker's house: he remained a shoemaker. The marriage, the family, the job, the town—people were born in the same town and they would die in the same town. Lao Tzu remembers, 'I have heard that in the ancient days people had not gone beyond the river.' They had heard dogs barking on the other side, the other shore. They had inferred that there must be a town because in the evening they had seen smoke rising—people must be cooking. They had heard dogs barking but they had not bothered to go and see. People were so harmoniously settled.

This constant change simply says that your mind is feverish. You cannot stay long at anything; then your whole life becomes a life of continuous change—as if a tree is being uprooted again and again and again, and never gets the right time to send its roots deep down into the earth. The tree will be alive only in name's sake. It will not be able to bloom, not possible, because before flowers come, the roots have to settle.

So, concentration means bringing your consciousness to one object and becoming capable of retaining it there—any object. If you are looking at a roseflower, you continuously look at it. Again and again the mind wanders, goes here and there; you bring it back. You tame the mind—you tame the bull. You bring it back to the rose. The mind goes again; you bring it back. By and by, the mind starts being with the rose for longer periods. Once your mind remains with the rose for a long period, you will be able for the first time to know what a rose is. It is not just a rose: God has flowered in it. The fragrance is not only of the rose; the fragrance is divine. But you never were in rapport with it for long.

Sit with a tree and be with it. Sit with your boyfriend or girlfriend and be with him or her, and bring yourself again and again. Otherwise, what is happening? Even if you are making love to a woman, you are thinking of something else—maybe moving in a totally different world. Even in love, you are not focused. You miss much. A door opens, but you are not there to see it. You come back when the door is closed again.

Each moment, there are millions of opportunities to see God but you are not there. He comes and knocks at your door, but you are not there, you are never found there. You go on roaming around the world. This roaming has to be stopped; that's what is the meaning of dharana. Dharana is the first step of the great synthesis of samyama.

The second step is dhyan. In dharana, in concentration, you bring your mind to a focus: the object is important. You have to bring again and again the object in your consciousness; you are not to lose track of it. The object is important in dharana. The second step is dhyan, meditation; in meditation, the object is not important anymore; it becomes secondary. Now, the flow of consciousness becomes important—the very consciousness which is being poured on the object. Any object will do, but your consciousness should be poured in a continuity; there should not be gaps.

Have you watched? If you pour water from one pot to another, there are gaps. If you pour oil from one pot to another, there are not gaps. Oil has a continuity; water falls discontinuously. Dhyana means, meditation means, your consciousness should be falling on any object of concentration in a continuity. Otherwise, it is flickering. It is constantly flickering; it is not a continuous torch.

Sometimes it is there, then it disappears; then again is there, then it disappears; then again is there. In dhyan, you have to make it a continuity, an absolute continuity.

When consciousness becomes continuous, you become tremendously strong. For the first time, you feel what life is. For the first time, holes in your life disappear. For the first time, you are *together*. Your togetherness means the togetherness of consciousness. If your consciousness is like drops of water and not a continuity, you cannot be really there. Those gaps will be a disturbance. Your life will be very dim and faint; it will not have strength, force, energy. When consciousness flows in a continuous river-like phenomenon, you have become a waterfall of energy.

This is the second step of samyama, the second ingredient; and then is the third ingredient, the ultimate—that is samadhi. In dharana, concentration, the object is important because you have to choose one object amidst millions. In dhyan, meditation, consciousness is important; you have to make consciousness a continuous flow. In samadhi, the subject is important: the subject has to be dropped.

You dropped many objects. When there were many objects, you were many subjects, a crowd, a polypsychic existence—not one mind, many minds. People come to me and they say, 'I would like to take sannyas, but . . .' That 'but' brings the second mind. They think they are the same, but the 'but' brings another mind. They are not one. They would like to do something and, at the same time, they would not like to do it—two minds. If you watch, you will find many minds in you—almost a marketplace.

When there are too many objects, there are too many minds corresponding to them. When there is one object, one mind arises—focused, centred, rooted, grounded. Now, this one mind has to be dropped, otherwise you will remain in the ego. The many has been dropped; now drop the one also. In samadhi, this one mind has to be dropped. When one mind drops, the one object also disappears because it cannot be there. They are always together.

In samadhi, only consciousness remains as pure space.

These three together are called samyama. Samyama is the greatest synthesis of human consciousness.

Now you will be able to understand the sutra: *'By performing samyama on the two types of karma, active and dormant, or upon omens and portents, the exact time of death can be predicted.'* Now if you concentrate, meditate, and get in tune in samadhi, you can be capable of knowing the exact time of death. If you move your samyama, this great synthesis of consciousness, this great power that has arisen in you; if you move it towards death, you will be able to know immediately when you are going to die.

How does it happen? When you go into a dark room, you cannot see what is there. When you go with a light, you can see what is there, or what is not there. You move in darkness almost your whole life, so you don't know how much prarabdha is still there—prarabdha, the karma that you have to fulfil in this life. When you go with samyama, with light burning bright, you bring the flame in; you know how much prarabdha is left. You see the whole house is empty, just in the corner a few things are left, and soon they will disappear. Now you can see when you are going to die.

It is said about Ramakrishna that he was much too interested in food, in fact obsessed. That is very unlikely. Even his wife, Sharda, used to feel very embarrassed, because he was such a great saint, with only one flaw—and the flaw was that he was much too interested in food. He was so interested that while he was giving *satsang* to his disciples, just in the middle, he will say, 'Wait, I am coming,' and he will go to look in the kitchen, what is being cooked. He will just go there and ask, 'What is being prepared today?' and then will come back and start his satsang again.

His closest disciples became worried. They said, 'This doesn't look good, *Paramahansa*. And everything is so perfectly beautiful—never has there walked such a beautiful and perfect man—but this small thing, why can't you drop it?' He would laugh and would not say anything.

One day his wife Sharda insisted too much. He said, 'Okay, if you insist, I will tell. My prarabdha is finished; and I am just clinging with this food. If I drop that, I am gone.'

The wife could not believe this. It is very difficult for wives to believe in their own husbands—even if the husband is a paramahansa it makes no difference. The wife must have thought that he is befooling, or he is trying to rationalize. Seeing that, Ramakrishna said, 'Look, I can see that you are not trusting me, but you will know. The day I am going to die, just three days before that day, three days before my death, I will not look at food. You will bring my *thali* in, and I will start looking in another direction; then you can know that only three days more am I to be here.'

That too was not believed; they forgot about it. Then, just three days before Ramakrishna died, he was resting, Sharda brought his thali, his food: he turned over, started looking to the other side. Suddenly, the wife realized, remembered. The thali fell from her hands and she started crying. Ramakrishna said, 'Don't cry now. Now my work is finished—I need not cling.' And after exactly three days he died.

He was clinging in compassion, just trying to create a bondage with one chain. The imprisonment is gone; the prison has disappeared. Out of compassion, he was trying to cling, to linger a little longer on this shore, to help those who had gathered around him. But it is difficult to understand a paramahansa. It is difficult to understand a man who has become a *siddha*, a buddha, one who has emptied all his sanchit, all accumulated karmas. It is very difficult—he has no gravitation. So Ramakrishna was clinging to a rock; the rock has gravitation. He was clinging to a rock so that he could linger on this earth a little longer.

When you have samyama, a consciousness fully alert, you can see how much karma is left. It is exactly like when a physician comes and he sees and touches the pulse of a dying man, and he says, 'Not more than two or three hours.' What is he saying? By long experience he has come to know how the pulse beats when a person is going to die. Exactly like that, exactly that way, a man who is alert knows how much prarabdha is left—how much pulse—and he knows when he has to go.

This can be done in two ways. The sutra says either to focus on death, which is prarabdha karma . . . *'By performing samyama on the two types of karma, active and dormant, or upon omens and portents, the exact time of death can be predicted.'* This can be done in two ways: either you look at the prarabdha, or there are a few omens and portents that can be watched.

For example, almost always before a person dies, nearabout nine months before, something happens. Ordinarily, we are not aware, because we are not aware at all, and the phenomenon is very subtle. I say almost always nine months because it differs, it depends: it will be the time between the conception and the birth: if you were born after nine months of being in the womb, then nine months; if you were born after being ten months in the womb, then ten months; if you were born after seven months in the womb, then seven months. It depends on the amount of time between the time of conception and birth.

Exactly the same time before death, something clicks in the hara, in the navel centre. It has to click because between conception and birth, there was a gap of nine months: nine months you took for birth; exactly the same time will be taken for death. As you prepared nine months in the mother's womb for birth, you will have to prepare for nine months to die. Then the circle will be complete. Something in the navel centre happens. Those who are aware, they will immediately know that something has broken in the navel centre; now death is coming closer. Approximately, nine months.

Or for example, there are other omens and other portents. A man, before he dies—exactly six months before he dies—becomes by and by incapable of seeing the tip of his own nose because the eyes start turning upward, very slowly. In death, they turn completely upward, but they start the turning, the returning journey, before death. This happens: when a child is born, the child takes almost six months, that is usual—there may be exceptions—the child takes six months to have fixed eyes. Otherwise, the eyes are loose. That's why children can bring both their eyes together near the nose, can take them far away to the corners very easily. Their eyes are still loose. The day a child's eyes become fixed: if that day comes after six months or nine months or ten or twelve months after birth, then exactly the same will be the time; again the eyes will start becoming loose and moving upward. That's why in India, villagers say—they must have come to know from yogis—that before a man dies, he becomes incapable of seeing the tip of his own nose.

And there are many methods in which yogis continuously watch the tip of their nose. They concentrate on it. Those who have been concentrating on it, suddenly one day realize they cannot see their own nose. Now they know death is approaching near.

According to yoga physiology, there are seven centres in man. The first is the genital organs, and the last is the *sahasrar*, in the head; between these two, there are five others. Whenever you die, you die from a particular centre; that shows your growth that you have been doing in this life. Ordinarily, people die through the genital organs, because the whole of life people live around the sex centre, continuously thinking of sex, fantasizing about sex, doing everything about sex—as if the whole of life seems to be centred around the sex centre. These people die through the sex centre. If you have evolved a little and you have attained to love, gone beyond sex, then you will die from the heart centre. If you have evolved completely, if you have become a siddha, you will die from the sahasrar.

The centre you will die from will have an opening because the whole life energy will be released from there . . .

Just a few days before, Vipassana died. Her brother, Viyogi, was asked to hit her head; that has become symbolic in India. When a person dies and is put on the funeral pyre, the head has to be hit. Just symbolic, because if the person has attained to the ultimate, then the head will break on its own; but the person has not attained. But we hope and pray, and break the skull.

The point of release becomes open—this can be seen. Some day or the other, when Western medical science will become aware of yoga physiology, this also will become part of all postmortems—how the person died. Just now, they see only whether he died naturally or was poisoned or killed or committed suicide—all ordinary things. The most basic thing they miss, which has to be there on the report—how the person died: from the sex centre, from the heart centre, or from the sahasrar—from where he died. And there is a possibility—yogis have done much work on it—it can be seen in the body because that particular centre breaks, as if an egg has broken and something has gone out of it.

When somebody who has attained to samyama becomes, just three days before he dies, aware from what centre he is going to move, almost always he moves from the sahasrar. A certain activity, a movement, just at the top of the head, starts working three days before one dies.

These indications can prepare you to receive death, and if you know how to receive death in a great celebration, in great joy, in delight—almost dancing and in ecstasy—you will not be born again. Your lesson is complete. You have learned whatsoever was to be learned here on this earth; now you are ready to move beyond, for a greater mission, for a greater life, for more unlimited life. Now you are ready to be absorbed by the cosmos, by the whole. You have earned it.

One thing more about this sutra: the kriyaman karma, the day-to-day karma, is just a very small fragment. In modern psychological terms we can call it the 'conscious.' Below it is prarabdha; in modern psychological terms we can call it the 'subconscious.' Even below that is sanchit; in modern psychological terms we can call it the 'unconscious.'

Ordinarily, you are not aware of your day-to-day activities, so how can you be aware of prarabdha or sanchit?—impossible.

So start by becoming aware of day-to-day activities. Walking on the road, be alert. Eating your food, be alert. Remain watchful of what you are doing. Remain with the activity; don't go here and there. Don't do things like a zombie. Don't move as if you are in deep hypnosis. Whatsoever you are saying, say everything fully alert, so that you are not going to repent ever.

When you say, 'I am sorry. I said something which I never wanted to say,' that simply shows you were asleep, not aware. When you say, 'I did something, I don't know why and how. I don't know how it happened, I have done it in spite of myself,' then remember, you were asleep. You are a somnambulist walking in sleep.

Make yourself more and more alert. That is the meaning of being herenow. Right now you are listening to me: you can be just the ears. Right now you are seeing me: you can be just the eyes, fully alert, not even a thought passing through your mind, no disturbance, no cloudiness inside. Just focused on me—totally listening, totally seeing—being with me herenow. That is the first step.

If you attain to that, the second step becomes available; then you can move into the subconscious. Then when somebody insults you, you will not become aware only when you become angry. You will become aware immediately somebody has insulted—there, a certain anger has moved into the subconscious depth of your being, just a small wave, very subtle. If you are not very sensitive and aware, you will not know it—unless it erupts into the conscious, you will not know it. By and by, you will become aware of subtle nuances, subtle shades of emotions—that is prarabdha, the subconscious.

When you become aware of the subconscious, another step will become available to you. The more you grow, the more growth becomes possible to you. You will be able to see, now, the third step, the final step, of becoming aware of sanchit, the accumulated past. Once you move into the unconscious—that means you are taking the light of consciousness into the deepest core of your being—you will become enlightened. That is the meaning of becoming a buddha—nothing is in darkness now. Every nook and corner is lighted. Then you live, you act, but you don't accumulate any karma.

The second sutra:

By performing samyama on friendliness, or any other attribute,
great strength in that quality is obtained.

First one has to become aware, and immediately the second step is to bring your samyama on the feeling of friendliness, love, compassion.

Let me tell you one story:

It happened, a great Buddhist monk—Tamino was his name—persevered, worked hard, and entered the state of satori, the state of samyama. And there he was aware of nothing.

When you are really aware, you are not aware of anything. You are only aware of awareness. That too is not good to say, because then awareness looks like an object. No, you are simply aware of nothing—just aware.

. . . And there he was aware of nothing, and his soul was like nothing. And this state was beyond even peace, and he would have been glad to remain in it forever . . . .

Remember it, when one attains to samyama, one would like to remain forever in it, one would not like to go out of it—but this is not the end of the journey. This is only half the journey; unless your samadhi becomes love, unless you bring whatsoever you have found within you to the greater world, unless you share your samadhi with others, you are proving yourself a miser. Samadhi is not the goal; love is the goal. So whenever it will happen to you, any of you, you will also come to a point when one wants not to move out. It is so beautiful, it is so tremendously blissful—who bothers?

. . . And this stage was beyond even peace, and he would have been glad to remain in it forever. But as it happened, on that day he had gone out to meditate in the little wood that surrounded his monastery. And as he sat there by the way, lost in meditation, there passed a traveller, and thieves leapt upon him and wounded and robbed him and left him for dead. He cried for aid to Tamino, but Tamino sat there unconscious, seeing and hearing nothing . . . .

Tamino was sitting there, and the man was dying there, and the man was calling for help; but he was so deep within himself that nothing reached him. He could not hear, he could not see— the eyes were open, but he was not there in the eyes, he had gone to the very rock-bottom of his being. Just the body was breathing, but he was not there on the periphery.

. . . And so the man lay bleeding on the ground, and there he was when Tamino returned to earth—came back to his body, came back to his senses. Tamino was dazed and for a long time did not understand what he saw nor knew what he had to do . . .

It takes a little time to put yourself together again on the periphery. The centre is so totally different. You move in an almost absolutely unknown territory. And when you come back, it is difficult to again get in tune with the periphery. It is almost like people who have been to the moon: when they come back, for three weeks they have to be put in a special house prepared for them—to get ready again to move on the earth. If immediately after coming back from the moon they would go to their home, they would get crazy or mad; because the moon is so different. The gravitation is not much there—one eighth of the earth. One can just jump sixty feet, seventy feet, easily. One can jump on anybody's terrace, no problem; the gravitation is almost nil. And the moon is so empty . . . one is dazed. And the silence is so tremendous, uninterrupted for millions of years—so heavy—that when one comes back from the moon, one is coming as if after one has died and is again coming back to the earth.

When the first man walked on the moon, he was not a theist,

but suddenly he fell on his knees and started praying; the first thing that has been done on the moon is prayer. What happened to him?—the silence was such, it was so deep, and he was so alone, suddenly he remembered God. In that loneliness, in that aloneness, in that solitude, he forgot that he didn't believe in God, that he is a sceptical mind, that he is a doubter. He forgot all. He immediately fell down and started praying.

When one comes from the moon, he has to be re-acclimatized to the earth; but this is nothing compared to when you go to the centre of your being and come back.

. . . Tamino was dazed and for a long time did not understand what he saw nor knew what he had to do. But presently, as the current of his life in the flesh set in again, he went up to the man and bound up his wounds as best as he could. But the man's blood had flowed for too long. He looked at Tamino and died— and those eyes Tamino could not forget. Those eyes haunted him, and he was so much disturbed—the whole satori was lost—he forgot all about the centre. He was puzzled.

And in the man's eyes, before he died, Tamino saw the look he had seen once on the battlefield; and all his peace, so painfully won, fled from him. He went back to the monastery, passed over onto the island and mounted the topmost terrace, and there sat down beside one of the images of Gautam Buddha. It was evening, and the setting sun alone shone on the stone face, till it seemed to flush into life.

And Tamino looked into the eyes of the face and said, 'Lord Buddha, was your gospel true?'

And the image answered back, 'True and false.'

'What was true in it?' asked Tamino.

'Compassion and love.'

'And what was false in it?'

'Flight from life, escape.'

'Must I go back to life?'

But the light had faded from the face and it turned to stone again.

It is a beautiful story. Yes, Tamino had to come back to life; one has to come back to love from samadhi. Hence, Patanjali's sutra immediately after samadhi, in which death is experienced: *'By performing samyama on friendliness, or any other attribute,'* compassion, love, *'great strength in that quality is obtained.'*

Contemporary psychologists will also agree, up to a certain limit. If you constantly think about something, it starts materializing. You must have heard the name of Emile Coue, or if you have not heard the name, you must have heard his slogan: Every day, in every way, I am getting better and better. He treated thousands of patients in great trouble—people in great trouble—and he helped them tremendously. And this was his only medicine. He would just say to them, 'Repeat: every day, in every way, I am getting better and better. Just repeat it, just feel it, just surround yourself with this idea "I am getting better, healthier, happier."' And thousands of people were helped; they came out of their illnesses, they came out of their mental diseases, they came out of their troubles and anxieties. They thrived again, they became alive again, and there was nothing in it—just a small mantra.

But what happens: you create the world you live in. You create the body also you live in; you create the mind also you live in. You create with your ideas. Whatsoever you think, sooner or later becomes a reality; every thought becomes a thing finally, eventually.

And this is with such an ordinary mind, which goes on changing the object every moment, goes on jumping from here and there; what to think about samyama? When there is no mind and just the idea of friendliness arises, one becomes in rapport with it, one becomes it.

Buddha has said, 'The next time I come in the world, my name will be Maitreya, "the friend."' It is very symbolic—whether he is coming or not, that is not the point—but it is very symbolic: he is saying that after becoming a buddha, one has to become the friend.

After one has attained to samadhi, one has to attain to

compassion. Compassion is the criterion whether your samadhi is true or not.

Remember, don't be a miser because habits persist. If in the outside world you are a miser and you cling to things, to money and this and that, when samadhi arises in you, you will cling to samadhi. The clinging will continue—and the clinging has to be dropped. Hence immediately, after death, when you start feeling the deathless, Patanjali says bring friendliness in, now think of sharing.

There are two seas in Palestine. One is filled with fresh and sparkling water. Trees and flowers grow around it. Fish live in it, and its banks are green. The pure waters of this sea possess a healing quality, and are brought down by the river Jordan from the hills around Mount Hermon . . . .

Jesus loved this river; Jesus loved this sea. Many miracles happened around this place with him.

. . . The master loved this sea, and many of the happier moments of his ministry were spent beside it. It is a place filled to this day with serenity and power.

The river Jordan flows on south into another sea. Here there is no life, no song of birds, no children's laughter. The air hangs sinister and heavy above its water, and neither man nor beast nor bird will drink. This sea is dead . . . .

What makes so mighty a difference between these two seas of Palestine, one so alive, so tremendously alive; and another so dead, so deadly dead? This is the difference:

. . . The Sea of Galilee receives but does not keep the waters of river Jordan. For every drop that flows into it, another drop flows out. The more it gives joyfully away, the more it receives in return. This is the sea of life—the Sea of Galilee.

The other sea hoards every drop of water reaching it and gives nothing in return. The Sea of Galilee gives and lives. The other sea gives nothing and does not live. It is truly named 'The Dead'—the Dead Sea.

And the same is true about human life. You can become the Sea of Galilee or you can become the Dead Sea. If you become the Sea of Galilee, sooner or later, you will attract the consciousness of Jesus to you. The master will walk around you again; again he will be seen with his disciples near you; again you will be in a totally different world, you will have the touch of the divine. Or you can become the Dead Sea; then go on receiving and don't give, then go on hoarding and don't give. How did it become dead? A miser is a dead person; a miser dies every day. Share, whatsoever you have, share, and you will receive more. That is the meaning of friendliness.

And Patanjali says, bring your samyama to compassion, love, and friendliness; and they will grow. Not that you will become friendly: you will become the friend. Not that you will become friendly: you will become friendship, friendliness. Not that you will love: you will become love, you will be the very quality of love.

The third sutra:

> By performing samyama on the strength of an elephant,
> the strength of an elephant is obtained.

Whatsoever you want, you bring your samyama to it and it will happen, because you are infinite. Whatsoever form you want to take, you can take after samyama. All miracles are possible; it depends on you. If you want to become so powerful like an elephant, you can become. Just by keeping the idea as a seed inside you and showering it with samyama, you will become that. Because of this sutra, many people have done many wrong things. It is a key, but if you want to become something devilish, you can become. You can misuse yoga as much as you can misuse science. Science has released atomic energy. Now, you can use it by dropping it on cities and killing people. You can create more Hiroshimas and Nagasakis—you can make the whole earth a dead, burned place, a cemetery.

The same atomic energy can be used creatively. All the poverty that exists on earth can disappear within minutes. All the food that is needed can be created, and all the luxuries that are available only to a very few can become part of the normal life of everybody. Nobody is barring the path, but somehow man does not have that creative understanding.

Yoga has been misused in the same way. All knowledge brings power, and power can be used positively or negatively.

I have heard an anecdote:

A drunk shuffled up to a rich banker and asked for sixpence for a cup of coffee. Being an extremely generous man, the banker handed him a ten-shilling note.

'Here,' he said, 'You can buy yourself twenty cups of coffee with that.'

Next evening, the banker saw the drunken tramp again.

'How are you today?' he asked cheerfully.

The tramp glared at him. 'Why don't you get lost?' he said rudely. 'You and your twenty cups of coffee. They kept me awake all last night.'

It depends; a blessing can become a curse. What Patanjali is saying is pure white magic, it is a magical formula. You can make it into devilish black magic. Then you will be destructive to others—and destructive to yourself. Remember that. That's why first he says to become friendly then he talks about power.

People like Patanjali are so cautious; they have to be cautious because of you. They watch their every step. First he tells how to attain to samyama; immediately he talks about compassion and friendliness; then he talks about power. Because when you have compassion, then power cannot be misused.

By directing the light of the superphysical faculty,
knowledge is gained of the subtle, the hidden, and the distant.

Every dimension becomes available—'*of the subtle, the hidden, the distant*'—once you know how not to be. Once you know how to be without any ego, once you know how to be a pure consciousness with no subject and no object, everything becomes possible. You can know all. By knowing one, all is known.

> *By performing samyama on the sun,*
> *knowledge of the solar system is gained.*

This sutra is a little complicated—not in itself, but because of the commentators. All the commentators of Patanjali talk about this sutra as if Patanjali is talking about the sun out there. He is not talking about that sun; he cannot talk about that; he is not an astrologer and he is not interested in astrology. He is interested in man. He is interested in mapping man's consciousness. And the sun is not of the 'out.'

In yoga terminology, man is a microcosm. Man is in a subtle way a small universe, condensed into a small existence. Existence, the whole of existence, is nothing but man expanded. This is yoga terminology: microcosm and macrocosm. Whatsoever exists outside, also exists exactly inside man.

Just like the sun, man has a sun inside; and just like the moon, man has a moon inside. And Patanjali is interested in giving you the whole geography of the inner world, of inner man. So when he says, '*Bhuwan gyanam surya samyamat*'—'*By performing samyama on the sun, knowledge of the solar system is gained,*' he does not mean the sun that is without. He means the sun that is within.

Where is your inner sun? Where is the centre of your inner solar system? It is exactly hidden deep in the reproductive system. That's why sex is hot; it is a sort of heat. We have the expression for animals: whenever a female is ready to be impregnated, we say she is in heat. That phrase is exactly accurate. The sex centre is the sun. That's why sex makes you hot and feverish; when you move in a sex act, you become hotter and hotter and hotter. You touch an almost feverish peak; you perspire; your breathing is disturbed, and after it, you feel exhausted. Then you fall into sleep.

When sex is exhausted, immediately the moon starts functioning. When the sun sets, the moon comes up. That's why after the sex act, you immediately fall into sleep. The function of the sun is gone; the function of the moon starts.

The sun is the sex centre. By performing samyama on it, you will be able to know the whole solar system inside. By performing samyama on the sex centre, you will become capable of going beyond it. You will know all the secrets of it; but it has nothing to do with the outer sun.

But if you know the inner sun, by reflection, you can understand the outer sun also. This sun is the sex centre of the solar system. That's why everything alive needs sun. Trees go higher and higher—in Africa, they go higher than anywhere else because the forests are so dense and there is much competition—because if you don't go high, you will die. You will not be able to reach to the sun. You will not be available to the sun and the sun will not be available to you. You will not be showered by the energy of life.

Sun is life; sex is life. All life arises out of sun; all life arises out of sex. All life.

Trees try to reach higher so that they can become available to the sun and the sun become available to them. Just watch. The same trees are on this side. These pine-like trees, the same trees are on this side—they have remained small. This side, they are throbbing high. The sun is more available on this side; on that side, the sun is not available.

Sex is the inside sun; the sun is the sex organ of the solar system. By reflection, you will be able to understand the outer solar system also, but the basic thing is to understand the inner solar system. So I will insist on this: remember that Patanjali is mapping the inner ground. And of course it can be started only from the sun because the sun is the centre. Not the goal, but the centre. Not the ultimate, but the centre. One has to rise above it, one has to move above it, but it is the beginning. It is not the omega, but it is the alpha.

Once Patanjali has said how to attain to samyama, how to transform into compassion, love, and friendship, how to become powerful for compassion, for love; he comes to the inner territory, the inner topography: *'By performing samyama on the sun, knowledge of the solar system is gained.'*

The whole world can be divided between two types of people: the sun people and the moon people, or you can call them yang and yin. The sun is the male; the moon is the female. The sun is aggression, the positive; the moon is receptive, the passive. You can divide the whole existence between the sun and the moon. And you can divide your body also between the sun and the moon; yoga has divided.

It has divided so minutely that it has divided even your breath, your breathing: one nostril is sun-breath; the other is moon-breath. If you become angry, you will breathe from the sun side. If you want to become silent, you will breathe from the moon side. The whole body is divided: one of your sides is male; the other side is female. The mind is divided: one part of the mind is male; another part of the mind is female.

And one has to move from the sun towards the moon, and then beyond both.

Enough for today.

Two

And a Perfect Liar at That

The first question:

Osho, will your disciples attain by sudden enlightenment, or by a slow, step-by-step growth? And is your pathless path for anybody, or only for rare exceptions?

The first thing to be understood is that the very word *attainment* is nonspiritual. It is part of your greed. The idea to attain is very worldly. Whether you want to attain prestige, power, wealth, or God, or nirvana does not make any difference. The desire to attain is worldly; it is materialistic.

The spiritual revolution happens only when you drop this greed, when you drop the very idea of *becoming*. You are that. You are already that—so then don't hanker for attainment. You have never been anything else other than that which you are trying to attain.

God is within you this very moment—healthy and kicking, because God is not something separate from you or from life. But your greed has been a problem, and because of your greed, exploiters have existed who go on showing you ways how to attain.

My whole effort here, my whole work here is to help you to see that you already have it. There is no question of any attainment. There is no question of any future. The moment you think in terms of attainment, tomorrow comes in, time comes in, future comes in. It is a desire. You would like to be somebody else other than you are—which is impossible. You can only be that which you are.

Becoming is dreaming; being is truth. But because of your greed, people have given you many ideas of how to attain—and you accepted. Not because what they say is truth, but because it enhances your greed.

To be close to me, all that you have to learn is: unlearn your greed. Drop it, right now. Don't postpone it, don't say, 'Yes, we will drop it somewhere in the future—tomorrow.' Just try to understand the very misery of greed, the very hell of it. If you see that greed brings hell, then why tomorrow? In that very vision, understanding, it drops. In fact, you don't drop it; it drops on its own accord.

And, if the very idea of attainment is stupid, then what is the point of asking whether you are going to attain in a sudden way or in a gradual way? They become irrelevant.

You are already that. Let this be your constant remembrance. Never for a single moment forget that you are gods and goddesses. Don't think in terms of ladies and gentlemen—forget all that nonsense. Remember, you are gods and goddesses. Never settle for less.

So, I have to annihilate your wrong ideas. They have been oversold to you—centuries and centuries of salesmanship in the name of spirituality.

Let me tell you one anecdote:

A Catholic girl and a Jewish boy fell madly in love. But their religion and their beliefs interfered. The Irish-Catholic mother advised her daughter, 'Sell him a bill of goods. Teach him the beauty and joys of Catholicism. Make him a Catholic first.' The girl did. She sold him and sold him and the wedding date was set. One day before the marriage, the girl came home, sobbed, cried, and said to the mother,

'The marriage is off.'

'Why?' the mother asked. 'Didn't you sell him?'

'I think I oversold him. Now he wants to be a priest.'

These salesmen of spirituality, from one century to another, for millennia, have oversold you the idea of attainment. They have exploited you. Just see the point: you can be only that which you already are—nothing else is possible. It is a given fact; it is a gift. So spirituality is not an attainment; rather, it is a recognition—a remembrance. You have forgotten, that's all . . . you have misplaced it somewhere, that's all, but it is there all the same.

And the second part of the question is: *'Is your pathless path for anybody, or only for rare exceptions?'*—only for rare exceptions—but everybody is a rare exception, because I have never come across any person who is not a rare exception. I have never come across a common man or a common woman. I have been searching hard, looking into everybody who comes to me; I always come across something unique, something incomparably unique, something absolutely unique.

God never repeats. His creativity is original—he does not believe in carbon copies. He never creates anybody again. He does not believe in the common and the ordinary. He creates only the extraordinary and the unique.

Try to understand it, because the society has again forced on you an idea that you are just a common man. A few people want to prove themselves uncommon. They can prove that only if they prove the whole lot common. Politicians—they cannot believe that everybody is unique. If everybody is unique, then what are they doing by being presidents and prime ministers? Then they will look just foolish. They are unique, the chosen, and the whole lot is common—the mass. Their egos, just to prove themselves extraordinary, have proved another thing also, simultaneously, that everybody is ordinary.

And they say you have to prove your extraordinariness—become rich, become a Rockefeller; or become powerful in terms of power politics, become a Nixon or a Ford; or at least become a great poet, an Ezra Pound or Cummings; become a painter, a Picasso, a van Gogh; an actor. Prove yourself! Become somebody in some direction; prove your talent and genius and your mettle. And, then those who have not proved in any way are the common mass. You are exceptional.

But I want to tell you that everybody is *born* exceptional, there is no need to prove it. And those who prove, they simply prove that they are uncertain about their uniqueness. Try to understand it: only inferior people, who have an idea of deep inferiority, try to prove themselves to be superior. Inferiority complex helps you to compete and prove so that you can prove you are superior. But basically, you are born unique and there is no need to prove it.

Enjoy if you enjoy creating poetry, but don't make it an ego trip. Enjoy if you enjoy painting, but don't make it an ego trip. Look at your painters, poets; they are so egoistic, almost crazy. What has happened? They are not enjoying their painting, their poetry. They are using their poetry and painting as steps to come to the top so that they can declare, 'I am unique, and you are not.'

Because of these ill people . . . they are pathological; they need psychological treatment. All politicians need, all power-oriented, ego trip people need treatment; they need to be hospitalized. Because of their madness, their feverish competition, their tremendous effort to prove that they are somebody, you start feeling that you are nobody, that you are not special, that you are there just to vegetate—live an ignoble life and die an ignoble death.

This is a very dangerous, poisonous idea, deeply planted in you. Throw it out.

But remember, when I say you are unique, I don't mean in any relative way. I don't say that you are more unique than somebody else. When I say you are unique, I say it in an absolute way—not in a relative, comparative way. I am not saying that you are more unique than anybody else. You are simply unique, as unique as the other—as unique as your neighbour. Uniqueness is your nature.

You ask: 'Is your pathless path for anybody, or only for rare exceptions?' It is only for rare exceptions, but everybody is a rare exception.

I would like to tell you one anecdote:

It happened, there was once a wicked king who could not bear to think that anyone was his superior . . . .

Must have been a pure politician—a pure poison.

. . . So he summoned all the pundits of the realm as was the practice on momentous occasions and put to them this question: 'Which of us two is the greater, I or God?'

Because when you start on an ego trip, the ultimate fight is against God—the final. The final has to be with God because one day or another the problem is going to arise: who is superior, God or you? Friedrich Nietzsche has said, 'I cannot believe in God because if I believe in God, I will always remain inferior.' Always . . . then there is no possibility to become superior. So Nietzsche says, 'Better to drop the very idea of God.' Nietzsche says, 'How can there be two superior beings, I and God?' This wicked king must have been a Nietzschean.

. . . The pundits shook with fear—because they knew if they said God is superior, they would be killed immediately, murdered, butchered. Being wise by profession, they asked for time, and then through old habit they clung to their position and their lives. But they were worthy men who would not displease God. They were therefore deep in grief, when the oldest pundit reassured them, 'Leave it to me, tomorrow I shall speak with the king.'

The next day when the court was gathered, the old man quietly arrived; his hands humbly joined together, his forehead smeared with white ashes. He bowed down low and pronounced these words: 'O Lord, undoubtedly you are the greater'—the king twirled his moustache which he wore long and tossed high his head—'You are the greater, King, for you can banish us from your kingdom while God cannot; for truly all is his kingdom and there is nowhere to go outside him.'

There is no way to go outside God. That's your uniqueness—that is everybody's uniqueness. There is no way to be something else other than part of God. That's your uniqueness and that is everybody else's uniqueness. Respect yourself and respect others also. The moment you start proving yourself superior, you are disrespectful to yourself because the very effort shows that you have accepted the idea that you are not unique—hence the effort to prove—and you are disrespectful to others also.

Respect yourself, respect others also, because deep down we are not separate. We are one whole. We are members of each other. We are not like islands; we are the vast continent of God.

The second question:

Osho, Patanjali says that through ignorance one accumulates ignorance, one accumulates karma; and previously we have heard you say that until one attains to a certain crystallization, one is not responsible for one's actions—rather, the divine is the doer, the one responsible. Would you please clear these seeming contradictions?

They appear contradictions to you. Rather than clearing the contradictions, I would like to clear *you*. I would like to clean you so completely that you are not there; then you won't see any contradictions.

To see contradictions is to see through the intellect. Once the intellect is not there interfering and your vision is clear—no thought floats in your consciousness; you are in a state of *samyama*, absolutely empty—you will never see any contradiction anywhere. All contradictions will look complementary. They are, but the mind has been trained by intellectuals, logicians, by Aristotle. You have been taught to divide things into polar opposites—day and night, life and death, good and bad, God and devil, man and woman. Watertight compartments.

Then if I say, that in every woman there is a man and in every man there is a woman, you will immediately say, 'Wait, there is a contradiction. How can a man be a woman, and how can a woman be a man? A man is man, a woman is woman— clear cut.' It is not so. Life does not believe in Aristotle; life is bigger than Aristotle. Man and woman are complementaries, not contradictions.

Have you seen the Taoist symbol of yin and yang?— Contradictions meeting into each other, dissolving into each other: day into night, night into day; life into death, death into life. And that's how it is. Life and death are not two separate entities. There is no gap between them, no interval. It is life that becomes death, and it is death that again becomes life.

You see a wave rising and moving in the ocean. Just in the wake of the wave, there is a hollow, upside down wave following. They are not two separate things. You see a great mountain: just by the side there is a great valley—they are not two things. The valley is nothing but the mountain upside down; the mountain is nothing but the valley downside up.

Man and woman, and all contradictions, are seemingly contradictory. Once you can see this fact, you will always be able to know that I have to talk in contradictions because I have to talk about the total, the whole. Whatsoever I say covers only part; then the other part is left: I have to say that part also. When I say that other part, you say, 'Wait, you are being contradictory.'

Language is still Aristotelian, and I don't think there will ever be a possibility of a non-Aristotelian language. It will be very difficult because for day-to-day, utilitarian purposes we have to divide things into black and white.

Black and white look so separate, but real life is like a

rainbow—the whole spectrum. Maybe on one side is white, on the other side is black, but in between there are millions of steps, all joined together. Life is a spectrum. If you drop the mid-steps, then things look contradictory. It is your vision that is not yet clear.

I have heard, it happened one day:

One drunkard burst into the office for registration of births and deaths.

'Gentlemen,' he hiccuped, 'I want to register the birth of twins!'

'Why do you say "gentlemen"?' inquired the registrar. 'Can't you see I am here all alone?'

'You are?' gasped the new father, staggering back. 'Maybe I had better go back to the hospital and have another look.'

Maybe they are not twins, only one. It is your unconsciousness that is giving you a very distorted view of life. And again and again you will come to feel contradictions in me. They are there, but only in appearances; deep down they meet.

Now, this particular contradiction: *'Patanjali says that through ignorance one accumulates ignorance, one accumulates karma; and previously we have heard you say that until one attains to a certain crystallization, one is not responsible for one's actions— rather, the divine is the doer, the one responsible.'*

These are two seemingly contradictory paths. One is, that you leave all to God—but *all*, total. Then you are not responsible. But remember, it has to be total; it is a total sacrifice, surrender, submission. Then if you do good, God is the doer; if you do bad, of course, God is the doer.

Remember the totality. That totality will transform you. Don't be clever and cunning, because the possibility is there that whatsoever you don't feel is good, you will say God is responsible. Whatsoever makes you feel guilty, you will throw it on God, and whatsoever enhances your ego, you will say, 'It is I.' You may not say so visibly, but deep inside you will say so. If you write a good poem, you will say, 'I am the poet.' If you paint a beautiful painting, you will say, 'I am the painter.' And if a Nobel Prize is going to be given to you, you will not say, 'Give it to God.' You will say, 'Yes, I have been waiting for it, already it is too late. The recognition—the *due* recognition—has been delayed too long.'

When Bernard Shaw got the Nobel Prize, he refused, saying, 'I have waited too long. Now it is below my prestige.' He was one of the most egoistic persons ever: 'Now it is below my prestige. When I was young, I was hankering for it, dreaming for it. Now I am old enough; I don't need it. My recognition in the world is already so great; my applause from people is so great, now I don't need any Nobel Prize. It is not going to give any more credit to me.'

He was persuaded that it would be an insult to the Nobel Prize committee, so he accepted, and then immediately he donated the money that comes with the Nobel Prize to some organization. Nobody had ever heard about that organization. He was the only member and the chairman of that organization.

And when asked later on what he had been doing, he said, 'If you get a Nobel Prize, your name goes in the corner of the newspapers once. I rejected it; so another day I was in the headlines. Then I accepted it again; another day I was again in the headlines. Then I donated it; again I was in the headlines. Then I donated it to myself; again I was in the headlines. I used it to its fullest.' He took the whole juice of it.

So the possibility is your ego will go on choosing. Whatsoever you feel guilty about, you will say God is responsible. Whatsoever you feel good about, you will say, 'Yes, here I am. I have done it.' Totality is needed in that too.

Now, look; and now this is another path, of Patanjali, Mahavira, Buddha. They say you are responsible—total responsibility; again. Patanjali does not really believe in God. He is too scientific for that. He says God is also a method to attain to nirvana, to enlightenment. That too is a way—just a way, not the goal. He is exactly like Buddha, Mahavira, who denied God completely, who said, 'There is no God, there is no need; only man is responsible.' But *total*: not only for good, but for bad also.

Now see how these two contradictions are joined together in the concept of totality. Both demand totality; that is their link. Really, totality works: whether you surrender everything to God or you take the whole responsibility on your own shoulders does not matter. That which is really significant is that you are total. So whatsoever you do, be total, and that will become your liberation. To be total is to be liberated.

So these two look contradictory, but they are not. They are both based in the same idea of being total.

There are two types of people; that's why two types of methods are needed. It is very easy for the feminine mind to surrender, to submit, to sacrifice; it is very difficult for the male mind to submit, to surrender, to sacrifice. So the male mind will need Patanjali, a path where the total responsibility is yours; the feminine mind will need a path of devotion—the path of Narad, Meera, Chaitanya, Jesus—all is God's: Thy kingdom come, thy will be done. Everything is his. Jesus goes on saying, 'I am his.' That is the meaning when he insists, 'He is the father and I am the son. As a son is nothing but an extension of the consciousness of the father, so am I.'

For the feminine mind, for the receptive mind, for the passive mind, Patanjali will not be of much help. Something of love is needed—something of putting oneself totally down, effacing oneself completely, sacrificing oneself completely. Dissolving and disappearing is needed for the feminine mind; but for the male mind Patanjali is perfect. Both are right because both are the mind; and the whole of humanity is divided into these two minds.

The contradiction appears because you cannot understand the whole mind. But through these two paths, whatsoever you choose, whichever you choose, you will become total; and, by and by, the total mind will flower in you.

The third question:

Osho, Ramakrishna used food as an anchorage to remain on the periphery. Is not compassion enough for returning to the periphery? And, pardon me for putting a personal question: what is your anchorage?

First, compassion is not enough, because compassion is so pure you cannot make an anchorage out of it. It is so pure that the earthly gravitation cannot function on it. The earth needs something more material. The body needs something more material; the body is part of the earth. When you die, the earth returns to the earth—dust unto dust. To remain in the body, just compassion is not enough.

In fact, the day compassion arises, you are ready to leave the body. Compassion gives you a totally different pull—the pull from the high, the pull from the above. You start being pulled from the above. It becomes almost impossible to remain in the body. No, that purity won't be of much help. A little impurity is needed to remain on the earth and in the body, something more material. Food is perfectly good; food is part of the earth, material, it can give you a weight. People have used different things in different ways, but pure compassion cannot be used. In fact, pure compassion is the cause that starts helping you to move upward. Let me introduce one word to you: *grace*. Gravitation is the pull of the downward and grace is the pull of the upward. The moment you are full of compassion, overflowing, grace starts functioning. You are so weightless, you can almost fly. No, a paperweight will be needed to force you here on the earth. Ramakrishna used that; food was his paperweight. He has become weightless: something was needed to give him a little weight so the gravitation goes on working.

Now you ask me, I will tell you one anecdote:

Four men of the cloth were having a confidential talk and discussing their vices.

'I like pork,' said the rabbi.

'I drink a bottle of bourbon a day,' said the Protestant minister.

'I have a girlfriend on the side,' confessed the priest.

They all turned to the Baptist minister, who shrugged and said, 'Me? I like to gossip.'

That's my answer also—I like to gossip. That's my weight. All these talks are nothing but gossips. If it hurts your ego, call them cosmic gossips, divine gossips—but they are gossips.

The fourth question:

Osho, I humbly wish to put the following question and sincerely hope you will answer this tomorrow. I have come from Singapore and would soon go back.

This morning, sir, you stated that the ego is the stumbling block and, that only by overcoming or transcending the ego the fulfilment of our essential nature could be achieved. Thence you said that by concentrating on the sex impulse, one can be enlightened. Don't you think the two statements are contradictory, for if you concentrate on the sexual act or impulse, you have become the doer and the egoist?

We think that only by being detached to the sensual desires, we can achieve the object. I humbly pray you enlighten the issue and clear the misunderstanding in my mind.

The question has to be from an Indian. I want it to be noted by you that it is from an Indian because it shows all the qualities of the Indian mind. Try to dissect the question step by step.

'*I humbly wish to put the following question and sincerely hope you will answer this tomorrow.*' No need to say these things, but the Indian mind is formal, it is not sincere, it is not direct, it is always hiding behind rituals, words. It looks polite; it is not, because a polite mind is direct, immediate. There is no need to hide oneself behind a screen of formalities, etiquette—at least not here.

God is not a formality, and etiquette is not going to help you in any way to solve life's problems. It may create trouble. *'This morning, sir, you stated that the ego is the stumbling block and only by overcoming or transcending the ego, the fulfilment of our essential nature could be achieved.'* First, you have heard something that I have not said. That too is part of the Indian mind. It is very difficult for the Indian mind to hear that which is said. He has his own ideas already; in fact too many—he has a philosophy, a religion, a great tradition, and all that nonsense. And he goes on mixing everything with his own.

Now, I have told you that one can transcend, but I have not said 'overcome.' Now this gentleman says, *'You stated that the ego is the stumbling block and only by overcoming or transcending . . .'* They are not synonymous. Overcoming is a repression: it is 'conquering over.' It is forcing something violently; it is a struggle and a fight. And whenever you fight, the ego cannot be transcended, because the ego lives by fight, struggle. So by overcoming, ego is never overcome. The more you try, the more you will become egoistic. Of course, now your ego will be religious, holy, pious. And, remember, whenever ego becomes pious it becomes more subtle and more dangerous—it is purified poison.

Overcoming is not the same as transcending. What is the difference? Transcending comes through understanding and overcoming comes through struggle. You fight, you force it down, you jump on the chest of it and you sit there, you wrestle with it; then it is overcoming. But it is always there and you are caught in a trap; now you cannot leave it, because the moment you get down, it will get up.

So an egoistic person who tries to overcome his ego will become humble, but now the ego will be there in his humility, in his humbleness; and you cannot find more egoistic people than humble people. They say, 'We are nothing,' but look in their eyes. They say, 'We are just dust of your feet, sir,' but look into their eyes, look what they are saying.

Let me tell you one anecdote:

'Doctor,' complained the patient, 'I have been having severe headaches. What can you do about it?'

'Been smoking much?' asked the doctor.

'No,' replied the patient, 'I never touch tobacco. Furthermore, I never take a drink and I have not had a date in twenty years.'

'In that case,' said the doctor, 'the only thing that could be the matter with you is that your halo is getting too tight.'

That will happen by 'overcoming'—your halo will get too tight and you will have headaches.

That happens to all religious people. They become uptight, false, inauthentic. When anger arises, they go on smiling; their smile is a painted smile, of course. They go on forcing the anger deep into the unconscious; and whatsoever you repress, spreads in your being. It becomes part of you. It happens that a religious man may not be found guilty of being angry, the incident of anger may disappear from his life, but anger will become his very style of life. You may not be able to catch him red-handed angry, but you will be able to see and feel that he is always angry. Anger will circulate into his blood; ego will circulate as an undercurrent in whatsoever he is doing. In fact, he will become much too concerned with whatsoever he has overcome and he will always be defending. He will remain in a defensive mood.

No, overcoming is not transcending. Transcending has a beauty; overcoming is ugly. When you transcend, you have understood the foolishness, the idiocy of the ego; you have understood the illusion of it; you have understood the baseless desire of it. And then it drops on its own accord—not that you drop it, because if you drop it then you will attain to another ego, that 'I have dropped the ego.' It drops through understanding. Understanding functions like a fire; it burns the ego.

And, remember how you will know whether the ego is overcome or transcended. If it is overcome, the person will become humble. If it is transcended, he will be neither egoistic nor humble, because the whole point is gone. Only an egoist can be humble. When the ego is not there, how can you be humble? Who will be humble? Then the whole base has disappeared from underneath. So whenever ego is overcome, it becomes humbleness. When ego is transcended, a man is simply liberated from that trap. He is neither humble nor egoistic. He is simple. He is true. He is authentic. He will not exaggerate either this way or that.

Exaggeration is part of the ego. First you exaggerate that, 'I am the greatest man'; then you exaggerate that, 'I am the humblest, the last.' First you exaggerate that 'I am somebody,' but special; then you exaggerate 'I am nobody'—but special.

First you want the world to recognize your somebodiness and praise you. When you find that is not being done . . . Because all are on the same trip and nobody is worried about your being somebody, they are all somebodies, and they are trying their ways. And when you feel the competition is too tough, and when you feel there seems to be no go in it, then you start the other—the more cunning way, the more sly way. You say, 'I am nobody,' but you wait: now they will recognize your nobodiness, they will come—you are a great sage. You are so humble, you have dropped the ego completely. And you will smile deep down and the ego will feel buttressed, flattered, and you will say, 'Now, so they have come.'

Remember, overcoming is not transcending.

'This morning, sir, you stated that the ego is the stumbling block and only by overcoming or transcending . . .' Never use 'or' between 'overcoming' and 'transcending'; they are totally different phenomena, absolutely different phenomena. *'. . . the ego, the fulfilment of our essential nature could be achieved.'*

'Thence you said that by concentrating on the sex impulse . . .' I have never said that: I said samyama—not 'concentration' only. Samyama is concentration, meditation, *samadhi*—ecstasy—all

together. That's how you go on hearing whatsoever you want to hear. I have to repeat so many times; still you go on missing.

If you remember, yesterday I repeated so many times the word samyama and I tried to explain to you what it is. It is not only concentration. Concentration is only the first step towards it. The second step is meditation; in meditation, concentration is dropped. It has to be because when you move on a further step, the lower step has to be dropped; otherwise how can you move? When you go up a staircase, you go on leaving steps behind you. The first step is left in the second; the concentration is dropped in meditation. *Dharana* is dropped in *dhyan*. And then the third step: samadhi, ecstasy. Then meditation is also dropped; then you attain to samadhi. And all these three are called samyama.

When you bring samyama to sex, yes, *brahmacharya* comes out of it—but not only by concentration. *'Thence you said that by concentrating on the sex impulse, one can be enlightened.'* Yes, by bringing samyama to any impulse, one can be freed from it. Because in deep samadhi, you are a tremendous understanding—and only understanding frees. And for an understanding mind, there is no need to avoid and escape. You can face it. The problem disappears: your fire of understanding is such, the problem is burned.

Yes, if you bring your samyama to the sex desire, the desire will disappear. Not overcome: you will transcend it.

'Don't you think that the two statements are contradictory...?' No, I don't think that. You are absolutely confused, and the confusion comes because of your ideology. Ideologies are always confusing; you always listen hiding behind your ideology and scripture. And it is very difficult to find an Indian who can listen directly—the Bhagvadgita goes on inside continuously, the Vedas, the Upanishads. The Indians have become like parrots; they go on repeating without understanding, because if you understand there is no need for any Bhagvadgita. Your own divine song arises; you start your own singing. You start doing your own thing—Krishna did his, why should you be doing it? Who is he to

be carboned and copied and imitated? And then you will become just an imitation. All Indians, almost all, have become imitators; they have false faces, masks. And they go on thinking the country is very religious. It is not: it is one of the most cunning countries in the world.

'Don't you think the two statements are contradictory, for if you concentrate on the sexual act or impulse you have become the doer and the egoist?' Who has told you that if you do samyama on sex you will become a doer? Samyama means witnessing—pure witnessing. You become a watcher, not a doer. How can you become a doer when you are seeing the sex impulse? When you see it, the seen becomes different from the seer.

You are seeing me here. Certainly, you are separate and I am separate. I am seeing you: you are the object of my vision and I am the capacity of my vision. You are separate; I am separate.

The known is separate from the knower, the seer is separate from the seen; and when you bring samyama to any impulse whatsoever—sex, greed, ego—suddenly you are separate because you see it. It is there like an object, and you are there, the onlooker. How can you become the doer? A person becomes a doer when the witnessing is lost; he becomes identified with the object of vision. He starts saying, 'This sex, it is me, it is I,' 'This hunger in the body, it is me, it is I.' If you watch the hunger, hunger is there in the body and you are far away on the stars.

Just try it: when you feel hungry, sit, close your eyes and watch the hunger. You cannot be identified with the hunger. If you feel identified, in that very moment witnessing is lost; you have become a doer.

The whole art of witnessing is to help you to feel separate from all that with which you are clinging.

No, the doer never arises out of samyama. The doer drops, disappears. Suddenly you see that you have never done anything—things have been happening, but you have not done anything. You are not the doer. You are a pure witness, *sakshin*. And this is the ultimate of all religion.

'*We think that only by being detached to the sensual desires, we can achieve the object.*' This is creating the trouble, that you have some ideas—you 'think.' If you have some ideas, practice them, and you will come to know their falsity. And you have been having them for so long, you are not fed up yet; and what has happened to you through those ideas? What transformation has come to you? What liberation has come to you? Be a little intelligent. Just see: these ideas you have been carrying for your whole life—what has happened? It is like a junkyard inside you. Nothing has happened. Now clean your inner space.

Here I am not trying to give you other ideas and substitutes. My whole effort is to annihilate you utterly, to destroy you utterly—to destroy your mind so completely that you become a state of no-mind, a clear vision, that's all. I don't believe in any ideology, and I don't want you to believe in any. All ideologies are false. And I say *all* ideologies—mine included—because ideas cannot bring you to the real. The real is known only when you have no ideas about it.

The real is there, and you are so full of ideas, you go on missing it. When you listen to me, if you listen through your ideas, you will get more and more confused.

Please, for a few minutes while you are here, put your ideas aside. Just listen to me. I am not saying believe what I say. I am saying just listen, give it a chance, and then later on think. But what happens: I am saying something and you are repeating something else inside you—stop that tape. Stop all old tapes; otherwise, you will not be able to understand me, what I am saying. And in fact I am not saying much; rather, I am being here. My saying is just a way of being with you.

So if you put your ideas a little aside—I am not saying throw them forever—just put them by the side, listen to me, then you can bring them up again if you feel they are better. But don't get mixed.

One anecdote:

One Jew, a very old man, came to see his son in America. He was shocked to find that the young man did not follow the Jewish laws. 'You mean,' he asked, 'you don't keep the dietary laws?'

'Papa, I eat in restaurants, and it is not easy to keep kosher.'

'Do you keep the Sabbath, at least?'

'Sorry, Papa, it is tough in America to do that.'

'Tell me, son,' the old man sneered, 'are you still circumcised?'

This is how the old mind goes on working. Put it aside; only then can you understand me. Otherwise, it is impossible.

The fifth question:

Osho, yesterday, you explained samyama as the synthesis of concentration, meditation, and samadhi. Please explain the difference between samyama and the final enlightenment.

How come Patanjali has not talked about catharsis whereas you strongly emphasize catharsis?

Please explain the preparatory antidote for the misuse of psychic powers.

How can one differentiate if one is undoing his prarabdha karma, destiny, or one is creating new karmas?

If the time for the death of a person is fixed by seconds, does it mean that man has no freedom to die earlier or prolong his life span?

First: *'Please explain the difference between samyama and the final enlightenment.'* Don't be worried about final enlightenment. And there is no way to explain it or even to describe it. If you are really interested, I am ready to give you final enlightenment, but don't ask explanations about it. That is easier—to give it to you—rather than describe it, because no description will do justice. Nobody has ever described it. Samyama can be described because samyama is the method. Enlightenment cannot be described. It happens out of samyama.

Samyama is like planting a seed, watering the plant, protecting the tree; samyama is like that. Then come flowers, they bloom. It is difficult to say anything about the flowers. Everything can be said before the flower comes into being because everything else is just a method, technique.

I can talk to you about technique and methods. If you follow those techniques and methods, one day you will wake into enlightenment. That can happen just now also, if you are ready to sacrifice yourself completely. What do I mean when I say sacrifice yourself completely?—it means to surrender yourself completely.

If you allow me, it can happen right now, because the light is burning within me. The flame can jump to you, but you don't allow. You are so defensive—as if you have something to lose. I can't see that you have anything to lose; you have nothing to lose, but you are so defensive, as if treasures are hidden there and if you open your heart, those treasures may be stolen. And there is nothing—just darkness, just the dirt of many, many lives.

If you open to me, if you become vulnerable to me, you sacrifice yourself; and unless a disciple sacrifices himself to the master, the contact has not been made. And the sacrifice has to be utter; you cannot withhold anything. If you are ready for enlightenment, then don't waste time: sacrifice yourself utterly, become vulnerable to me.

Difficult. One feels lost. One feels, where is one going? One feels as if all of one's treasures are being taken away. And there is nothing—no treasure—even you are not there to be lost. And one who is there cannot be lost. The one that can be lost is not you; that which cannot be lost is you. By becoming vulnerable, you will lose something that is your ego; you will lose something, but you will not lose yourself. In fact, by losing all else, you will for the first time attain to your authentic being.

So don't ask about final enlightenment. Buddha has said, 'Buddhas can only indicate the path; nobody can tell you.' I can show you the water, but don't ask me how it feels when water quenches the thirst. How can I tell you? The water is here—why not taste it? Why not drink it? Drink me, and let your thirst be quenched. Then you will know how it is, how it feels—it is a *feel*, and there is no way to describe it. It is like love: if you have fallen in love, you know what it is, but if somebody asks what is love, you will get puzzled.

There is a famous saying of Augustine: 'I know what time is, but when somebody asks me, "What is time?" suddenly I don't know.' You also know what time is, and if somebody asks you, it will be difficult to say.

I have heard about one Russian, Leo Tolstoy, a great novelist. He was in London, and he didn't know much English, and he wanted to know what time it is, so he asked a gentleman, 'Please, tell me, what is time?' The Englishman shrugged and said, 'Go and ask some philosopher.' What is time? You can say, 'What is the time?' but you cannot say, 'What is time?' You know, you feel it, because you live in time. Continuously, it is there and passing, passing by you. You live in time as a fish lives in water, but even a fish cannot define what water is.

In fact, I have heard a story that once a philosophic fish became very much worried because she heard the talk, too much talk, about the ocean, and she had never come across it. So she was meditating. The king fish came and looked at the fish, and he thought that there seems to be some trouble, she was very much worried. So the king fish asked, 'What is the matter with you? What has gone wrong?' And the fish said, 'I am very much worried—I want to know what this ocean is. So much talk about it and I never come across it.' And the king fish laughed and said, 'You fool, you are in it!'

But when something is so close, it is difficult to know. You never come across it. You are in time, but you never come across it; you cannot grasp it, becomes difficult to define it.

You are in God: becomes difficult to define God. You are in enlightenment already. Just a turning, just a clarity, a recognition, a remembrance. That's why I say, I am ready to give it to you, because it is already there. Nothing is to be done: just if you allow me to hold your hand for a while . . .

The second thing: *'How come Patanjali has not talked about catharsis whereas you strongly emphasize catharsis?'*

Let me tell you one anecdote:

A staggering drunk stopped a passer-by and asked the time. The passer-by looked at his watch and told him.

The drunk looked bewildered, and shook his head. 'I just can't work it out,' he said drunkenly. 'All night I have been getting different answers.'

All night! When you start thinking about me and Patanjali, remember the difference of 5,000 years. And all night you have been getting different answers?

When Patanjali was here on the earth, man was a totally different being. A totally different quality of humanity existed; catharsis was not needed, people were primitive, simple, childlike. A child does not need catharsis; an old man needs. A child has not accumulated anything.

Watch a child. When a child is angry, he becomes angry—he jumps, screams, yells. And then the anger is gone and he is smiling and he has forgotten—he has been through catharsis. When he feels loving, he comes and hugs you and kisses you. And he is not worried about etiquette and manners and things like that. And you are also not worried; you say, 'He is a child, not yet civilized'— that is, not yet poisoned, not yet educated; that is, not yet conditioned.

When the child wants to scream, he screams. He lives in total freedom; there is no need for catharsis. He is already every moment throwing whatsoever comes up; he never accumulates. But an old man?—the same child will become old after fifty, sixty, seventy years. He has accumulated too much; when he wanted to be angry, he could not be.

There are a thousand and one situations when you would like

to be angry but you cannot be—it is 'uneconomical,' or 'financially dangerous.' When your boss yells at you, you go on smiling. You would like to kill him, but you go on smiling. Now what will happen to the anger that has arisen? It will be repressed.

The same happens in the life of a society. Patanjali was here when people were primitive. If you go to interior parts of India, where primitive tribes still exist, they will not need Dynamic Meditation, remember. They will laugh at you; they will say, 'What are you doing? What is the point?' Every night after the day's work is over they dance, they dance to orgasm. Twelve, one o'clock in the night, they will continue dancing with their drums, primitive, with great energy, with ecstasy. And then they will fall asleep under the trees. And the whole day their work is such . . . chopping wood; then how can you collect anger inside you? They are not clerks in an office. They are not yet civilized. They live life as it comes by. Chopping wood they become nonviolent—they need not any Mahavira to teach them. They need not any philosophy of Jainism to be nonviolent.

Yes, a businessman needs the philosophy of nonviolence; that's why all the Jainas are businessmen. Just sitting on the *gaddi* the whole day, smiling and smiling—one gets almost crazy. Then one needs a philosophy of nonviolence to keep oneself in control; otherwise one will jump on anybody—for no excuse, for no reason. But when a man is chopping wood, what need has he of any philosophy of nonviolence? When he comes home, he has thrown violence so completely, he *is* nonviolent.

That's why Patanjali never talked about catharsis; it was not needed. Society was just in the childhood stage: people were childlike, innocent; they were living their life without any repression. Catharsis is needed when repression enters into the human mind. The more repressive a society, the more cathartic methods will be needed. Then you will have to do something to bring it out.

And I tell you it is better to do Dynamic Meditation than to throw your anger on somebody else, because if you throw it on somebody else, your *sanchit* karma will become bigger and bigger. If you throw it in a Dynamic Meditation, your sanchit karma is being emptied. You are not throwing at anybody, you are simply angry—not at anybody. You are simply yelling—not against anybody. You are simply crying. This simple crying, yelling, screaming, being angry, violent, cleanses you, and it creates no chain in the future.

So what Patanjali says about samyama, I will make catharsis also a part of it, because I am not worried about Patanjali, I am worried about *you*—and I know you well. If you don't throw it to the sky, you will throw it on somebody somewhere, and then it will create a chain of karma.

Catharsis is a must for the days to come: the more man will become civilized, the more catharsis will be needed.

The third thing in the question: *'Please explain the preparatory antidote for the misuse of psychic powers.'* The only antidote for the misuse of psychic powers is love; otherwise power corrupts. All power corrupts. It may be wealth, it may be prestige, it may be politics, or it may be psychic—it makes no difference. Whenever you feel powerful, if you don't have love as an antidote, your power is going to become a calamity to others, a curse, because power blinds the eyes. Love opens the eyes, love cleanses the eyes; your perception becomes clear. Power clouds.

Let me tell you one anecdote:

A wealthy miserly man never gave to the needy. His rabbi asked him to help a poor family in need of food and medicine. He refused.

The rabbi handed him a mirror and said, 'Look into this. What do you see?'

He said, 'I see my face in it, nothing else.'

'Now,' replied the rabbi, 'look through that window. What do you see?'

He said, 'I see men and women. I see two lovers engrossed in each other, and children playing. Why? Why do you ask me?'

'You answered your own question,' replied the rabbi. 'Through the window, you looked at life; in the mirror, you saw yourself. A mirror is of glass like the window, but coated on the back with silver. As this silver concealed your view of life, you saw only yourself; so has your silver, your wealth, concealed all else from your sight, so you see and think of yourself.'

The rich man hung his head. 'You are right,' he said. 'I have been blinded by silver.'

But all power blinds. Whether it is of silver or gold or psychic achievement, all power blinds. Then you go on seeing only yourself. Hence, Patanjali's insistence; the moment samyama is achieved, immediately bring friendliness, love. Let that be the first thing after samyama, so that your whole energy becomes a flow of love, of sharing, so whatsoever you have, you go on sharing. Then there is no possibility of any misuse.

The sixth question:

Osho, as one drunkard to another, your wine is the sweetest of all.

I have only one thing to say: I have given you only the appetizer. The wine is still waiting—get ready. Don't get too drunk by the appetizer.

All that I say to you is just the appetizer.

And the last question:

Osho, do you ever tell lies?

I am a liar, and a perfect liar at that—and this too is a lie.

Enough for today.

Three

Witnessing the Inner Astronomy

By performing samyama on the moon,
knowledge concerning the arrangement of the stars is gained.

By performing samyama on the polar star,
knowledge of the movement of the stars is gained.

By performing samyama on the navel centre,
knowledge of the organization of the body is gained.

By performing samyama on the throat,
there comes a cessation of the feelings of hunger and thirst.

By performing samyama on the nerve called kurma-nadi,
the yogi is able to be completely motionless.

Patanjali is not a speculator. He is not an airy, fairy philosopher; he is very down to earth. He means business, as I mean business. His approach is scientific. The very approach makes him totally different from others: others have been thinking about the truth; he is not thinking about the truth, he simply prepares you to receive the truth.

The truth cannot be thought; it can only be received. It is already there and there is no way to think about it. The more you think, the farther away you will wander from it; thinking is a wandering, a rambling in the clouds. The moment you think, you are already going away—the truth has to be seen, not thought.

Patanjali's basic approach is how to create the clarity, the eyes, which can see it. Of course, it is going to be hard work; it is not just poetry and dreaming. A man has to become a lab, a man has to transform his whole life into an experiment—only then can the truth be realized.

So while listening to Patanjali's sutras, never forget it, that he is not handing you some theories, he is giving you a methodology that can transform you. But then it depends on you.

There are four types of people who become interested in religion. The first, the majority, is only curious, is in search of something amusing, something outlandish, something interesting, something fascinating. Patanjali is not for those, because a curious person is never so deeply interested that he can be convinced to transform his life. He is looking for a sensation. Patanjali is not for those people.

Then there is a second type we will call the student. He is interested intellectually; he would like to know what this man Patanjali is thinking, saying—but he is interested in knowledge. Not in *knowing*, but knowledge. He is interested in gathering more information. He is not ready to change himself; he would like to remain himself and gather more knowledge. He is on an ego trip. Patanjali is not for that type either.

Then there is the third type, the disciple. A disciple is one who is ready to discipline his life, who is ready to transform his whole being in an experiment, who is courageous enough to go on this inner adventure—which is the greatest, which is the most daring, because nobody knows where one is moving. One is moving into the unknowable. One is moving into the abyss. One is moving into the uncharted. Yoga is for the disciple; the disciple will be able to get in tune with Patanjali.

Then there is the fourth state, or the fourth type; I will call it the devotee. The disciple is ready to change himself, but still not ready to sacrifice himself. The devotee is ready to sacrifice himself.

The disciple will go far enough with Patanjali, but not to the very end, unless he becomes a devotee also, unless he comes to recognize that the transformation that religion is concerned about is not a modification. It is not just modifying you, making you better and better; it is a death, and one has to sacrifice oneself totally. It is a discontinuity with your past.

When the disciple is ready, not only to transform himself but to die, he becomes a devotee. But a disciple can go far enough, and if he goes, one day or another he will become a devotee. If he becomes a devotee, only then will he understand the whole of Patanjali, the whole beauty of it, the whole grandeur of it, the tremendous door that Patanjali opens into the unknown.

But, many people who were just curious have written many books about Patanjali. Many people who were just students have created great tomes of learning, scholarship, and they have done much harm. They have interpreted and reinterpreted Patanjali these 5,000 years. Not only that, there are interpretations of interpretations of interpretations. The whole thing has become almost like a jungle and it is very difficult to find where Patanjali is.

This calamity has happened in India to everybody who has brought any truth to human consciousness. People have been continuously interpreting, and they create more clouds than clarity, because in the first place they are not disciples. And even if they are disciples, they are not in that state of mind where they can rightly interpret. Only a devotee . . . but devotees ordinarily don't bother.

Hence, I have taken Patanjali to talk about. The man needs great attention because there are very, very rare people who can be compared to the height of Patanjali, to his scientific attitude. He has made religion almost a science. He has brought religion out of all mystifications, but the interpretations have been trying to force all his sutras back again into the world of mystifications. That is a vested interest. If Patanjali comes back and looks at the interpretations that have been done on his sutras, he will not be able to believe it.

And words are very dangerous things. You can play with them very easily. And words are like whores; you can use them but you can never trust them. And they change meaning with every new interpreter—just a slight change, just a comma from here to there. And Sanskrit is a very poetic language—each word has many meanings, so it is very easy to mystify a thing, very easy.

I have heard, once two friends stayed in a hotel. They were travelling in the mountains and they wanted to go early in the morning—very early, nearabout three o'clock—to the nearest peak to see the sunrise, so they had fixed the alarm. When the alarm rang, one, who was an optimist, said, 'Good morning, God.' The other, who was a pessimist, said, 'Good God, morning?'

They both used the same words, but with a tremendous difference.

I have heard a Sufi story:

Two disciples of a master were sitting in the garden of the monastery, meditating.

One said, 'It would be good if we were allowed smoking.'

The other said, 'It will not be possible; the master will never allow it.'

They said, 'Why not try? There is nothing to lose. We should ask him.'

The next day, they asked the master. To the first, he said, 'No, absolutely no.' To the other, he said, 'Yes, certainly yes.'

When they met, they could not believe—what type of man is this? Then the one asked, 'Please, tell me how you had asked.'

The first, to whom was said no, absolutely no, said, 'I asked him, 'Sir, can I smoke while meditating?' He said, "No, absolutely no!"' Then he asked, 'And what had you asked?'

He said, 'Now I know. I had asked, "Sir, can I meditate while smoking?" He said, "Yes, certainly yes!"'

It makes a lot of difference. Words are whores, and one can go on playing infinitely with words.

I am not an interpreter. Whatsoever I am saying is on my own authority—I am not saying it on the authority of Patanjali. Because my experiences and his experience correspond, that's why I am speaking on him. But I am not trying to prove the authority of Patanjali. How can I prove that? I am not trying to prove that Patanjali is true. How can I prove that? I can only say something about myself. What am I saying then?—I am saying this: that I have also experienced the same. And Patanjali has given it beautiful language and expression. It is difficult to improve upon Patanjali as far as scientific explanation, scientific expression, is concerned. Remember this.

If he comes back, he will be almost in a state . . . I was reading one story and I remembered him. It happened on a road:

On a road, three thieves saw a man on a donkey entering the town. Following the donkey was a goat with a tinkling bell around its neck.

One of the thieves said proudly, 'I am going to steal his goat.'

The second thief said, 'That's not such a big thing. I am going to steal the donkey he is sitting on.'

The third thief said, 'I will steal the clothes he is wearing.'

The first thief followed the man and on a street corner fastened the bell onto the tail of the donkey and stole the goat. The bell kept tinkling, and the villager thought the goat was still following.

The second thief, who was waiting by another corner, faced the man and said, 'A new custom, huh? Hanging the bell on the donkey's tail?'

The man looked behind and exclaimed, 'My goat is gone!'

The thief said, 'I just saw someone with a goat going by that road.'

'Keep an eye on my donkey,' the man said and ran to get the goat.

The thief then rode away on the donkey.

The man searched the road in vain for the thief who stole his goat. Then he came back for his donkey and saw what had happened. He walked a while in distress until he came across someone who was sitting by a well, crying.

'What is the matter with you? They have stolen my goat and donkey; why are you wailing like this?'

'I had a treasure chest that fell into the well. I am too afraid to go in. If you get the chest, I will go fifty-fifty with you.'

Anxious to compensate for his losses, the villager quickly undressed and went into the well. When he came out, empty-handed, he saw his clothes gone. He began to wield a big stick, whirling and whirling around. People gathered to watch.

'They stole everything I had. Now I am afraid they might try to steal me, too!'

That will be the situation if Patanjali comes back: interpretations have taken everything away. They have stolen all: they have not even left his clothes on. And they have done it so beautifully that you would never even suspect. In fact, after 5,000 years, things that I am saying will look very strange to people who have been reading Patanjali's interpreters, commentators. My things will look very strange. They will think I am giving new meanings. I am not giving new meanings, but Patanjali has been misinterpreted so long that if I exactly say what he meant, my sayings will look very strange, outlandish—almost unbelievable.

The last sutra was about the 'sun.' It looks natural to think about the sun in the solar system; that's how all the commentators have interpreted it. It is not so: the 'sun' is concerned with your sex mechanism—the source of all vitality, energy, heat within you.

In English, you have the expression and the name for a certain combination of nerves: you call it *solar plexus*. But people think that the solar plexus exists inside the navel. That is wrong. The solar energy exists in the sex centre, not in the navel, because it is from there that your whole body gets the heat, the warmth. But the explanation may look far-fetched; so let me explain it to you more. And then there are others—the moon, the stars, and the polestar.

The words simply indicate as if Patanjali is talking in astrological or astronomical terms about the solar system. He is talking about your inner cosmos. Man is a whole system, and corresponding to everything outside, there exists something within man: man is almost a miniature universe.

Man can be divided into two types: the sun type and the moon type. The sun type is aggressive; the sun type is violent, outgoing, extrovert. The moon type is introvert, ingoing, nonaggressive, passive, receptive. Or you can call them yang and yin; or you can call them the male and the female. The male is outgoing, the female is ingoing. The male is positive; the female is negative. Their functioning is different because they function from different centres. The man functions from the sun centre, the woman functions from the moon centre.

So, in fact, when a man becomes mad, he should not be called a lunatic. Only when a woman becomes mad, she should be called a lunatic; the word *lunatic* comes from *lunar*—moonstruck. When a man becomes mad, he is sunstruck; he is not moonstruck, and when a man becomes mad, he becomes aggressive, violent. When a woman becomes mad, she goes simply crazy, eccentric.

When I use the words *man* and *woman*, I don't mean exactly all men and all women, because there are men who are more feminine than male and there are women who are more male than feminine. So don't get confused. A man can be moon-oriented and a woman can be sun-oriented; it depends from where their energy is getting its supply, from what source. The moon has no energy source of its own; it simply reflects the sun. It is a reflective mechanism, that's why it is so cool. It transforms the energy from hot to cool. The woman also gets energy from the sex centre, but it passes through the moon.

The moon is the hara. Just below the navel, two inches below the navel, there is a centre; Japanese call it hara. Their word is perfect. That's why they call suicide 'hara-kiri' because the moon centre is the centre of death—just as the sun centre is the centre of life. All life comes from the sun; all death from the moon.

Gurdjieff used to say that man is food for the moon. In fact, he was saying something very close to Patanjali—and he was one of the men who was very close, but in the West, people could not understand what he meant. He used to say that everything is food for something else. Everything has to be food for something else in the ecology of existence. You eat something: you have to be eaten by something else, otherwise the continuity will be broken and the circle will be broken. Man eats fruit; fruits are eating the solar energy, the earth, the water. Man must be eaten in his own turn by something. Who eats man? Gurdjieff used to say that the moon eats man. He was a very eccentric man. His expressions are not scientific; his expressions are apparently very absurd. But if one goes deep in them, one will find pure diamonds there.

Now the first sutra:

Chandre tara vyuha gyanam.

*By performing samyama on the moon,
knowledge concerning the arrangement of the stars is gained.*

So the moon is the hara, just two inches below the navel. If you hit hard there, you will die; not even a single drop of blood will come out, and you will die. And there will be no pain. That's why Japanese can die so easily; nobody else can do that. They simply strike a knife into the hara—but they know exactly where it is—and they disappear. The body is disconnected from the soul.

The moon centre is the death centre. That's why men are so much afraid of women. They come to me—so many men—and they say that they are afraid of women. What is the fear? The fear is because woman is the hara, the moon—she eats man.

That's why men have always tried to keep women under control; otherwise she will eat, she will destroy them. Women have always been forced to remain in a certain bondage. Try to understand the phenomenon.

Why, all over the world, has man always been putting women into forced slavery? Why? There must be some fear, some deep fear of women, that if women are allowed freedom, men will not be able to live. And there is truth in it.

Men can have only one orgasm at a time; a woman can have multiple orgasms. A man can make love to only one woman at a time; a woman can make love to as many people as she wants. If a woman is allowed total freedom, no man will be adequate enough to satisfy her—no man. Now the psychologists agree with this. All the recent research of Masters and Johnson and the reports of Kinsey, they all have come to one point that is absolutely certain: that no man is adequate enough to satisfy a woman sexually. If they are allowed freedom, a group of men will be needed to satisfy a woman.

One man, one woman, cannot live together—if total freedom is allowed. Then the woman will demand that she is not satisfied yet, and that will become a death.

Sex energy gives you life. The more you use sex energy, the more death comes closer. Hence, yogis became so afraid of releasing sex energy, and they started conserving it; because they wanted to prolong life so their work on themselves is completed, so they don't die before their work is complete, because then they have to start it again.

Sex gives you life. The moment sex energy leaves your body, you are going towards death. There are many small insects that die in one sexual orgasm. There are a few spiders who die on their girlfriend; just making love they die. They make love once, and not only that, you will be surprised, when they die—and they die coupled together—the girlfriend starts eating them. She actually eats them. Because what to do with a dead boyfriend? And this is true that in all sex relationships the man becomes by and by afraid.

Woman gets energy out of sexual love, man loses energy, because woman's hara is functioning: she transforms the hot energy into cool energy. She is a receptivity; she is a passive opening, a welcome. She absorbs energy; man loses energy.

This hara centre, or call it the moon, exists in men also, but is nonfunctioning. It can function only if much effort is put to transform it, to bring it to activity.

The whole science of Tao is nothing but to make the moon centre function fully. That's why the whole Tao attitude is receptive, feminine, passive. Yoga is also on the same way, but from a different angle. Yoga tries to bring solar energy—the sun energy—inside the body, works on the sun energy and the path on which the sun energy has to move, and brings it to the moon. Tao and tantra work on the moon, make it more receptive, more magnetic, so it pulls the solar energy toward itself. Yoga is a sun method, Tao and tantra are moon methods, but the work is the same.

All the yoga exercises are to channel the sun energy towards the moon, and all the Tao and tantra exercises are to make the moon so magnetic that it pulls all the energy that is created by the sun centre and transforms it.

That's why a Buddha or a Mahavira or a Patanjali or Lao Tzu, when they attain to their total, absolute flowering, look more feminine than like men. They lose all corners that men have; they become more round. Their body becomes more feminine. They attain to a certain grace, which is feminine. Their eyes, their faces, their walking, their sitting—everything becomes more close to feminine. They are no longer aggressive, no longer violent.

'By performing samyama on the moon, knowledge concerning the arrangement of the stars is gained.' If you bring your samyama, your witnessing, to the hara centre, you will become able to know all the stars within your body—all the centres within your body— because when you are focused on the sun centre you are so excited, you are so feverish, that you cannot attain to clarity. To attain to clarity, one has to come first to the moon. The moon is a great phenomenon of transforming energy.

Just see. In the sky, also, the moon gets the energy from the sun; then it reflects it. It has no energy of its own, it simply reflects, but changes its quality so totally. Look at the moon and you will feel peace; look at the sun and you will start getting mad. Look at the moon and you will feel a calmness surrounding you. Buddha attained to his final enlightenment on a full moon night.

In fact, all those who have attained have always attained in the night. Not a single human being has become enlightened in the day: Mahavira became enlightened in the night, it was the no moon night, *amawas*; the night was totally dark. Buddha became enlightened on the full moon night, *purnima*. But both became enlightened in the night. As yet it has not happened that a man has become enlightened in the day. It will not happen, because for enlightenment the energy has to move from the solar to the lunar, because enlightenment is a cooling down of all excitement, of all tensions: it is a great relaxation—the ultimate relaxation. There is no movement in it.

Try to do it: whenever you have time, just close your eyes . . . In the beginning, press the point just two inches below the navel with your fingers to feel it, and become aware of it. Your breathing goes up to that point. When you breathe naturally, your belly goes up, falls down, goes up, falls down. By and by, you will see that your breathing exactly touches the hara; it has to touch it. That's why when breathing stops, you die: the breathing is no longer touching the hara, the hara is disconnected. Once the hara is disconnected, you die; death comes from the hara.

When a man is young, he is solar, when a man is old, he becomes lunar. When a woman is young, she is lunar, when she becomes old, she becomes solar. That's why many women will start growing moustaches when they become old; they are becoming solar. The wheel turns. Many men, when they become old, become nagging. Old people are very nagging, irritated, continuously in anger—angry at each and anything. They are becoming lunar. They have not transformed their energies; they have lived an accidental life. Women become more aggressive in old age because their lunar is exhausted, they have used it. Now their solar part is still fresh, new, can be used.

Men in their old age start taking the style of women and they start doing things that were never expected of them. For example, in everything woman and man differ. If a man becomes angry, he would like to hit; if a woman becomes angry, she will talk and nag and . . . but she will not hit. She is not aggressive; she is passive.

I have heard one anecdote:

A woman lecturer was going great guns. 'Yes,' she cried, 'women have suffered in a thousand ways!'

She paused for effect.

A meek little man in the front row raised his hand. 'I know one way in which they have never suffered,' he said.

The lecturer fixed a stern eye upon him. 'What way is that?' she demanded.

'They have never suffered in silence,' said the man.

The passive energy becomes a nagging. Have you observed? Girls start talking before boys. Almost always they are ahead as far as language is concerned; in schools and colleges, universities, they are always ahead of the boys as far as language is concerned. A girl starts talking six or eight months before a boy starts talking. And a girl becomes very proficient in talking, very soon—almost perfect. She may talk nonsense, but she talks efficiently. The boy lags behind. He can fight, he can run, he can be aggressive, but he is not so articulate.

The energies function in different ways: the moon energy, if life is not going well, becomes sad; the sun energy, if life is not going well, becomes angry. So women become sad; men become angry. If a man feels something is wrong, he would like to do something about it. A woman will wait.

If a man is angry, he would like to kill somebody. If a woman is angry, she would like to commit suicide. The first thing that comes to a man in anger is to murder, to kill. The first thing that comes to a woman in anger is to commit suicide, to destroy oneself.

Have you seen husbands and wives fighting? The husband starts beating the wife; the wife starts beating herself. The functioning is different.

But a perfect man needs to have a synthesis of both the energies—solar and lunar. When both the energies are fifty-fifty and balanced, one attains to tranquility. When man and woman are balanced within you, you come to have a stillness that is not of this earth. The sun cancels the moon, the moon cancels the sun, and you remain there undisturbed . . . you remain there in your absolute being, with no movement, with no motivation, with no desire.

And once you can feel the hara functioning and your sun energy being transformed by the hara, you will see many things within you. You will see all the stars. What are these stars?—your centres are the stars.

Each centre is a star in your inner sky, and each centre has to be known and you have to bring your samyama on it, because it has many mysteries hidden behind it. It will reveal them to you. You are a great book—the greatest—and unless you read yourself, all reading is useless.

When Socrates and men like Socrates say, 'Know thyself,' they mean this. They mean that you have to know the whole territory of your inner being, in every bit. Every nook and corner has to be travelled, light has to be brought, and then you will see what you are—a cosmos as infinite as the outer cosmos, and in one way greater than it because you are conscious also; because you are not only alive, you know that you are alive because you can become a witness also.

Dhruva tadgati gyanam.

By performing samyama on the polar star,
knowledge of the movement of the stars is gained.

And what is the polar star in your inner being? The polar star is very symbolic. Mythologically, it is thought that the polar star is the only star that is absolutely unmoving. It is not true—it moves, but very slowly. But it is symbolic: something in you has to be found which does not move at all. Only that can be your nature, only that can be your being: something like a polestar—*dhruva*—unmoving, absolutely unmoving, because when there is no movement, eternity is there, when there is movement: time.

Movement needs time; no movement needs no time. If you move, there will be a beginning and an end. All movement starts and ends; there will be a birth and death. But if there is no movement, then you are beginningless, endless; then there is no birth, no death.

So where is the polestar within you? That's what yoga call *sakshin*, the witness. The witness is the polestar. First bring your samyama on the solar energy because that is where you exist ordinarily, biologically. That is where you find yourself. That is already given. Transform it to lunar energy: become more cool, collected, calm. Let the excitement, the feverishness, the heat be gone, dispersed, so that you can watch the inner sky. And then the first thing to find is: who is the watcher. That is the polestar because the watcher is the only thing that is unmoving within you.

Now let me explain it to you. You are angry, but you cannot remain angry forever. Even the angriest man laughs sometimes, has to. It cannot become a permanent state of affairs, being angry. Even the saddest man smiles, and even the man who laughs continuously sometimes cries and weeps and tears come to his eyes. Emotions cannot be permanent, that's why they are called *emotions*; the word comes from *motion*, movement. They move, hence they are emotions. From one to another, you continuously change. This moment you are sad, that moment you are happy;

this moment you are angry, that moment you are very compassionate; this moment you are loving, another moment full of hatred; the morning was beautiful, the evening is ugly. This goes on.

This cannot be your nature, because behind all these changes, something is needed like a thread which holds all of them together. Just as in a garland you see flowers, you don't see the thread; but the thread is the one which is holding all the flowers. So these are all flowers: sometimes anger flowers, sometimes sadness flowers, sometimes happiness, sometimes pain, sometimes anguish. But these are all flowers, and your whole life is the garland. There must be a thread; otherwise, you would have fallen apart long before. You continue as an entity, so what is the thread, the polestar? What is permanent in you?

That is the whole search of religion: what is permanent in you. If you go on being concerned and engaged with the non-permanent, you are in the world. The moment you change your attention toward that which is permanent in you, you are becoming religious.

Sakshin: the witness. You can witness your anger. You can witness your sadness. You can witness your anguish. You can witness your blissfulness. The witness remains the same. Or, for example, in the night you sleep. The day is gone and the image that you carried the whole day, of who you are, is also gone. You may have been a very rich man in the day. In the night, in a dream, you may become a beggar.

Emperors tend to become beggars in their dreams; beggars tend to become emperors in their dreams, because a dream is a completion. Even an emperor sometimes feels jealous of beggars because they move on the street so free, unconcerned, as if they have nothing to do and the whole world to enjoy. And he watches them sitting in the sun and enjoying sunlight, sunrays. He cannot do that; he has too many other things to do. He is so occupied. He sees them singing in the night under the stars. He cannot do that—it won't look good for an emperor. He feels jealous. In the night, emperors dream they have become beggars. Beggars dream they have become emperors because they are jealous. They see the palaces, the riches, the merriment that goes on. They would also like to have it.

So whatsoever is lacking, comes into your dreams; your dream is a complementary thing. If you study your dreams, you will know what is lacking in your life. The moment nothing is lacking, dreams disappear. So an enlightened person never dreams, he cannot dream. It is impossible for him to dream because nothing is lacking. He is contented, absolutely contented. If he is a beggar, he is so contented that he is already an emperor in his beggarliness.

Once it happened, a great Sufi mystic, Ibrahim, used to live with a beggar. Ibrahim renounced his throne because he saw the falsity and the foolishness of it, and he was a courageous man. He left his kingdom and he became a beggar. Then one beggar accompanied him for a few days. The beggar would pray every night to God, 'God, do something. Why have you made me so poor? The whole world is enjoying. Just I am left out of it. Not even bread enough to eat, no clothes to wear, no shelter to live. Do something! Sometimes, I start suspecting whether you are there or not because my prayers remain unfulfilled.'

Ibrahim listened to this prayer once, twice, thrice; then one day he said, 'Wait. It seems you have got your poverty without paying the price.'

The beggar said, 'Price for poverty? What do you mean? What are you talking about? Has poverty also to be paid for?'

Ibrahim said, 'Yes, I have paid for it with my whole kingdom and then I know the beauty of it. You have got it free of charge, so you don't know what poverty is. You don't know the freedom that it brings; you don't know the weightlessness that it brings. You don't know what poverty is. First you need to suffer like a rich man; then you will know. I have known both; I am contented.'

'In fact,' Ibrahim said, 'I cannot pray because I cannot find anything to pray for. At the most, I can say, "Hello, God. Thank you." Finished. There is nothing to say. I am so contented.'

An enlightened person cannot dream: he is so contented. And I say to you, he will not even say, 'Hello, God. Thank you.' Why disturb him? Or he will say it once, and every day he will say, 'Ditto.' What is the point of saying it? And, in fact, he knows already that your whole heart is saying hello, thank you. What is the point of saying it?

In the night, you dream and you forget your image that you carried the whole day. You may be a great scholar in the day, then you forget. You may be a king, and you forget. Or you may be a great ascetic, who has renounced the world, and in dreams beautiful women surround you and you forget that you are an ascetic, a monk, and this is not good . . . . All that is good and bad in the day is gone because you are absolutely someone different; the mood has changed, the climate has changed. But one thing remains permanent: in the day if you watch your activities—walking on the street, eating food, going to office, coming home, being angry, being loving—if you watch, in the night also you can watch, and you can go on watching that this is a dream. So, in a dream, I have become an emperor? Good. You can go on watching.

In twenty-four hours, only one thing can be permanent, and that is the watcher, the witness. That is the polestar inside you.

'By performing samyama on the polar star, knowledge of the movement of the stars is gained.' And remember, first Patanjali says performing samyama on the moon, the arrangement of the stars is gained—which star is which, and where. By performing samyama on the polar star, sakshin, the movement of the stars is known, because the movement can be known only against something that is permanent. If nothing is permanent, movement cannot be known; and if everything is moving and you don't have a permanent base, unmoving base, how can you know movement?

That's why you cannot feel the movement of the earth. The

earth is moving, as fast as you can imagine. It is a spaceship. It is continuously moving: whirling on its centre and at the same time, running fast around the sun. Day in, day out, year in, year out, it goes on and on and you never feel it—because everything else is running with the same speed: the trees, the houses, you, everything. It is impossible to feel it because there is no point of contrast. Just think of yourself as if you had a small thing to stand on—the whole earth moves, you are not moving—then you will know. You will get almost dizzy; it is going so fast. Then you will not be able to be in Pune; sometimes it is Philadelphia passing, sometimes it is Tokyo passing, sometimes . . . and continuously the earth is moving, revolving.

And it is moving so fast, but to know it, to feel it, you need a non-moving base. That's why man lived for so many centuries on the earth and just 300 years ago, through Galileo and Copernicus, we came to know that the earth moves. Otherwise, for millennia we had been thinking that the earth is the centre, unmoving centre, everything else moves in the world—all the stars, the sun and moon—only the earth is unmoving: this is the centre.

Inside, also, everything is moving except the sakshin, the witness. Except your awareness, everything is constantly moving. Once you know this witness, you will be able to see how fast everything else is moving.

Now a very complicated thing has to be understood. For example, I talked up to now in terms as if the centres are static. They are not. Sometimes the sex centre is in the head, moving; that's why the mind becomes so sexual, you go on thinking and fantasizing. Sometimes, the sex centre is in your hands, and you would like to touch a woman. Sometimes, the sex centre is in your eyes, and whatsoever you see, you turn it into a sexual object; you become pornographic—whatsoever you see, immediately it turns into a sex object. Sometimes, the centre is in the ears; whatsoever you hear makes you sexual. It is possible to go to a temple and listen to *bhajans*, divine, devotional singing, and feel sexual if your centre is at that moment in the ears. And you will be very worried, 'What is happening? I am in the temple; I have come as a devotee. And what is happening?'

And sometimes it is possible, you may be sitting by your girlfriend, your wife, and she is available—not only available, welcoming, waiting—and you don't feel sexual at all: the sex centre is not at the sex centre where it should be. Sometimes, it happens when you fantasize about sex, you enjoy much; when you make love to a woman, you enjoy nothing—nothing at all. What happens? You don't know where your centre is. When one becomes sakshin, one becomes alert where the centre is, and then much is possible.

When it is in your ears, it gives energy to your ears; those are the moments when you can train the ear and you can become a musician. When it is in your eyes, those are the moments you can become a painter, an artist; then you look at the trees and they will be greener than they are; then the roseflowers will have a different blooming quality to them, you will project. When the sex centre is on the tongue, you can become a great orator—you can hypnotize people; a single word from you, and it goes to the very heart of your listeners, they are hypnotized. There are right moments . . . . If your sex centre is in your eyes, you can just look at someone and he will be hypnotized; you can become a hypnotist, you will have hypnotic power. When the sex centre is in your hands, touch anything and it becomes gold, because sex is energy and life.

And the same is for the moon.

Up to now, I talked about their static locations. Ordinarily, they are found there, but nothing is static, everything is revolving.

If your death centre is in your hands and you are a physician, give the medicine and the patient will die. Do whatsoever you will and you will not be able to save your patient. In India, they say, 'That doctor has the hands of a physician: whatsoever he touches, becomes medicine.' And some other doctor, 'Don't go near him: you bring a small disease to him, and he will magnify it and you will come back worse than you had gone there.'

The yogi becomes alert. In ayurveda, which evolved by the side of yoga in the ancient India, a physician had to be a yogi also; unless you are a yogi, you cannot be a real physician, you cannot be a real healer. The physician had to watch his own inner arrangement before he would go to the patient to see and treat him. If the death centre is in the hands, he will not go. If the death centre is in his eyes, he will not go. The death centre should be in the hara and the life centre in his hands, then he will go: a right arrangement of things.

Once you know your inner world, many things become possible. You have also observed it sometimes, but you don't know what is happening. Sometimes you don't do anything, and you go on being successful. And sometimes you do such hard work and nothing succeeds, everything fails. Your arrangement is not right. You are functioning through a wrong centre.

When a warrior goes to the war, to the war front, he should go when the death centre is in his hands. Then . . . then he can kill very easily. Then he is death incarnate. That is the meaning of an 'evil eye'—the man whose death centre has got fixed into the eyes. If he looks at you, you will be in trouble; his very look is a curse.

And, there are people whose eyes have become fixed with the life centre. They look, and you feel a blessing; they look, and you feel blessed. They look at you, and something, something *alive*, showers on you.

'By performing samyama on the polar star, knowledge of the movement of the stars is gained.'

Nabhi chakre kaya vyuha gyanam.

By performing samyama on the navel centre, knowledge of the organization of the body is gained.

The navel centre is the centre of your body, because it is through the navel centre that you were fed by your mother in the womb. For nine months you existed only by the navel centre; you were connected with the navel, it was the passage, the bridge. And when the navel centre was disconnected from the mother and the cord was cut, you became an independent being. Your navel is tremendously significant as far as the body is concerned.

'*By performing samyama on the navel, knowledge of the organization of the body is gained.*' And the body is a great, complicated mechanism, very delicate. In your single body, there are millions of cells; in your small head, there are millions of nerves. Scientists have developed many complicated mechanisms, but nothing to compare with the human body—and there seems to be no possibility that they will ever be able to create such a complicated mechanism, functioning so well. It is a miracle. And functioning so automatically; and continuously, it functions for seventy or even a hundred years.

Everything is made as if perfect. It is a self-perpetuating system: eats, whenever you are hungry, creates hunger; when you have eaten well, gives you an indication—stop; digests, makes blood and bones and marrow; and continuously goes on cleaning itself, because so many cells are dying every moment that have to be thrown out. Creating, cleaning, maintaining itself; and everything is automatic.

If you follow a natural way of life, the body functions so beautifully, it hums so beautifully.

By knowing the navel centre, you will be able to know the whole mechanism of the body; that's how yoga physiology was known. It has been known not from the outside; it has not been known by post-mortem reports. Because yoga says when a man is dead, whatsoever you know about him is not true about a man who is alive, because a dead man is totally different from an alive man. Now scientists are coming to guess it, that the post-mortem at the most is a guess, because when a man is dead, the body functions one way and when a man is alive, it functions differently, so whatsoever we know about the dead body is, at the most, approximately true about the living body, but not exactly true.

Yoga came to know from the inside. Yoga discovered the physiology with full life and awareness. That's why there are many things which yoga talks about and modern physiology will not agree with, because modern physiology is of a dead man, of a corpse, and yoga is concerned with life.

Just think. When the electricity is flowing through the wires, you cut the wires; then you will have one experience. When the electricity has stopped flowing, then cut the wires; you will have another experience. And these are totally different.

You dissect a dead body. And you cannot dissect an alive body because by the time you dissect, it will be dead. So one day or another, physiologists have to agree with yoga research that if you want to know the alive body, when the electricity is flowing and one is vital, then somehow one has to go deep within oneself and from there, from that vantage point of view, one has to know what the body is, how it is arranged.

When you go into a dead body, it is going into a house whose owner has left it. You may come across furniture, but you will not come across the owner. When you go inside a house when the owner is there, he fills, his presence fills, the whole house. When you are present in the body, your presence is making every cell qualitatively different. When you are gone, then just a dead thing is left, just matter.

By performing samyama on the throat,
there comes a cessation of the feelings of hunger and thirst.

These are the inner investigations. Yoga came to know that if you are hungry, the hunger is not exactly in the stomach. When you are thirsty, it is not exactly in the throat. The stomach gives the information to the brain, and then the brain gives the information to you; it has some indications. For example, when you are feeling thirsty, the brain makes your throat feel thirsty.

When water is needed in the body, the brain creates a symptom in the throat, and you feel thirsty. When you need food, the brain creates something in the stomach, and you have hunger pangs.

But you can deceive the brain very easily: you can drink water with sugar—because the brain understands the language of the sugar only—so if you eat sugar, or drink sugar, immediately the brain thinks now there is no need; the hunger disappears. That's why people who eat too many sweets lose their appetite. Just a small quantity of sugar is not going to nourish you, but the brain has been befooled by you. Sugar is the language; immediately the brain thinks the sugar level has risen high, finished. It thinks you have eaten well and through the food the sugar level has risen high. You have simply taken a sugar pill; that is a deception.

Yoga came to know that by bringing samyama to certain centres, things can disappear. For example, if you bring samyama to the throat, you will feel that thirst has gone and hunger has gone. That's how yogis could fast so long. It is said about Mahavira that he fasted sometimes even three months, or four months, continuously. During the whole period of twelve years while he was meditating, he fasted almost eleven years. Three months he would fast, and then one day he would eat, then again one month he would fast, and two days he would eat; this way. In twelve years, he was eating only one year; that means in twelve days, one day of eating, eleven days of fasting, average.

How did he do it? How could he do it? It is almost impossible, humanly impossible. Yoga has some secrets.

If you concentrate on the throat—try: next time you feel thirsty, close your eyes, sit, and bring your total attention in the throat. Once the attention is there, you will see the throat is relaxing. Because whenever your total attention is at any point, you become separate from it. The throat is thirsty: you feel I am thirsty. If you bring your witnessing consciousness to it, suddenly you are separate. Your cooperation is broken. Now you know the throat is thirsty, not I. And how can a throat be thirsty without you?

How can the body be hungry without you? Have you ever

seen a dead man hungry or thirsty? Even if all the water disappears and evaporates from the body, a dead man will not feel thirst. Identification is needed.

Try it: next time you feel hungry, try it. Just close your eyes, go deep down into the throat . . . watch. You will see the throat as separate from you. The moment you will see the throat as separate from you, the body will stop saying that the body is hungry. The body cannot be hungry; only your identification with the body.

By performing samyama on the nerve called kurma-nadi,
the yogi is able to be completely motionless.

Kurma-nadi is the vehicle of *prana*: breathing. If you silently watch your breathing, not changing its rhythm in any way, neither making it fast nor slow, just leaving it natural and relaxed, and if you simply watch it, you will become absolutely still. There will be no movement in you. Why?—because all movement comes through breathing, prana. All movement comes through breathing. The movement exists in you through breathing. When breathing stops, a person is dead—he cannot move.

If you constantly bring your samyama to breathing, to kurma-nadi, by and by you will come to a state where you will see breathing has *almost* stopped. Yogis do this meditation facing a mirror because the breathing becomes so silent, they cannot feel it. They can only see whether there is some mist on the mirror from their breathing or not. Sometimes, they have become so silent that they cannot decide whether they are still alive or not. In deep meditation, this experience will happen to you also sometimes; don't be afraid. Breathing almost stops.

When consciousness is perfect, breathing almost stops. But don't be worried; that is not death. That is simply stillness. The whole effort of yoga is to bring you to such stillness that it cannot be broken by anything, to such a state of consciousness that cannot be disturbed.

I have heard:

A madman of the way, called at a shop and asked the businessman, 'What makes you sit here day in, day out?'
'In order to make profit.'
'What is profit?' asked the madman.
'It is the making of one into two,' said the businessman.
'This is not profit,' the madman said. 'Profit is when you can make two into one.'

That madman was not an ordinary madman; he must have been a realized man. He was a Sufi master.

Yes, profit is when you make two into one. Profit is when all duality disappears, when only one remains. The word *yoga* means the method of becoming one. Yoga means how to join together that which has fallen apart. The very word *yoga,* means 'joining together.' The word *yoga* means *unio mystica*. The word *yoga* means 'union.' Yes, profit is when you can make two into one.

And the whole effort is how to find the permanent, how to find the one behind the many, how to find the unmoving behind all the changes, the flux—how to find the deathless, how to find the beyond. Your habits will create trouble because you have lived with wrong habits for so long. Your mind is conditioned for wrong habits—you always divide. Your whole intellect has been trained to divide and dissect and make many out of one. Man has lived up to now through the intellect, and he has forgotten how to put them together.

A man came to a Mohammedan mystic, Farid, with golden scissors as a present; the scissors were really very beautiful and very valuable. But Farid laughed and said, 'What am I going to do with scissors, because I never cut a thing in two? You take them. Rather, bring me a needle—and no need to bring a golden needle, any needle will do—because my whole effort is to sew things together.'

But old habits are of dissecting. Old habits are of finding that which is continuously changing. The mind is excited about something new and the changing; the unchanging seems uninteresting. You will have to be aware of these habits, otherwise they will assert themselves in some way or the other—and the mind is very cunning.

Let me tell you one story:

Maulana Arshad Va'ez was a great preacher, very eloquent, but he was also a beggar.

Once the king called him to his court and said, 'Maulana, on the recommendations of my ministers, I am sending you as a delegate to Shah Shoja's court in Shiraz. However, I want you to promise me that you will refrain from begging during your stay abroad—because I would not like my representative to beg, so you have to promise.'

Maulana did as asked and set out for Shiraz.

After bringing his mission to a successful termination, he was addressed by the Shah of Shiraz, 'The fame of your preaching has reached to our land and has made us desirous of listening to one of your sermons.'

Maulana consented.

On the appointed day, Friday, he climbed to the pulpit and delivered a moving sermon, bringing tears to the eyes of his audience. But before he had left the pulpit, suddenly, he could not resist his begging habit any longer.

He said, 'O Muslims! Until several weeks ago I used to beg. But before coming here, they made me take an oath that I would not beg during my stay in your city. I ask you, my brothers, if I have sworn to refrain from begging, have you too sworn not to give me anything?'

Mind is very cunning. It will find ways and means: 'If I cannot beg, you can give.'

Remember, that the mind is very much accustomed to analysis, and yoga is synthesis. So whenever the mind comes to analyse, put it aside, set it aside. Through analysis, you will reach the last, the minutest, the atomic; through synthesis, you will reach the greatest, the total. Science has come to discover the atom, and yoga came to discover *atma*; atom means the minutest, and atma means the biggest. Yoga came to know the whole, to realize the total; and science has come to know the smaller and the smaller and the smaller, and they go on.

First, science divided matter into molecules, and then they thought that the molecule is difficult to divide; then they succeeded in dividing it, then they called it the 'atom.' The word *atom* means indivisible, which cannot be divided anymore—but they divided that too. Then they came to electrons and neutrons and they thought now it cannot be divided because it has become almost invisible, it cannot be seen. Nobody has ever seen any electron, so how can you divide it? But now they have succeeded in dividing it also. Without seeing it, they have succeeded in dividing.

They will go on and on and on . . . . Everything has slipped out of hand.

Yoga is just the opposite process of synthesizing, of joining and joining and joining, so you come to the total. The total is one.

The mind is also divided into the sun mind or moon mind. The sun mind is scientific; the moon mind is poetic. The sun mind is analytical; the moon mind is synthetical. The sun mind is mathematical, logical, Aristotelian; the moon mind is totally different—illogical, irrational. They function so differently that there exists no language between them.

A gypsy was having a quarrel with his son. He said to the boy, 'You lazy, do-nothing idler! How many times shall I tell you that you should work and not let your life pass in indolence? How many times shall I tell you that you should learn juggling and clowning so that you can enjoy your life?'

Then he raised his finger in threat, saying, 'By God, if you don't listen to my words anymore, I will throw you in a school; then you will gather lots of stupid knowledge, become a learned man, and spend the rest of your life in want and misery.'

That's a gypsy mind—moon mind. A gypsy thinks: become a wanderer, be a clown, but enjoy. And the gypsy says, 'I will throw you in a school so that you will gather all sorts of stupid knowledge and become a learned man—and then your whole life will be wasted. You will live in misery.'

Try to see where you are: in the sun mind—rational, arguing, argumentative, logical; or in the moon mind—poetic, imaginative, dreaming. Where are you?

And, remember, both minds are half-half. One has to go beyond both. If you are in the sun mind, come to the moon mind first, because the way passes through that. If you are a householder, first become a gypsy.

That's what sannyas is. I make you gypsies, wanderers. If you are too logical, I say trust, surrender, sacrifice, submit. If you are too argumentative, I say to you I have no argument, just look at me, and fall in love—if you can. It is a love affair. If you can trust, you will shift your energy from the sun to the moon.

Once you shift your energy from the sun to the moon, then there opens a new possibility: you can go beyond the moon also. Then you become a witness. That is the goal.

Enough for today.

Four

Man Means Mind

The first question:

Osho, is it possible to be conscious of enlightenment, and be enlightened? Can the thought of being enlightened create ego in one? Kindly explain.

The first thing to be understood is: what is ego. The ego is not very substantial. In fact, it is not. It is just an idea, a substitute without which it will be difficult for you to live. Because you don't know who you are, you have to create a certain idea about yourself; otherwise, you will simply go mad. You have to fix some indicators so that you can know, 'Yes, this is me.'

I have heard, once a fool came to a big city. He stayed in a *dharmashala*. There were many people there—he had never slept before with so many people; he was a little worried and scared. The fear was that when he falls asleep, in the morning when he awakes again, how he will recognize that he is really himself? So many people . . . he had always slept in his room, alone, so there was no problem because there was no possibility. Of course, he was always himself, but here with so many people sleeping around, a crowd, he may get lost. It's okay while you are awake, you can continue remembering yourself, but while asleep, you may miss, you may forget, and in the morning you may be confused; you may be lost in the crowd.

Seeing him so worried and sitting on his bed, somebody asked, 'What is the matter with you? Why don't you go to sleep?' He explained his problem. The man laughed; he told him, 'This is very simple. Look in that corner; some child has left his balloon. Bring it and tie it to your foot so in the morning you will know perfectly that it is you if the balloon is there.'

The fool said, 'That's right.' And he had to sleep, he was so tired, so he fastened the balloon with a string to his foot and went to sleep.

The man played a joke: in the night, when the fool was snoring, he took the balloon off his foot and fastened it to his own foot. In the morning, when the fool looked around, he started crying and weeping. A crowd gathered, and they asked, 'What is the matter?'

He said, 'Now I know perfectly that he is me, but who am I?'

Now this is the problem.

The ego is because you don't know who you are. So a name, an address, a certain face that you have seen reflected in the mirror, in the photographs, the album—these all help. They are balloons fastened to you.

If suddenly, one day in the mirror you see that this is not the face you have always been accustomed to seeing, you will go mad—the balloon is missing. The face is constantly changing, but the change is so slow that you never recognize it. Just go back home and look at the album of your childhood. You know that it is you, which is why you don't see much difference, but just ponder over it, how much you have changed. The face is not you, because deep down something has remained permanent in you. And your name can be changed; I do it every day. I go on changing your names just to give you the feeling that the name is just a balloon fastened to you, it can be changed, so that you get disidentified with the name.

The ego is nothing but a false substitute for the self. So when you know who you are, there is no possibility of the ego arising again.

You ask me, '*Can the thought of enlightenment create an ego?*' The thought can create it if it is only a thought. Then, in fact, it is not good to say that it can create it: the ego is already there, the thought is already thought by the ego. If the ego has disappeared and you have really become enlightened—and that is the meaning of enlightenment: the shift from the ego to the self, the shift from the unreal to the real, the shift from the mind to no mind, the shift from the body to the embodied—once you know who you are, I cannot see that somebody can persuade you to tie a balloon to your feet to remember yourself. It is impossible.

An enlightened person cannot be egoistic, whatsoever he says. Their assertions may look very egoistic to you. Krishna says in the Gita to Arjuna, to his disciple, 'Leave everything and come to my feet. I am the very God who has created this world.' Very egoistic . . . Can you find a more egoistic person? Listen to what Jesus says: 'My father in heaven and I are both one.' He is saying, 'I am God.' Very egoistic . . . Mansoor declared, 'I am truth, the very truth, the ultimate truth'—'*ana'l haq*.' Mohammedans were very annoyed; they killed him. Jews killed Jesus. Very egoistic assertions? The Upanishads say, '*Aham brahmasmi*'—'I am the whole, the total.'

But they are not egoistic; you misunderstand them. Whatsoever they are saying is *true*.

I have heard about one man who was worried very much about his inferiority complex, so he went to an Adlerian psychoanalyst. And he said to the psychoanalyst, 'I am suffering very much from an inferiority complex. Can you help me?' The psychologist looked at him and said, 'But you are inferior. It is not a question of inferiority complex; you *are* inferior, so what can I do?'

When Krishna says, 'I am God,' he *is*—he is not being egoistic. What he can do? If he says, 'I am not,' that will be untrue. If he behaves politely, as the so-called mahatmas do—that I am just dust underneath your feet—he will be untrue, he will be false. He will be hiding the fact. When Mansoor says, 'I am the truth,' he is.

But the problem is not with Mansoor, Krishna, or Jesus; the problem is with you. You cannot understand the language of no ego. You go on interpreting it in your own ways.

Let me tell you one anecdote:

A grocer had a beautiful parrot, which kept him company, amused his customers, and in his absence took care of the shop.

One day when he stepped out for ablutions and the parrot was watching the shop from a top shelf, the grocer's cat jumped on a mouse without any warning. The parrot was so frightened that he flew across the shop and knocked down a jar of almond oil.

When the grocer returned, he saw the scene and was seized with anger. He took a stick and hit the parrot on the head repeatedly until the poor bird's skull was stripped of all its feathers.

The parrot, bald and rejected, sat on a corner shelf. For days, he didn't open his mouth. The grocer, who was now very remorseful of his act, tried every trick on his abused companion. He even sought his customers' help.

But it was all in vain; the parrot didn't talk.

One day, as the bird was sitting in his usual silence, a bald dervish came to the shop. Immediately, the parrot landed down on the counter and said, 'So you too knocked down a jar of almond oil!'

He understands that he has become bald because he knocked down an almond jar. Now there comes a dervish who is also bald, immediately the interpretation . . . We understand the language that we have lived up to now.

An enlightened person has no ego—has no humbleness either. Humbleness is a very polished ego; when ego disappears, humbleness also disappears.

An enlightened person knows who he is, so there is no need to carry a false identity. It was needed before, otherwise you would have got lost in the crowd, it would have been impossible to live without it. The ego is a need while you are ignorant, but when you become enlightened, it simply drops on its own accord. It is as if a blind man gropes with his stick when he walks; he can ask, 'When one's eyes are cured, does one carry a stick to grope, or not?' What will we say? We will say, 'When the eyes are cured, the stick is dropped. Who carries the stick? Why? And why should one grope when the eyes are there?' The stick and the groping are a substitute—a very poor substitute at that—but it is needed when one is blind.

Now the question has to be understood. *'Is it possible to be conscious of enlightenment, and be enlightened? Can the thought of being enlightened create ego in one?'* If the ego is there, there is no need to create it; it is already there and the thought of enlightenment is created by it. If the ego has dropped and *really* the awareness, the consciousness, the self, has arisen out of darkness, the sunrise has happened; then nothing can create the idea of the ego, nothing whatsoever. You can declare you are God; even that will not create the egoistic old pattern—nothing can create it.

'Is it possible to be conscious of enlightenment...?' Enlightenment is consciousness. Again you use your language; I can understand it, but it is wrong. You cannot be conscious of consciousness; otherwise, you will become a victim of infinite regression. Then you will be conscious of your consciousness of consciousness, and so on, so forth, ad infinitum. Then there will be no end: one consciousness, you will be conscious of it; a second consciousness, you will be conscious of it; a third consciousness . . . and you can go on. No, that is not needed; one consciousness is enough.

So when one is enlightened, *one is conscious*, but one is not conscious of consciousness. One is perfectly conscious, but there is no object in it. One is simply conscious, as if a light goes on enlightening the emptiness around it. There is no object; there is nothing the light can fall upon, it is pure consciousness. The object has disappeared; your subject has flowered into totality. Now there is no object—and hence, there can be no subject. The object and subject both have disappeared. You are simply conscious. Not conscious of anything, just conscious. You *are* consciousness.

Let me explain it to you from some other dimension that may be easier to understand. When you love—if you have ever loved—you are not a lover; you become love. Not that you do something: you are not a doer, so how can you call yourself a lover? The right expression will be that 'you are love.'

When people come to me and I see great promise in their eyes, I don't say, 'You are promising.' I say, 'You are *promise*.' See the difference: when somebody says to somebody, 'You are promising,' it is not much. But, 'You are promise'—it has tremendous value in it. When you say to somebody, 'You are promising,' you mean that this man appears to have something that you would like, or may be used for some ambition of yours. When a father says to the son, 'You are promising' he means, 'I wanted to become very rich; I could not do that. You will be able to do it—you are promising.' It is the father's ambition that he is seeing can be fulfilled through the son.

When I say to you, 'You are promise', I have no ambition to fulfil through you. I simply make a statement about you; it has nothing to do with my ambition. I am fulfilled. I am not desiring of any fulfilment through anybody. When I say, 'You are promise,' I make a statement of fact about you. It simply shows your potentiality, your possibility.

And see: if you are a musician, and your son is not going to be a musician, has no tendency, no desire, no talent; you will not call him promising. The same son may be promising to a father who is a mathematician, but he is not promising to you. If you are after money, and the son wants to renounce the world, he will not be promising to you; he will be just the opposite. When you call somebody promising, you relate him to your own desires.

When I say, 'You are promise', I mean you have a tremendous potentiality to grow, to flower—whatsoever the direction, whatsoever direction you choose to move.

Whenever you are in love, you will not feel that you are a lover. You will feel you are love. That's why Jesus says, 'God is love.' He should have said, 'God is very loving'; his language is not right. What do you mean by 'God is love'? He is saying 'God' and 'love' are synonymous. In fact, he is saying, 'God is love' is a tautology. It can be said that he is saying, 'Love is love,' or 'God is God.' Love is not an attribute of God; love is his very being. He is not loving, he is simply love.

The same happens when one becomes enlightened. He is not conscious about enlightenment; he is simply conscious. He lives in consciousness, he sleeps in consciousness, he moves in consciousness, he lives, he dies in consciousness. Consciousness becomes an eternal source in him, a non-flickering flame, a non-wavering state of being. It is not an attribute, it is not accidental, it cannot be taken away. His whole being is conscious.

The second question:

Osho, I am usually in two minds—sun and moon. Please comment.

Mind usually is in two minds, that's how mind functions. You will have to understand the whole mechanism of the mind, how it functions.

The functioning of the mind is to divide; if you don't divide, the mind disappears. The mind needs division. The mind creates opposites: the mind says, 'I like you; I don't like you. I love you; I hate you.' The mind says, 'This is beautiful; that is ugly.' The mind says, 'This has to be done; that has to be dropped.' The mind is choice; hence Krishnamurti's insistence that if you become choiceless, you will become no-mind. To become choiceless means to drop dividing the world.

Just think. If man disappears from the earth, will there be anything beautiful? Will there be anything ugly? Will there be anything good, anything bad? All divisions will simply evaporate with humanity. The world will remain the same. The flowers will flower, the stars will move, the sun will rise—everything will continue the same. But division will disappear with man; man brings division into the world. Man means mind.

That's the whole meaning of the Biblical story. God told Adam not to eat the fruit of the tree of knowledge. It would be better if we can translate the 'tree of knowledge' as 'tree of mind.' The whole story will become Zen. And that is exactly the meaning. The tree of knowledge is the tree of mind; otherwise, why should God want his children to be ignorant? No, he wanted them to live without mind; he wanted them to live without division, to live in unity, in unison. That's the meaning of the Biblical story. If a Zen master is to comment on it, or if I am to comment on it, I will say, 'Better to say the "tree of mind."' Then the whole thing becomes very clear.

God wanted Adam to live without mind. To live, but without dividing life—then life has a tremendous intensity. Division divides you also. Have you ever watched? Whenever you divide, something shrinks in you, something breaks in you. The moment you say, 'I like somebody,' a hand is extended towards that somebody. The moment you say, 'I don't like,' the hand shrinks back. You are not open to life in its totality. God wanted Adam to remain total.

And the Biblical story says that unless man drops his knowledge again, he will not be received back into the garden of God. Jesus dropped knowledge. That's why Jesus looks absurd, paradoxical. What Adam did against God, Jesus washed out, cleaned it away from human consciousness. Adam came out of the garden; Jesus entered again. How did Jesus enter again?—dropping the mind, the division.

Mind always functions through division. Just try not to divide. You see a flower: don't say it is beautiful, there is no need—it is beautiful without your saying so. You don't add any more beauty to it by saying so. So what is the point?

There is a small story about Lao Tzu. He used to go for a morning walk. A neighbour used to follow him. Knowing well that Lao Tzu doesn't want to talk much, he always kept himself silent. But once a friend was staying with the neighbour, and he also wanted to come, and he came. Lao Tzu and Lao Tzu's neighbour remained quiet, silent. The friend was a little embarrassed, but he also kept silent because the neighbour had told him not to say anything. Then the sun was rising, and it was so beautiful, and he forgot and said, 'So beautiful a morning.' Only this much . . . Nobody commented on it—neither his friend nor Lao Tzu.

Back home, Lao Tzu told the neighbour, 'Don't bring this man again. He is too talkative.'

Too talkative? Even the neighbour said, 'He has not said anything; he simply said, "How beautiful a morning."'

Lao Tzu said, 'I was also there, so what was the point of saying it? And it was beautiful without saying it. Why bring the mind in? No, this man is too talkative; don't bring him.'

He destroyed the whole morning? He divided the world: he said the sunrise was beautiful. Whenever you say something is beautiful, something has been already condemned, because the beauty cannot exist without the ugly. The moment you say something is beautiful, you have said that something else is ugly. The moment you say, 'I love you,' you have said that you hate somebody else.

If you live without dividing . . . just watch the flower, let it be there, whatsoever it is. Let it be in its reality, don't utter anything. Just see it: not only that you don't utter, don't say it inside also. Don't formulate any idea about it. Let it be there, and you will come to have a great realization.

When sadness comes to you, don't call it sadness. I have given this meditation to many people, and they become surprised. I tell them, 'Next time you feel sad, don't call it "sad," just watch it.' Your calling it sadness makes it sad. Just watch it, whatsoever it is. Don't bring the mind in, don't analyse, don't label it. The mind is such a great divider, and goes on continuously labelling things, categorizing. Don't categorize. Let the fact assert itself, let the fact be there, and you simply be a witness. Then, by and by, you will say, 'See, sadness is not sadness,' and happiness is not so much happiness as you used to think.

By and by, the boundaries merge, meet, and disappear. And then you will say, it is one energy: happiness, unhappiness, both are one. Your interpretation makes the difference, the energy is one. Ecstasy and agony are one. Your interpretation makes them two. The world and God are one. Your interpretation makes them two.

Drop the interpretation and see the real. The uninterpreted is the real; the interpreted is the illusory.

The question is: *'I am usually in two minds . . . .'* Mind is always in two minds; that's the way the mind functions, thrives, and lives.

Sun and moon: that has also to be understood. Because every man is also a woman and every woman is also a man.

Now, this is possible: you can remain divided inside—the man separate from the woman, the inner woman separate from the inner man. Then there will always be a conflict, a certain tug of war. This is the ordinary state of humanity. If your inner man and woman can meet, in a deep embrace, merge into each other; for the first time, you will become one—neither man nor woman. Then you will be transcendental.

Let me tell you a story, one of the very daring and courageous stories. Such a courageous story is possible only in India. Not today's India, because today's India has become very cowardly.

You must have seen a *lingam*, Shiva's symbolic representation as phallus. There are millions of temples devoted to Shiva's lingam. In fact, you will never find a statue of him; his statues have completely disappeared, only the symbol has remained. The symbol is not only a lingam, it is a *yoni* also; it is both, man and woman. It is man into woman, it is sun into moon, it is the male meeting the female, it is yin and yang in deep sexual embrace. This is an indication of how the inner man meets with the inner woman, because the inner has no face. That's why Shiva's statues have disappeared. The inner is just energy, so the lingam has no form, it is just energy.

But the story is told . . . don't be shocked by it, because the Western mind has become much too afraid of reality.

The story is that Shiva was making love to Devi, his consort. And of course when a Shiva makes love to his consort, it is no ordinary love. And he does not make love with closed doors; the doors were open. There was some emergency in the world of the gods, and Brahma and Vishnu and the whole crowd of gods came to ask Shiva's solution for some urgent problem. So they came into the room—the privacy of Shiva became a marketplace—but he was so deeply in love that he was not aware that a crowd was watching. All the gods became voyeurs; they could not leave, because something tremendous was happening, the energy was so high; they felt it. They could not leave. They could not disturb, because it was almost sacred.

And Shiva went on making love, and on and on and on. The gods became worried whether he was ever going to end it, and they were in such a problem that an urgent solution was needed. But Shiva was completely lost. He was not there, Devi was not there—the man and woman had completely merged into each other. Some unity had happened, a great synthesis, a great orchestra of energies.

They wanted to stay, but then they become afraid of the other gods. That's how the puritan mind works. They were very interested in seeing and watching, but they were afraid if others saw them watching and seeing and enjoying it, their prestige was at stake. So they all cursed Shiva: 'From today your form will disappear from the world and you will always be remembered as a phallic symbol': lingam in yoni, sun in moon, the jewel in the lotus. 'Now you will be always remembered as sexual orgasm.' This was a curse.

This always happens. I have one friend who is very against pornography, and his whole library is full of pornography. So once I visited him, I said, 'What is this?' He said, 'I have to read all the pornographic books just to criticize them. I have to be aware of what is happening in pornography because I am so much against it.' He is eating his cake and saving it also.

The other *devas* cursed Shiva, but to me that curse seems to have proved to be a blessing, because the symbol is really beautiful. It is the only phallic symbol in the world worshipped as God, without any condemnation. Hindus have completely forgotten that it is phallic; they don't think that it is phallic. They have accepted it deeply. The symbol is beautiful because there is not only Shiva there; there is yoni also. Yin is also there. The lingam is placed in yoni; both are meeting. It is a symbol of meeting, of orgasm, of energy becoming one.

The same happens inside, but it will happen only when you drop the mind. Love is possible only when you drop the mind. But if you drop the mind, then not only love but God also is possible, because love is God.

If an inner conflict exists in you between sun and moon, you will always be interested in the outer woman. If you are a man, you will be interested in the outer woman, you will be fascinated by the outer woman. If you are a woman, you will be fascinated by the outer man. Once the inner conflict is resolved and your sun energy is moving into the moon energy and there is no longer any rift, they are bridged; you will not be fascinated by the outer woman or outer man. For the first time, you will be sexually content.

I am not saying that you will leave the outer woman. There is no need. Or that you will leave the outer man—there is no need. But now the whole relationship will be totally different, very harmonious. It will not be a relationship of need; rather, it will be a relationship of sharing. Right now, when a man approaches a woman, it is a question of need. He wants to use the woman as a means. The woman wants to use the man as a means. That's why all women and all men are continuously in fight: basically, they are fighting within themselves. The same fight is reflected outwards.

And when you are using a woman, how can you think the woman can be totally at ease with you, in harmony? She feels she is being reduced to a means. And no man or woman is a means. She feels she is being used like a thing, reduced to thing-hood. Her soul seems to be lost; that's why she is angry. And she tries to reduce the man to a thing. She turns the husband into a henpecked husband; she forces him. And this goes on.

This is more a conflict than love—a struggle. More like war than like love, more like hatred than like love.

Once you are in tune with your inner woman and man, suddenly, you are in tune with others also. Your inner conflict disappears, your outer conflict disappears; the outer is just a shadow to the inner. Then you can be related, or you may not be related; you are totally independent. Then it is whatsoever you choose it to be. If you want to be related, you can be related, but there will be no conflict. If you don't want to be related, if you want to be alone, you can be alone and there will be no loneliness. This is the beauty, when one comes to an organic unity inside.

That's what Patanjali's whole effort is: how to transform the solar energy into lunar energy. And then, how to be a witness to both: meeting, merging, becoming one: how to be transcendental to them.

The mind will never allow you. Unless you drop the mind . . . the mind always is divided because that is its very blood; it depends on division. So you are a man, you are a woman—this is division, this is mind. Who is a buddha, a man or a woman? We have a symbolic representation of Shiva as Ardhanarishwar—half man, half woman. That's perfect. It has to be so because you are born of a father and a mother; half of you comes from your father, half of you comes from your mother. So, at the most, the difference between a woman and man is a difference of emphasis, it is not a difference of quality. The woman is consciously woman, unconsciously man; the man is consciously man, unconsciously woman. That's all the difference is.

Very difficult, because your minds have been conditioned to be a man or to be a woman and society emphasizes the roles too much. It does not allow a fluid being, it makes solids of you. When the boy and the girl can understand, the parents start emphasizing, 'You are a boy. Don't play with dolls. That's not good for a boy; you are going to be a man. This is for girls.' Men don't count girls at all. 'Sissy, girlish. Don't do it; be a man.' And the small boy, not knowing where he is being led, starts focusing more and more on being a man. He goes far away from his original unity, the pure unity of his being. He becomes a man, which is half his being. And a girl becomes a woman, which is half her being. She is told not to climb trees; that is only for boys. What nonsense. Trees are for all. 'Don't go swimming in the river; that is for boys.' Rivers are for all.

That's how humanity is impoverished. The girl is given a certain role and the boy is given a certain role, their totality is completely lost. They become fixed in their windows; they cannot see the whole sky; the frame of the window becomes too much.

Man is a frame, woman is a frame—it is not your being. Don't be too identified with the frame, get out of it.

Once you start loosening, relaxing, and once you start reabsorbing the rejected, the denied part, you will become so enriched, you cannot even imagine, dream. Then your being will be whole.

And that's what I mean when I want you to be 'holy'. I don't mean become a Catholic monk or become a Buddhist monk or a Jaina monk. All stupid. I want you to become holy, holy in the sense of being whole. Become total. Reclaim whatsoever has been denied by society; don't be afraid of reclaiming it. Don't be afraid—if you are a man, don't be afraid of being a woman sometimes.

Somebody has died; you cannot weep because you are a man and tears are only meant for women. What a beautiful thing—

tears—denied to man. Then man becomes more and more hard, violent, anxious, then there is no wonder if Adolf Hitlers are born. A man whose tears have disappeared is bound to become Adolf Hitler some day or the other. He is bound to become a Genghis Khan, whose tears have disappeared. Then he will become incapable of feeling sympathy, then he will become so hard that he will not be able to feel what he is doing to people. Hitler killed millions with not even a small prick of his conscience. He was really the man; the woman had completely disappeared— the compassion, the love, all disappeared. The tears had disappeared.

I would like men also to cry like women. Tears flowing, they will soften your heart. They will make you more liquid and flowing. They will melt your window frame, and they will allow you to have a bigger sky.

Women are not allowed to laugh uproariously, like Gurudayal—no woman is allowed to laugh. That is against feminine grace. What nonsense. If you cannot laugh deeply, you will miss much. The laughter must come from the belly; the laughter must be so hilarious that the whole body shakes with it. It should not be heady. But women smile, they don't laugh; an uproarious laugh is so unladylike. Then ladies live a very feverish life. By and by, they become more and more filmy, more and more dreamlike, not real, not authentic.

Don't become ladies and gentlemen. Become holy. And the whole integrates all and everything. And the whole integrates God and Devil both. Then there is no division; then the mind drops. A holy man has no mind.

If the holy man is still Catholic, he is not holy, because he has a Catholic mind. If the holy man is still Hindu, he is not holy; he has a Hindu mind.

Just the other day I was reading a book of Pagal Baba. His name means 'Crazy Daddy.' And he must be crazy, and not crazy in the sense of the Sufis, because they call enlightened people 'mad,' but crazy in the sense of psychoanalysts. He is neurotic.

He says in his book—I was simply surprised to come across it, and he is thought to be a holy man—he says in the book, 'Many Westerners tell me they would like to be converted to Hinduism, and I have to tell them that this is not possible. A Hindu is born, nobody can be converted into a Hindu.' A Hindu is born—you have to earn it for many lives, if you do good karmas for many lives, you are born a Hindu. You cannot be converted—it is not as cheap as becoming a Christian.

And this holy man Pagal Baba says, 'I have to refuse them because for many lives they will have to earn it: it is the pinnacle to be a Hindu.' And he says that even if you are born a Hindu, and if you don't follow good karmas and continue becoming more and more religious and virtuous, you will fall back to a lower class of humanity—for example, you may become an American. This man says so. And the beauty of it is that he has found an American publisher; Simon & Schuster has published his book.

These are not holy men. These are Hindu chauvinists, stupid people, neurotic.

If you have a mind, you cannot be holy. Howsoever virtuous, the mind remains unholy because the mind cannot be whole. Remember it.

One evening, Mulla Nasruddin said to his wife, 'Bring us some cheese to eat, for cheese enhances the appetite and makes the eyes bright.'

'We are out of cheese,' the wife said.

'That's good,' Mulla replied, 'for cheese is injurious to the teeth and gums.'

'Which of your statements is true then?' she asked. Mulla answered, 'If there is cheese in the house, the first one; if not, the second.'

This is the way the mind functions.

You love a woman if she becomes available to you, if not,

you hate. If the cheese is in the house, the first; if the cheese is not in the house, the second . . .

Drop divisions; drop dividing. Live life as a whole. It will be difficult, I know, because for centuries the mind has been conditioned to divide. And unloosening it, unhinging it, is going to be difficult, but it is worth it, because you are missing so much.

Psychologists say that 98 per cent of life is being missed: 98 per cent. Only 2 per cent is being lived because the window frame does not allow more than that.

Break the window, break the frame—burn it! Your Hinduism, your Christianity, your Jainism—burn them! And come out of them. If you can come out of all your ideologies, attitudes, prejudices, you will become whole.

The third question:

Osho, you have often said that the enlightened ones never dream. But you have told us that once Chuang Tzu dreamt that he has become a butterfly. Please comment.

This is from Yoga Chinmaya. It seems he cannot even understand humour, and I know why he cannot understand it: he has been too much in wrong company—Indian yogis and sadhus—and he has forgotten the very quality of humour, and humour is a basic quality of being holy. A holy man is a humorous man. But he is too fixed.

When I said that Chuang Tzu dreamt, Chuang Tzu himself had related that dream. Not that he dreamt. He is creating a beautiful joke about himself—he is laughing about himself. It is very easy to laugh about others, difficult to laugh at oneself. But the day you become capable of laughing at yourself, you become egoless, because the ego enjoys laughing at others' cost. When you start laughing at yourself, the ego cannot exist.

Yes, no enlightened person ever dreams, but enlightened

persons have humour. They can laugh, and they can help others to laugh.

It happened, three men were travelling; they were in search of truth. One was a Jew, another a Christian, and the third was a Muslim. They were all great friends.

One day, they found a coin with which they bought a piece of halvah. The Muslim and the Christian had just eaten, so they were a little worried the Jew will eat the whole halvah; and they were so full, they had stuffed themselves so much. So they suggested—they conspired against the Jew—they suggested, 'Let us go to bed now. In the morning, we will tell our dreams. Whoever has had the best dream, eats the halvah.' And because two were in favour of it, the Jew had to agree, just to be democratic, there was nothing else to do.

The Jew, who was very hungry, could not sleep much. And it is very difficult to sleep when the halvah is there and you are hungry and these two people have conspired against you . . . .

In the middle of the night, he got up and ate the halvah and went back to bed.

In the morning, the Christian was the first to relate his dream. He said, 'Christ came, and when he was ascending to the heavens, he took me with him. It was the rarest dream I have ever seen.'

The Muslim said, 'I dreamt of Mohammed, who took me on a tour of paradise . . . and beautiful women dancing, and streams of wine flowing, and trees of gold and flowers of diamonds. It was tremendously beautiful.'

Now it was the Jew's turn. He said, 'Moses came to me and said, "You old idiot, what are you waiting for? Christ took one of your friends to heaven, Mohammed is entertaining the other in paradise—at least get up and eat the halvah!"'

Humour is part of holiness; wherever you find a holy man serious, escape from there, because he can be dangerous. He must be ill inside; seriousness is a sort of disease, one of the most fatal diseases—and it is very chronic in religion.

Just try to understand. Don't become too clever, because that simply proves to be foolishness and nothing else. Always allow a little foolishness also in you, then you will be wiser. A fool is against wisdom, but a wise man absorbs foolishness also. He is not against it; he uses that too.

Chuang Tzu is one of the most absurd men who have ever been here on the earth. That's why I have named this auditorium 'Chuang Tzu Auditorium.' I love the man; he is so absurd. How can you avoid loving this man?

Buddha will not say, 'I dreamt.' He was a little serious. Patanjali will not say, because he will be afraid of Chinmaya.

Some swami is bound to raise the question: 'You and dreamt? Enlightened people never dream. What are you saying?' Chuang Tzu is not afraid of anybody; he says, 'I dreamt.' He is a very loving man. He is holy. He can laugh and help others to laugh; his holiness is full of laughter.

The fourth question:

Osho, what is Patanjali's methodology or your technique of becoming a self-contained individual? In this connection, kindly explain how such a spiritual man literally lives from moment to moment. How to cultivate this habit of living from moment to moment in practical, everyday life?

This whole question must be from someone who has not understood me at all. It seems to be from somebody absolutely new. But, still, many people are new, and it will be helpful to understand it.

'*What is your technique of becoming a self-contained individual?*' I am not interested in making you a self-contained individual at all, because that is impossible. You are so interconnected with the whole, how can you become self-contained? That is the ego's effort, to become self-contained. To become absolutely independent of all, that is the ego trip, the ultimate ego trip.

No, you cannot become self-contained. You can become the whole contained, but not self-contained. You can contain the whole and you can be contained by the whole, but you cannot become self-contained. How can you divide yourself from the universe, separate? You cannot exist even for a single moment.

If you don't breathe, you will not be able to be alive. And you cannot contain your breath in; it has to go out. It has to come in again. It is a constant movement between you and the whole. Those who know, they say it is not that *you* breathe; on the contrary, the whole breathes you.

Just silently watch your breath sometimes. There may come, one day, one moment when suddenly your attention shifts to a new mysterious experience. First when you watch your breath—your *kurma-nadi*, what Buddha calls Anapanasati yoga—when you watch your breath, you think *you* are breathing. By and by, you see, you will *have* to see because that's truth: you are not breathing. You are not needed to breathe; that's why even in sleep you go on breathing, even if you become unconscious, even if you are in a coma, you go on breathing. You are not breathing; otherwise, sometimes you will forget and you will drop dead. You never forget, because it is not needed.

The breathing goes on by itself, on its own accord. One day, you will see that, 'I am breathing' is nonsense; on the contrary, 'breathing is breathing me'.

And then one day you will have another revolutionary, radical, turn of your consciousness. You see that you exhale out, you inhale in: one day you will see your exhalation is God's inhalation, your inhalation is God's exhalation. The whole exhales; that is the moment when you feel you are inhaling. The whole inhales; that is the moment when you feel you are exhaling.

Who are you? And what nonsense are you are asking—how to become self-contained. Without the sun, you will not be. If the sun disappears, you will disappear, all life will disappear. We are interconnected; the whole existence is one. Everything is interconnected; independence is not possible. I am not for dependence, because when independence is not possible, how can dependence be possible? My word is *interdependence*; that's what is true and real.

So the first thing, don't think in terms of self-containment. Self is your disease. Drop it! So the whole becomes available to you. And only then can you live from moment to moment, otherwise you cannot. If you are protecting, guarding, defending yourself, how can you live moment to moment? You will have to prepare for the future. You will have to prepare for tomorrow, who will take care of you? You are a self-contained individual— who will take care of you tomorrow? You will have to look to the bank balance. You will have to prepare. You cannot live moment to moment.

Only a person who has come to realize, 'I am not, the whole is,' can live moment to moment, because then there is no other way to live. The future is not yet there, and if this moment the whole has been protecting me, mothering me, helping me, then the whole will take care tomorrow also, as it has taken care up to now. It will take care. And if the whole decides that I am not needed, and I dissolve—perfectly okay, because who am I to object?

This is what a religious man is: a deep surrender, a total surrender to the whole. Then he lives moment to moment.

'In this connection, kindly explain how such a spiritual man literally lives from moment to moment.' He does not live, he allows God to live through him. Then one is spiritual.

A worldly man lives his life, a spiritual man does not live his life; he allows God to live through him. He becomes a vehicle, he says, 'Come. Thy kingdom come, thy will be done. Come, pass through me, live through me, *be* through me. I am empty and ready. I am just like a hollow bamboo. Come, make a flute out of me, sing a song out of me. Sing your silence or your song, but celebrate through me. I am ready and waiting for you, and available.'

A spiritual man is a great availability. He says to God,

'Whenever you are willing, I am ready. I will wait, and I will keep patient. There is no hurry, also: if you are engaged somewhere else and much work is there, do it. I can wait for eternity.'

A spiritual man is not one who is living his life. But in India or in other countries also, that is the idea: that a spiritual man is one who lives a very disciplined life. This is not the definition of a spiritual man, and don't become a victim of it, because if you start living your life, you will be constantly in a fight with the whole. Don't swim in the river; don't try to push it. Float with it, go with it—go with it to the ocean. It is already going; there is no need to worry. Drop all worries, don't try to swim upstream, otherwise you will be exhausted. But that's what is thought about a religious man, a spiritual man—one who is giving great fight to God.

Gurdjieff used to say, 'All your so-called religions are against God.' And he was right. These are subtle strategies of the ego. Beware of them.

I am here not to make you enemies of God. I am here to teach you how to float with him, how to be friendly with him, how not to resist him. I am here to break down all your strategies, your morality, your ethics, your disciplines. These are all strategies; how you protect yourself, how you are trying to be independent and self-contained. I am here to destroy and annihilate you completely.

And when your strategies are taken away, you will disappear. In your disappearance appears the spiritual man. It is nothing that you can do by your efforts. It is your absolute, utter failure! . . . When the religious man enters in you, when you become religious and spiritual. You cannot succeed to be a spiritual man.

'How to cultivate this habit . . .?' Religion is not a habit. Spirituality is not a habit, it is awareness; and a habit is just the opposite of awareness. A habit is unconscious. But many people do that, for example, you smoke cigarettes, it becomes a habit. When do you say it has become a habit? When it has become so automatic, you cannot drop it; then you say it has become a habit. Now if you don't smoke, you feel great disturbance, you feel an urge so tremendous that you cannot withhold from it, you have to go with it—now it has become a habit. The same way, you try to make prayer also your habit. You pray every day; then by and by, it becomes just like smoking. If you don't pray, you feel something is missing. You call it religious; then why not call smoking religious? What is wrong with smoking?

Smoking is a mantra. What do you do in a mantra? You repeat a certain sound, you say, 'Ram, Ram, Ram, Ram . . . .' That's what smoking is: you take the smoke in, you take it out, you take it in, you take it out, you take it in, you take it out; it becomes a mantra. It is already a 'Transcendental Meditation,' TM.

No, religion has nothing to do with habits. You must be thinking that religion has something to do with good habits, not bad habits—smoking is a bad habit, prayer is a good habit. But all habits are unconscious, and religion is becoming conscious.

It is possible that you may become so habituated to doing good that it may become impossible for you to do bad, but that doesn't make you a spiritual man. It makes you a very convenient man, it makes you a very good citizen of the world, it makes you a very good member of the society, but not a religious man. Society played tricks with you. You can go on doing good, go on doing good . . . because you cannot do bad. It has become habitual. But habit is not virtue. Awareness.

And sometimes it happens that the situation is not the same, but you are habituated to doing something—you go on doing it, without looking at the situation. Sometimes, something is bad and the same thing can be good at other times. In one situation, one response is virtuous; in another situation, the same response can be a sin. But if you have become habituated, you behave like a robot, automaton.

I will tell you one story, one of the most beautiful ones I have ever come across:

Mr Ginsberg died and went to heaven and was greeted by the recording angel with great jubilation.

'We have all been waiting for you, Ginsberg, for you have been a good man. Look at your record here', and the recording angel opened a gigantic ledger and ran his finger down one page after another. 'Look at that: good deed, good deed, good deed, good deed. Ginsberg, you are loaded with good deeds.'

But as he turned the pages, the recording angel grew solemn and his face took on a look of anxiety. Finally, he closed the ledger and said, 'Ginsberg, we are in trouble.'

'Why?' asked Ginsberg in alarm.

'I had not realized it, but you have nothing but good deeds. You have no sins at all.'

'But isn't that the whole idea?' asked Ginsberg.

'In a manner of speaking, it is,' said the recording angel. 'But in actual practice, we always get a few sins. That fellow there— a good man—committed only one, but it was a real whopper. Now, if you come in with no sins at all, it will create envy and hard feelings, there will be murmurings and backbitings. In short, you will bring dissension and evil into heaven.'

'So what to do? What am I to do?' asked poor Ginsberg.

'I tell you what,' said the recording angel, 'this is irregular, but maybe I can get away with it. I will erase the last page of your record and you will have six more hours of life. You will have another chance. Please, Ginsberg, commit a sin—and a *real* one—and then come back.'

No sooner said than done, Ginsberg suddenly found himself back in his hometown. He had a few hours in which to commit a sin and get away from his perpetual good deeds, and he was desperately eager to do so for he wanted to go to heaven. But what kind of sin could he commit? He had been so virtuous, he scarcely knew what sin was.

After much thinking, he recalled that if one had sexual relations with a woman not one's wife that was sin. It also seemed to him that a certain unmarried woman past her first youth had often cast meaningful glances at him, which, being virtuous, he had, of course, ignored.

He would ignore them no longer. And time was running fast. With a determined step, he walked to the house of the young lady, a Miss Levine, and knocked. She opened the door, saw him standing there, and said in surprise, 'Why, Mr Ginsberg, I had heard you were sick, and feared you were dying, but you look completely yourself.'

'I am perfectly well,' said Ginsberg. 'May I come in?'

'Of course,' said Miss Levine eagerly, and locked the door behind him.

What happened afterwards was inevitable. In almost no time, they were clearly sinning and Mr Ginsberg, with the vision of a waiting heaven, made up in enthusiasm for what he lacked in experience.

Anxious to make the sin a real good one, and something that would thoroughly satisfy the recording angel, Ginsberg took pains not to hasten. He kept matters going till an inner feeling told him his time was nearly up.

Anticipating heaven with lyrical joy, Ginsberg rose and excused himself. 'Miss Levine,' he said, 'I must leave now. I have an important engagement.'

And Miss Levine, smiling up at him from bed, murmured softly, 'Oh, Mr Ginsberg, darling, what a good deed you have done for me this day.'

What a good deed! So, poor Ginsberg . . .

Don't get so habituated to good; don't get so habituated, don't become so mechanical. Don't ask, 'How to cultivate this habit of living from moment to moment?' It is not a habit at all; it is an awareness.

There is nothing else; the past is gone, the future has not come yet. Can you live in the past, that which is gone? How can you live in it? Can you live in the future, that which is not yet? How can you live in it? It is a simple understanding, a tacit understanding that the only possible life is in the present. There is no need to make a habit of it. It has nothing to do with religion; it has something to do with simple, mere intelligence. The past is gone, how can you live in it? The future has not come yet, how can you live in it? Just a little intelligence is needed.

Only the present is there. All that is there is the present; there is no other way. So live it if you want to live it. If you think of the past and the future, you waste it. And when it will become past, you will start thinking about it. And when it was future, you were planning for it, and when it comes, you are not there. You either move in memories or you move in your imagination.

Drop memory and imagination. Be herenow. And it is not a question of habit. How can you be herenow just by habit? Habit comes from the past; habit drags you to the past. Or you can make it a discipline, but then you are making it for the future. You are waiting: 'Today I will cultivate the habit, and tomorrow I will enjoy.' But again you are in the future.

Habit is not the question, not at all relevant. Just become alert. If you are eating, eat—just eat, let your whole being be absorbed in it. If you are making love, become a Shiva and let your consort be Devi. Love, and let all the gods watch and come and go—don't be worried. Whatsoever you are doing ... walking on the street, then just walk, enjoy the breeze, the sun, the trees— the present.

And, remember, I am not telling you to practise. It can be done immediately, without any practise. It can be done immediately; just a little intelligence is needed. Habits, cultivations, are for stupid people, because they cannot live intelligently, they have to take the help of habits, disciplines, this and that. If you are intelligent—and I can see you are intelligent, I see you are promise—there is no need. Just start! Don't ask how; right now start. You are listening to me? Just listen. Many of you will be thinking, not listening, comparing notes with your own prejudices.

The person who has asked the question is not listening. I can say it with absolute certainty, not knowing who has asked. From where does my certainty come?—because I can understand the mind from the question. He must be getting angry and annoyed.

People ask questions to be solaced, consoled, but I am not here to console you. I am here to disturb you so totally that you *drop*—out of sheer disgust with your strategies—you drop. And I am absolutely certain, as much certain as it happened once:

Sheikh Farid, a mystic, a Sufi mystic, was invited by the king. He went there, and the king said, 'I have been hearing many miracles about you, and if you really claim that you are a great saint and mystic, then show me some miracle, because spiritual men always are miraculous.'

Farid looked into the eyes of the king and said, 'I can read your thoughts, and just for an instance I can say that this is the thought right now in your mind: that you can't believe it. You are saying inside, "I can't believe it." Am I right or not?'

The king said, 'You caught me.'

The man who has asked the question must be feeling very much annoyed. Then you miss, because through annoyance, you cannot listen to me; you cannot be herenow.

The last question:

Osho, one says you told Ram he is enlightened—in the sense of realized. Another says you had both your tongues in both your cheeks. Ram says you were joking and that I should ask you. I tell myself, it is really none of my business, but still, is he? Has he?

If he has understood that I was joking, he must be enlightened.

Enough for today.

Five

The Meeting of Sun and Moon

By performing samyama
on the light under the crown of the head
comes the ability to contact all perfected beings.

Through pratibha, intuition, knowledge of everything.

Performing samyama on the heart
brings awareness of the nature of mind.

Man is evolution. Not only that man is evolving, he is the very vehicle of evolution itself, he is evolution—a tremendous responsibility, and something to be delighted about also, because that's the glory of man. Matter is the beginning, God the end. Matter is the alpha point, God the omega point. Man is the bridge: matter passes through man and is transformed into God. God is not a thing and God is not waiting somewhere. God is evolving through you; God is becoming through you. You are transforming matter into God. You are the greatest experiment that reality has made. Think of the glory of it, and think of the responsibility also.

Much depends on man, but if you think that you are already there because you have the form of man, then you will be misguided by your mind. You only have the form; you are only a possibility. The real is going to happen, and you have to allow it to happen. You have to open towards it.

That's what yoga is all about: how to help you to move upward towards the omega point where your whole energy is released, transformed, the whole of matter is transmuted into divinity. Yoga has mapped the whole journey, the whole pilgrimage of man; from sex to *samadhi*, from the lowest centre, *muladhar*, to the highest centre, the very peak, the pinnacle of evolution, the *sahasrar*.

These things have to be understood before we can enter into the sutras of today. Yoga divides man into seven layers, seven steps, seven centres. The first is muladhar, the sex centre, the sun centre, and the last, the seventh, is the sahasrar, the God centre— the omega point.

The sex centre is intrinsically moving downward. It is your connection with matter, what yoga calls *prakriti*—nature. The sex centre is your relation with nature, the world that you have left behind, the past. If you go on confining yourself to the sex centre, you cannot evolve. You will remain where you are; you will remain in contact with your past, but you will not be connected with the future. You are stuck there; man is stuck at the sex centre.

People think they understand everything about sex. Nothing much is yet known, at least not to those who think they know— the psychologists. They think that they know, but the basic thing is yet lacking: the knowledge that sex can become an upward movement, that there is no necessity that it should move only downward. It moves downward because the mechanism to move downward exists in man, already exists in man. It exists in animals also; it exists in trees also. There is nothing much significant about it that it exists in man. The significance of man is that something more exists in man that doesn't exist yet in the plants, in the birds, in the animals. They are bound to move downward; they don't have a staircase within them.

That is what we mean by seven centres: the staircase of evolution. It exists in you. You can fall upward—if you choose to. If you don't choose, you will go on falling downward.

So now, with man, the evolution is going to be conscious. Up to now, you have been helped. Nature has brought you to this point; from hence onwards, you will have to take your own responsibility. You will have to become responsible. Man has matured; man has come of age; now nature can no longer take care of you. So if you don't move consciously, if you don't make a conscious effort to evolve, if you don't accept the responsibility, you will remain stuck.

So many people feel the 'stuckness,' but they don't know from where it is coming. Thousands of people come to me and they tell me they are feeling stuck. They know something is possible, but they don't know what it is. They know that they should move, but they don't know how to move, where to move. They know that they have been in the place where they are long enough, and they would like to explode into new dimensions, but they are stuck. This stuckness is coming from the muladhar, from the sex centre, the sun centre.

Up to now, there has been no problem for you. Nature has been helping; nature has mothered you up to now. But you are no longer a child, no longer a baby, and nature cannot go on feeding you on her breast. Now the mother says, 'Leave the breast; be on your own.' The mother has said so long ago. Those who have understood it, they have taken the responsibility and have become *siddhas*, buddhas, those who have achieved.

Now the path is going to be your decision. Now you have to move on your own. This possibility exists in the muladhar centre: it can open upward. So the first thing to be understood today is, don't think that you understand sex in its totality. You don't understand it.

I have heard one anecdote:

One man, accompanying his son to the classroom, told the teacher that his youngster would like to know all about the birds and the bees.

'Do you have reference to elementary sex instructions?' inquired the teacher.

'Heck, no,' replied the father. 'The kid knows all about sex. He wants to know about the birds and the bees.'

But I would like to tell you that nobody knows all about sex yet. Unless God is realized, you cannot know all about sex, because God is the final possibility of sex energy—the ultimate transformation of sex energy. Unless you know who you are, you will not be able to know what sex really is in its totality. You will not be able to comprehend it. Only a part of it is known, the sun part. The moon part is not even known yet; the psychology for the feminine energy has yet to evolve. Freud and Jung and Adler and others, whatsoever they have been doing is more or less centred around man. Woman as yet remains an uncharted territory. The moon centre, even the moon centre, is not yet a known fact.

A few people have had a few glimpses . . . for example, Jung had a few glimpses. Freud remained completely sun-oriented. Jung moved a little towards the moon, of course, very hesitatingly because the whole training of the mind is scientific, and to move towards the moon is to move in a world totally different from science. It is to move in the world of myth, it is to move in the world of poetry, imagination, it is to move in the world of 'irreason,' illogic.

Let me tell you a few things; Freud is sun-oriented, Jung is leaning a little towards the moon. That's why Freud was very angry with his disciple Jung. And Freudians are very much annoyed by Jung; it seems he betrayed his master.

The sun-oriented person always feels that the moon-oriented person is dangerous. The sun-oriented person moves on the clean-cut superhighways of reason, and the moon-oriented person starts moving in labyrinths. He starts moving in the wilderness, where nothing is clear-cut—everything is alive, but nothing is clear-cut.

And the greatest fear for man is woman. Somehow, man

suspects that death is going to come from woman, because life has also come from her. Everybody is born out of a woman. When life has come from woman, then somehow death is also going to happen through her, because the end always comes to meet the beginning; only then is the circle complete.

In India, in Indian mythology, we realized it. You must have seen pictures or statues of Mother Kali, who is the symbolization of the feminine mind, and she is dancing on the body of her husband, Shiva. She has danced so terribly that Shiva is dead, and she goes on dancing. The feminine mind has killed the male mind; that is the meaning of the myth.

And why is she painted black? That's why she is called Kali; *kali* means black. Why is she so dangerous? In one of her hands she is carrying a freshly cut head with blood dripping from it— almost a personification of death. She is dancing wildly, on the chest of her husband, and the husband is dead and she goes on dancing in great ecstasy. Why is she black? Because death has always been thought of as black, as a dark, black night.

And why has she killed her husband? The moon always kills the sun. Once the moon arises in your being, logic dies; then logic cannot remain, then reason cannot remain. Now you have attained a totally different dimension.

You never expect logic from a poet. You never expect logic from a painter, from a dancer, from a musician. They move in a totally dark world; they move in darkness.

Reason has always been afraid, and man has always been afraid because man is reason-oriented. Have you not observed it, that always man feels it is difficult to understand a woman and the mind of a woman? And the same is the feeling of women— they cannot understand men. A gap exists, as if they are not part of one humanity, as if they are different.

Let me tell you one anecdote:

An Italian debated with a Jew, 'You Jews are so proud. There is tremendous propaganda claiming that you are the most intelligent people in the world. Sheer nonsense! In Italy, excavations have been made, and in some strata of the earth at least two thousand years old, wire has been found, which proves that our Roman ancestors at that time already had the telegraph.'

The Jew answered, 'In Israel, excavations have been made in parts of the earth four thousand years old and nothing has been found, which means that we had the wireless before you had the telegraph.'

This is how logic functions. It is a hair-splitting, but it can go on and on. Even in love man remains rational, argumentative. Man is always trying to prove something.

Watch. A woman takes it for granted that everything is proved, and man goes on trying to prove something—always defensive. Somewhere deep in their sexuality is the root cause of it. When a man and a woman make love, the woman need not prove anything. She can just be passive, but the man has to prove his manhood. From that very effort to prove his manhood, man is continuously defensive and always trying to prove something or the other.

The whole of philosophy is nothing but finding proofs for God. Science is nothing but finding proofs for theories. Women have never been interested in philosophy; they take life for granted, they accept it, they are not defensive in any way, as if they have proved already. Their being seems to be more circular; the circle seems to be complete. That may be the cause of their body being so round. It has a shape of roundness. Man has corners, and is always ready to fight and argue, even in moments of love.

I was reading about Somerset Maugham:

When Somerset Maugham, the writer, was nearly ninety, he had a bout of influenza. One day a lady admirer phoned and asked if she might send fruit and flowers.

'It is too late for fruit,' Maugham replied, 'and too early for flowers.'

Such a simple gesture of love . . . Logic enters immediately.

One very famous woman, a dancer, an actress, and one of the most beautiful, asked Bernard Shaw, 'Would you like to marry me?'

Bernard said, 'For what?'

The woman said, 'I always think that my beauty—my body, my face, my eyes—and your intelligence, both will make a beautiful child. It will be a beautiful gift to the world.'

Bernard Shaw laughed and said, 'Wait. It could be just otherwise: it may have your intelligence, which means nothing, and it may have my beauty, which is almost ugliness. The child could be just the other way.'

The male mind always goes on dissecting.

Jung reports in his memoirs that he was sitting with Freud, and that day he suddenly felt a great strain in his stomach, and he felt as if something was going to happen, and suddenly there was a sort of explosion in the cupboard. Both became alert. What had happened? Jung said, 'It has something to do with my energy.' Freud laughed and scoffed and said, 'Nonsense, how can it have anything to do with your energy?' Jung said, 'Wait, within a minute it will come again' because he again felt his stomach getting strained. And within a minute—exactly within a minute— there was another explosion.

Now this is the feminine mind. And Jung writes in his memoirs, 'Since that day, Freud never trusted me.' This is dangerous because it is illogical. And Jung started to think about a new theory he calls 'synchronicity.'

The theory that is the base of all scientific effort is causality— everything is joined with cause and effect. Whatsoever happens has a cause, and if you can produce the cause, the effect will follow. If you heat water, it will evaporate. Heating is the cause: bring it to a hundred degrees and it will evaporate. Evaporation is an effect. This is the scientific base.

Jung says there is another principle, which is 'synchronicity.'

It is difficult to explain it because all explanations are from the scientific mind, but you can try to feel what he means. If you make two clocks so similar that they are synchronized with each other: when on one clock the hand comes to twelve, the other clock chimes the twelve bells. One clock simply moves, shows the time; the other clock chimes—eleven, twelve, one, two. Anybody listening to it will be surprised because the first clock is not the cause of the second chiming. They are in no way related. It is only that the maker, the watchmaker, has synchronized them in such a way that something happens in one, and simultaneously something else happens in the other. They are not connected by any cause and effect.

Jung says just by the side of causality there is another principle. The maker of the world, if there is any, has made the world in such a way that many things happen, which are not cause and effect. You see a woman and suddenly love flowers. Now is this to be explained by cause and effect or by synchronicity? Jung seems to be more accurate and closer to the truth. The woman has not caused the love in you, you have not caused the love in the woman, but man and woman, or the energy of sun and moon, have been made in such a way that when they come close, love flowers. It is synchronicity.

But Freud became afraid; they were never close again. Freud had chosen Jung to be his successor, but that day he changed his will. Then never again, they went apart, farther and farther away.

Man cannot understand woman; woman cannot understand man. It is almost like sun and moon—when the sun is there, moon disappears; when the sun goes down, the moon appears. They never meet. They never come face to face. Your intellect, your reason, disappears when your intuition starts functioning. Women are more intuitive. They don't have a reason for something, but they can have a hunch, and their hunches are almost always true.

Many men have come to me and told me, 'This is strange. If we are having some affair and we have not told the wife, somehow or the other she comes to know. But we are never able to know whether the wife is having an affair or not.'

There was just such a case between Sheela and Chinmaya. Chinmaya was having an affair, and they both came to me. And Chinmaya said, 'This is strange. Whenever I have an affair, immediately Sheela comes. Wherever she is, she immediately comes back to the room. Otherwise, she never comes—she is working in the office or doing something. But whenever I am interested in a woman and I take any woman to my room—even just talking, then Sheela comes. And this has happened so many times.' And I inquired, 'Has it ever happened the other way?' He said, 'Never.'

A woman lives by hunches. She cannot reason it out. She simply feels it, and feels it so deeply that it is almost a truth to her. That's why husbands can never defeat any woman in argumentation. They don't listen to your argument. They go on insisting, 'This is so.' And you also know that this is so, but you go on protesting. The more you protest, the more they know that this is so.

It happened, there was a case in a court:

The day of the trial came, and the defendant lost his composure when twelve women were picked for the jury box.

'Do I have to be tried by a lady jury?' he asked his lawyer.

'Keep quiet,' said the lawyer.

'Keep quiet nothing!' the defendant exclaimed. 'If I cannot fool my wife, how can I hope to fool twelve women? Plead guilty.'

It is impossible. They have another way of knowing, a separate way of knowing: the moon way of knowing.

The feminine psychology has yet to be developed, and unless a moon psychology is developed, psychology will not have the status of a science. It will remain a prejudice; it will remain *male* prejudice. It will not say anything about human beings as such.

Freudian psychology is sun psychology; Jungian psychology is leaning a little towards the moon. And there is a man, Roberto Assagioli; his psychology is a synthesis between sun and moon, just the beginning of it. He calls his psychology 'psychosynthesis.' Freud calls his psychology 'psychoanalysis.' Analysis comes from the sun; synthesis comes from the moon. Observe, whenever there is light, things are separate. Then one tree is here, another tree is there, but everything is separate. And then comes the darkness of the night and everything disappears—the separation. Everything becomes one. The dark night, and all divisions disappear.

Moon psychology is going to be synthetic; sun psychology analytical, dissecting, arguing, proving. But there is a possibility of higher psychologies. I would like to give you a few hints, what I call 'the psychology of the buddhas'. Freud is sun, Jung moon, Assagioli, sun plus moon. A buddha is sun plus moon plus beyond, and later on I will explain to you what I mean by 'beyond.' And then that beyond can also be looked at, through many ways.

Sun plus beyond—you have Patanjali, you have Mahavira, yoga; the language is of the sun, the experience is of the beyond. Then, sun plus moon plus beyond—you have tantra, Shiva; the experience is of the beyond, but the expression is both sun plus moon. And then, you have moon plus beyond—Narad, Chaitanya, Meera, Jesus; the experience is of the beyond, but the expression is of the moon. And then there is just beyond—Bodhidharma, Lao Tzu, Chuang Tzu, Zen; they don't believe in expression so they don't need sun or moon expression, they say it cannot be said. Lao Tzu says, 'The Tao that can be said is no longer Tao. The truth that can be uttered is already a lie; it cannot be expressed.'

These are all the possibilities, but they have not yet been actualized. Here and there a man has attained, but that attainment and realization has to be codified in such a way, classified in such a way, that it becomes a part of the collective human consciousness.

Now the sutra:

> *By performing samyama*
> *on the light under the crown of the head*
> *comes the ability to contact all perfected beings.*

The sahasrar is just below the crown of the head. The sahasrar is a subtle opening in your head. Just as the genital organs are a subtle opening in the muladhar, from that subtle opening you move downward into nature, into life, into the visible, the material, into the form; exactly like that, you have a nonfunctioning organ in the crown of the head, there is also a subtle opening. When energy rushes there, that opening bursts open, and from there you come in contact with super-nature—call it God or perfected beings, siddhas, those who have already attained.

Through sex, you reproduce more bodies like you. Sex is creative; it gives birth to more children just like you, you reproduce yourself. When your energy moves through the sahasrar, the seventh chakra, you reproduce yourself; that is what resurrection is. That is what is meant by Jesus when he says, 'Be reborn.' Then you become father and mother to yourself. Your sun centre becomes your father, your moon centre becomes your mother, and the meeting of your sun and moon inside releases your energy toward the head. It is an inner orgasm—the meeting of the sun and the moon, or call it the meeting of the *anima* and the *animus*, the male and the female inside you.

Your whole body is divided into male and female. This has to be understood. Do you see how much left-handed people are suppressed? If a child writes with the left hand, immediately, the whole society is against him—the parents, the peers, the teachers. The whole society forces him to write with the right hand. Right is right and left is wrong. What is the matter? Why is right, right and left, wrong? What is wrong with left? Ten per cent of the people in the world are left-handed. Ten per cent is not a small minority; out of 10 there is always one person who is left-handed.

He may not have conscious awareness of it, he may have forgotten about it, because from the very beginning left-handed people are being forced to become right-handed. Why?

The right hand is connected with the sun centre, with the male inside you; the left hand is connected with the female inside you, with the moon centre. And the whole society is male-oriented.

Your left nostril is connected with the moon centre; your right nostril is connected with the sun centre. You can try it. Whenever you are feeling very hot, close your right nostril and breathe from the left, and within ten minutes you will feel a subtle coolness coming to you. You can experiment; it is so easy. Or, if you are shivering and feeling chilly, close your left nostril and breathe from the right; within ten minutes you will be perspiring.

Yoga has come to understand it, and yogis say—and yogis do it—in the morning, they will never get up breathing from the right nostril because if you get up breathing from the right nostril, there is more possibility that in the day you will get angry, you will fight, you will become aggressive—you will not be cool and collected. So in yoga it is part of the discipline that everybody getting up, first looks which nostril is functioning. If the left is functioning perfectly okay, that is the right moment to get out of bed. If it is not functioning, then turn over, close your right nostril and breathe from the left. By and by, the left takes over; then get up.

Always get up with the left nostril functioning and you will see a total difference in your whole day's activity. You will be less angry, less irritated, more cool, more collected, calm. Your meditation will go deeper. If you want to fight, then the right nostril is very good. If you want to love, then the left nostril is very good.

This breathing continuously changes; you may not have observed, but observe it. Modern medicine has to come to understand it because it can be used in treatment very, very significantly. There are diseases that can be helped by the moon, and there are diseases that can be helped by the sun. If you know exactly, then the breathing can be used to treat a person. But modern medicine has not yet stumbled upon the fact; continuously your breathing changes, forty minutes one nostril functions, then forty minutes the other nostril functions. Continuously within you the sun and moon change—you swing from sun to moon, from moon to sun.

That's why you change your moods so often. Sometimes you suddenly feel irritated—for no reason at all. Nothing has happened, everything is the same, you are just sitting in the same room—nothing has happened—suddenly you feel irritated. Watch. Bring your hand close to your nose and feel: your breathing must have changed from left to right. Just a moment before, you were feeling so good, just a moment after, you are feeling so bad, just ready to fight or do something.

Remember, the whole body is divided. Your brain is also divided into two brains. You don't have one brain; you have two brains—two hemispheres. The left side of the brain is the sun brain; the right side of the brain is the moon brain. You may be puzzled, because if everything left is the moon, why the right side of the brain is the moon. The right side of the brain is connected with your left side of the body. Your left hand is connected with the right side of the brain; your right hand is connected with the left side of the brain, that's why. Crosswise.

The right side of the brain is the seat of imagination, poetry, love, intuition. The left side of the brain is the seat of reason, logic, argumentation, philosophy, science.

And unless you attain to a balance between the sun and moon energy, you will not be able to transcend. Unless the left side of your brain meets with the right side of your brain and is bridged, you will not reach to the sahasrar. You have to become one to reach the sahasrar because the sahasrar is the omega point in your being. You cannot reach there as man, you cannot reach there as woman; you have to reach there just as pure consciousness—one, total, whole.

Man's sexuality is sun-oriented, woman's sexuality moon-oriented. That's why women have the monthly period in twenty-eight days, because the moon has a twenty-eight-day month. They are affected by the moon; the moon has a twenty-eight-day cycle of phases.

And many women feel, when the full moon night comes, a little crazy, a little berserk. Beware; when the full moon is there, beware of your wife or girlfriend. She becomes a little wild, just as the ocean becomes wild and is affected by the moon energy.

Have you seen? Men like to make love with open eyes. Not only that, but with the full light on. If there were not other troubles, men would like to love in the daytime. And they have started, particularly in America, because other troubles have disappeared. People are making love more in the morning than in the night. Women like to make love in darkness, and even in darkness, they want to close their eyes.

The moon shines in darkness, loves darkness, the night.

That's why women are not interested in pornography. Now because of the lib movement, a few magazines have started to compete with *Playboy* and that type of magazines: *Playgirl* has come into existence. But women are basically not interested in pornography. In fact, they can never understand why men like to see naked women's pictures so much. They have a certain difficulty in understanding the fact.

Man is sun-oriented, light-oriented. Eyes are part of the sun; that's why eyes can see. They correspond with the sun energy. So man is more eye-oriented. That's why man is a voyeur and woman is an exhibitionist. Men cannot understand why women go on decorating themselves so much.

I have heard:

One couple went to the mountains to celebrate their honeymoon. The young man was lying in bed and waiting for the wife. The wife was powdering her body and doing her hair and doing this and that, polishing her nails, and then she took a few drops of perfume and put them behind her ears. Then the young man jumped out of the bed. The wife asked, 'What is the matter? Where are you going?' He ran towards his suitcase, and said, 'If it is going to be a formal affair, at least I must put my clothes on.'

Women are exhibitionists—they would like to be seen. But that's perfectly okay because that's how men and women fit: man wants to see; woman wants to show. They fit, perfectly; it is absolutely okay. If women don't want to exhibit, then they will create trouble, and if man is not a voyeur, for whom will women prepare so much—for whom? Nobody will look at them.

Everything fits in nature in a perfect way. It synchronizes.

But to reach to the sahasrar, you have to drop this duality of functioning. You cannot reach God as man or woman. You have to reach God as a simple, pure being. *'By performing samyama on the light under the crown of the head comes the ability to contact all perfected beings.'* The energy has to move upward, and samyama is the methodology to do it. First, if you are a man, you have to be fully conscious of your sun, your solar energy centre, your sex centre. You have to be there at the muladhar, showering your consciousness on the muladhar. When the muladhar is showered by consciousness, you will watch and you will see that an energy is arising and moving into the hara centre, into the moon.

And you will feel so blissful when the energy moves into the moon centre. All your sexual orgasms are nothing compared to it—absolutely nothing; there is ten thousand times more intensity when your sun energy moves into your own moon energy. Then the real man meets the real woman. When you meet a woman outside, howsoever close you come, you remain separate. It is a very superficial meeting—just two surfaces meet, that's all, just two surfaces rub each other: that's all. But when your sun energy moves into the moon energy, then two centres of energy meet. And the man whose sun and moon are meeting remains cheerful, blissful—continuously, because there is no need to lose this orgasm. This is permanent orgasm.

If you are a woman, bring your consciousness to the hara centre and you will see your energy moving toward the sun centre.

One centre is nonfunctioning; one is functioning. The functioning has to be joined to the nonfunctioning: immediately, the nonfunctioning starts to function. And when the energy is meeting—sun and moon are becoming one—you will see that now the energy goes on rising upward. You start falling upward.

I have heard:

A madman was the guest of a distant relative who put him up in the basement where there was a bed. In the middle of the night the host was awakened to the sound of his visitor's laughter coming from upstairs.

'What are you doing here?' he asked. 'You are supposed to be sleeping in the basement.'

'I was,' the guest answered. 'I rolled off my bed.'

'And how did you fall upstairs?'

'That's what I am laughing at.'

Yes, it happens. Once the sun and the moon meet, then you are like that madman; you fall upward. And then you will laugh because it is really something ridiculous. Falling upward? One has never heard of it.

You have heard the story, Newton was sitting in a garden and one apple fell. This apple seems to be connected with humanity too much—the same apple was there when Adam was trapped by the snake—and again, this poor Newton was sitting and one apple fell, and he discovered the theory of gravitation. But when your sun and moon meet, you go, suddenly, into a different reality, a separate reality: you start falling upward. You defy Newton—gravitation is meaningless. You gravitate upward! And, of course, the whole training has been this: that if you throw a thing, it falls downward, everything falls downward. Then the laughter is reasonable.

It is said about Hotei, a Zen monk, that once he became enlightened he never stopped laughing. He continued, continued, till he died. He moved from one village to another laughing and laughing. It is said about him that even when he was asleep you could hear his laughter. People used to ask, 'Why do you laugh?' He would say, 'How can I say? But something has happened, something very ridiculous. Something which should not happen— is not *supposed* to happen—has happened.'

Yes, the madman was doing right. If one day you fall from your bed and suddenly you find yourself upstairs, you will laugh. But this happens, and the madman is no ordinary madman. This is a Sufi story; the madman must have been a master.

This sutra says: '*Murdha jyotishi siddha darshanam*'; the moment your consciousness meets with the sahasrar, you suddenly become available to the world beyond, to the world of the siddhas.

In yoga symbolism, the muladhar, the sex centre, is thought to be like a red lotus of four petals. The four petals represent four directions; redness represents heat, because it is the sun centre. And the sahasrar is represented as a thousand-petalled lotus of all colours . . . a thousand petalled—*sahasrar padma*—a thousand-petalled lotus of all colours because it includes the whole. The sex centre is only red. The sahasrar is a rainbow, all colours included, the totality included.

Ordinarily, the sahasrar, the one-thousand-petalled lotus, hangs downward in your head. Once the energy moves through it, the energy makes it upward. It is as if a lotus is hanging without energy, downward—just the very weight of it makes it hang downward—then energy rushes in it, makes it alive. It moves upward, opens to the beyond.

When this lotus moves upward and blooms, it is said in yoga scriptures, 'It is as resplendent as ten million suns and ten million moons.' One moon and one sun meet in your being. That becomes the possibility of the meeting of ten million suns and ten million moons. You have found the key of the ultimate orgasm, where ten million moons meet ten million suns—ten million females meet ten million males. You can think of the ecstasy . . . .

Shiva must have been in that ecstasy when he was found making love to his consort Devi. He must have been at the sahasrar. His lovemaking cannot be sexual; it cannot be from the muladhar. It must have been from the omega point of his being. That's why he was completely oblivious of who was watching, who was standing; he was not in time, he was not in space. He was beyond time, beyond space. This is the goal of yoga, of tantra, of all spiritual effort.

The meeting of the male and female energy creates the possibility of the ultimate meeting of Shiva and Shakti, life and death. In this way Hindu gods are tremendously beautiful, and tremendously humane. Think of the Christian God—with no consort, with no woman. Looks a little rigid, looks a little alone, looks a little empty, looks a little too male-oriented, too sun-oriented, hard; no surprise if the Jewish and Christian concept of God is of a very terrible God.

Jews say, 'Be afraid of God. Remember, he is not your uncle.' But Hindus say, 'Don't be worried, he is your mother.' Jews have created a very ferocious God, who is always ready to throw fire and thunder and destroy and kill. Just a small sin, maybe just an innocent sin, and he becomes terribly upset . . . seems to be almost neurotic.

And the whole Christian conception of the trinity—God, the Holy Ghost, and the son—the whole trinity seems to be like a boys' club: homosexual, no woman at all. And Christians are so afraid of the moon energy, the woman, so afraid, that they have no conception. Somehow, later on, they improved upon it a little by adding the Virgin Mary; somehow, because it is totally against their ideology, and then too they insist that she is a virgin . . . .

The meeting of the sun and moon is not allowed at all; even if they allow Mary to be respected . . . of course it is a secondary status because in the original trinity, there was no place for her. Somehow, feeling the incompleteness of it all, they have managed to bring the Virgin Mary in from the back door. But then too they insist she is virgin. Why this insistence? What is wrong in the meeting of male and female energy?

And if you are so afraid of the meeting of male and female energy in the outer world, how will you be ready for the same meeting in the inner world?

Hindu gods are more human, more down-to-earth, and of course, more compassion, more love flows through them.

Pratibhad va sarvam.

Through pratibha, intuition, knowledge of everything.

The word *pratibha* is a difficult word, it cannot be translated into English; 'intuition' is a very, very poor substitute for it, and I will have to explain it to you—it cannot be translated, I can only describe it.

The sun is intellect; the moon is intuition. When you transcend both, then comes pratibha, and there is no word for it. The sun is intellect, analysis, logic; the moon is intuition, the hunch, just a flash—suddenly you jump on the conclusion. Intellect moves through method, process, syllogism; intuition suddenly comes to the conclusion—with no process, no methodology, no syllogism. You cannot ask intuition why. There is no 'therefore' in intuition. A sudden revelation, as if lightning has happened and you have come to see something, and then the lightning disappears and you don't know how it happened and why it happened, but it has happened and you have seen something. All primitive societies are intuitive, all women are intuitive, all children are intuitive, all poets are intuitive.

But pratibha is totally different. It has been translated as 'intuition' in all the English translations of Patanjali's yoga sutras, but I would not like to translate it that way. Pratibha means: when the energy has moved beyond the duality of intellect and intuition. It is beyond both. Intuition is beyond intellect, pratibha is beyond both. Now, there is no logic in it, no sudden lightning in it, everything is eternally revealed. In pratibha, one becomes omniscient, omnipotent, omnipresent; everything is revealed simultaneously—the past, the present, the future—all. That is the meaning: *pratibhad va sarvam*—through pratibha, all.

When your energy moves through the sahasrar and ten million moons and ten million suns meet within you, and you become an oceanic experience of orgasm—which goes on and on and on, eternally; then there is no end to it—there is pratibha. Then you see; you see all through and through, you know all through and through. Then space and time both disappear, with all their limitations.

So, one psychology is sun-oriented, another is moon-oriented, but the real psychology—the real psychology of being will be pratibha-oriented. It will not be divided into man and woman. It will be the highest and the greatest synthesis, and transcendence.

Intellect is like a blind man: it gropes in the dark. That's why so much argumentation is needed. Intuition is not blind but is like a crippled man, it cannot move. Pratibha is like a healthy man, all limbs healthy.

There is an Indian story that once a forest caught fire. There was one blind man and one crippled man in the forest. The blind man could not see, he could run—but it was dangerous to run without knowing where you are running, when the fire is all over, all around. The crippled man could not walk, but he could see. They came to a tacit understanding: the blind man allowed the crippled man to ride on his back and to see for him—the crippled man agreed to see for him if the blind man was to run for him. In their synthesis, they could get out of the forest and the fire.

Intellect is half; intuition is also half. Intuition cannot run, it is just in flashes. It cannot be a continued source of revelation. And intellect goes on groping in the dark, continuously groping in the dark.

Pratibha is a synthesis and a transcendence.

If you are too intellectual, you will miss a few things in life that are very beautiful. You will not be able to enjoy poetry, you will not be able to delight in singing, you will not be able to celebrate in dancing. They will look a little foolish, a little below you. You will be uptight, you will hold yourself back, you will remain a little repressed. Your moon will suffer.

If you are just intuitive, you may be able to enjoy much, but you will not be able to help others much because the communication will be lacking. You may be able to live a beautiful life yourself, but you will not be able to create a beautiful world around you, because that is possible only through intellect.

When science and poetry meet, then a perfect world is possible. Otherwise, intellect goes on condemning intuition; intuition goes on condemning intellect.

I have heard:

A woman asked a new acquaintance, 'How long have you been married?'

'Twenty-odd years,' replied the other.

'Why do you call them odd?'

'Wait,' said the woman, 'until you see my husband.'

The intuition thinks the intellect is odd, the intellect thinks the intuition is odd. Separately, they are odd; together, they create a great orchestra, a great harmony.

The great Persian mystic, Rumi, in a beautiful poem tells us of how one day Moses, the prophet, sees a shepherd on the way, crying, 'O Lord, where art thou? I long to serve thee and comb thy hair and wash thy clothes and kill thy lice and bring milk to thee and kiss thy little hand and rub thy little feet and sweep thy little room at night before thou dost retire.'

Moses, the prophet, hearing these words, is greatly annoyed and quickly he speaks rough words to the shepherd, 'O foolish man! To whom are you speaking these foolish words? What blasphemy are you uttering? Better that you were stricken dumb than that you should speak thus to God the Most High. Thy words are a crime. A shepherd! Put cotton into your mouth and speak no longer a word of irreverence to the Lord, who in a moment can consume thee to ashes and dust.'

And the shepherd, we are told, rends his garment in agony and heaves a sigh and goes quickly forth into the wilderness.

Then, unto Moses comes a revelation at night. To Moses speaks the Lord, 'Moses, thou wert sent into the world to unite, not to sever. But you have parted from me my servant, my devotee. Dear to me is that shepherd. Forget not, Moses, that every mode of worship is mine. The modes are many; religions are many, yet all are mine. Each one has his own path, his own way, his own form, his own idiom. Moses, I look not at tongues and words, I look at the spirit and the inward feeling.'

And Moses goes out to meet the shepherd and says to him, 'I repent. And I ask thee to forgive me.'

The intellect always goes on thinking in its own idiom. The intuition remains incomprehensible to it. And the intuition cannot believe in intellect, it seems too superficial, with no depth.

You have to come to a synthesis within you. That's what Patanjali means when he says, 'pratibhad va sarvam.' You have to come to such a deep synthesis that pratibha arises in you; which is one where logic and prayer meet, where work and worship meet, where science is not antagonistic to poetry and poetry is not antagonistic to science.

That's why I say man is yet in the making, he is evolving. Man is yet a form without content. The content has to be achieved, that great alchemy has to be achieved. You have to make yourself a great experimental lab of evolution and you have to bring your energy from the muladhar, from the sex centre, upward to the sahasrar.

Hridaye chitta samvit.

*Performing samyama on the heart brings
awareness of the nature of mind.*

That too is not an adequate translation, but it is difficult; translators are in a difficulty.

'*Hridaye chitta samvit.*' First, when Patanjali uses the word *hridaye*, he does not mean the physical heart. In yoga terminology, just behind the physical heart is the real heart, hidden. It is not part of the physical body. The physical heart simply corresponds with the real heart, the spiritual heart; there is a synchronicity between them, but no causal relationship. And that heart can be known only when you have reached to the peak. When your energy has come to the omega point of the sahasrar, only then can you realize the real heart, the very abode of God.

'*Hridaye chitta samvit*'—*Performing samyama on the heart brings awareness of the nature of mind.*' That too is not true: *chitta samvit* means the very nature of *consciousness*, not of mind. The mind is gone, left behind, because the mind is either the sun mind or the moon mind. Once you have transcended sun and moon, mind is gone, left behind. In fact, chitta samvit is a state of no mind. If you ask Zen people, they will say no-mind. The mind is gone because it exists with the division; when the division is gone, mind is gone. They are together, two aspects of one phenomenon. The mind divides and the mind exists through division—they depend on each other, they 'interdepend.' When division is gone, mind is gone; when mind is gone, division is gone.

There are two ways to reach this state of no-mind: one is the tantra way—you drop the mind, division disappears; the other is the yoga way—you drop the division, and the mind disappears. You can do either. The ultimate result is the same: you become one, a unison arises.

'*Hridaye chitta samvit.*' Then you come to know what is the real nature of consciousness. Again, this word *consciousness* in English denotes as if it is an antonym to *unconsciousness*. Chitta samvit is not an antonym to unconsciousness. Consciousness includes all: unconsciousness is also a sleeping state of consciousness, so there is no antagonism. Consciousness, unconsciousness, all—the very nature of consciousness—is revealed when one brings one's awareness, samyama, to the heart.

In yoga, the heart centre is called *anahat chakra*—the anahat centre. You must have heard the famous Zen koan: when a disciple reaches to the master, the master gives something absolutely absurd to meditate upon. One of the famous absurdities is, the master says to the disciple, 'Go, and listen to the sound of one hand clapping.' Now this is absurd. The one hand cannot clap, and there cannot be a sound of one hand clapping. For a sound, two hands are needed to clap and create it. *Ahat* means 'by conflict'; anahat means 'without any conflict.' Anahat means the sound of one hand clapping.

When all sounds disappear in you, you hear the sound that is constantly there, which is intrinsic to nature, which is the very nature of existence—the sound of silence, or the sound of soundlessness. The heart is called anahat chakra, the place where constantly a sound is being created—without any conflict—an eternal sound. Hindus have called that sound *omkar*, *om*. It has to be heard. So people who go on repeating, 'Om, om, om . . .' are doing a foolish thing. By your repetition, you cannot come to the real omkar, to the real sound, because by your making it, you are creating it by clapping.

Become completely silent, drop all thinking, become unmoving, and suddenly it is there; it has always been there, but you were not available to listen to it. It is a very, very subtle sound. When you have dropped the whole world from your mind and you are alert only for it, then by and by, you become receptive to it—by and by, you start hearing it.

Once you can hear the sound of one hand clapping, you have heard God, you have heard all.

Patanjali is taking you step-by-step toward the omega point. These three sutras are very significant; ponder over them again and again, meditate on them. And try to feel them within your being. They can become keys that can open the doors of the divine.

Enough for today.

Six

You Can't Corner a Madman

The first question:

Osho, you are so tremendously superb and disarming that sometimes I wonder have you ever been in a corner?

To be in a corner, one needs to be logical in the first place. I am not logical; you cannot force me into a corner. I am so illogical that it is impossible to force me into a corner. Remember this, if you cling to the intellect, you can be forced into a corner anytime because you have something to cling to. Once it is proved that that is wrong, illogical, you will be in a corner. If you cannot prove your prejudice logically, you will be in a corner. But I am absolutely illogical—I have no prejudice to prove, I have nothing to prove. How can you put me in a corner?

Let me tell you one anecdote:

A man was claiming to be God. He was taken to the Caliph, who said, 'Last year someone was claiming to be a prophet—he was executed. Do you know about it?'
'Serves him right,' the man answered. 'I had not sent him.'

Now you cannot put such a man in a corner. It is impossible because the illogical approach is an open approach. In fact, there are no corners because there is no room—no walls around it. It is an open sky; one can move anywhere. You can be forced into a corner if you live in a room, walled, and there are corners. If you live under the sky, how can you be pushed into a corner? There are no corners at all.

And that's what I teach you: why cling to prejudices? If you are a Hindu or a Mohammedan or a Christian, you can be put in a corner. But if you are neither, corners have disappeared: there is no possibility to force you anywhere. Then the whole sky is yours, and the moment you understand the beauty and the freedom of the whole sky, you will drop all prejudices, all ideologies.

I have no ideology, nothing to prove. I am here just to give you a glimpse of me.

And I am very illogically here; in fact, I should have left before. Someone has asked, 'Why did you suddenly stop and put your hand to your head yesterday morning? Why?' It happens sometimes: I lose contact with my body. I should have gone, really. I am illogically here—trying somehow to put some weight on me so I can help you a little longer. You may not have been aware, but it has happened many times before. Mind is a mechanism: I am using it; sometimes I lose contact. Body is a mechanism: I am using it; sometimes I lose contact. Sometimes I start moving into the abyss so fast that I have to stop for a single moment.

Not only that I am illogical; I am illogically here.

And those who want to be argumentative with me will be at a loss. They cannot defeat me, because I am not trying to convince them and I am not trying to prove anything. I am not interested in converting you; I am just interested in giving you something that I have. If you are ready, open, en rapport with me, you can receive it. Otherwise, later on, you will repent very much.

It happened:

A drunk staggered into a crowded pub, pushed his way through the customers, and approached the bar. Finding a man and woman in his way, he brushed them aside, pushed the woman rudely aside, elbowed his way through to the counter and belched loudly. The man he had just pushed past turned to him angrily.

'How dare you push through like that and belch in front of my wife?' he asked indignantly.

The drunk looked apologetic.

'I am sorry to belch in front of your dear lady,' he said. 'I didn't realize it was her turn.'

I am like that drunk: you cannot corner me.

That's what I am doing with your questions. What answer I give is not important—try to see that I am destroying your question. My answer is not an answer but a strategy to destroy your question. There are people who answer your questions, they give you certain ideas, they fill you with certain ideologies, theories, dogmas, cults . . . I am not answering your question that way. If you watch, if you are aware, you will be able to see that I try to destroy your question. Not that you receive the answer, but that you lose the question.

If someday you become questionless, that will be the point of realization. Not that you will have any answer: you will not have any questions; that's all. You can call it 'the answer,' when there is no question.

A buddha is not a man who has all the answers; a buddha is a man who has no questions. The questioning has disappeared— the questioning has become absurd, irrelevant. He is simply there without any question. That's what I mean when I say he is a no-mind. Mind always questions, mind is a questioning; as leaves come out of the trees, questions come out of the mind. Old leaves fall, new leaves come; old questions disappear, new questions come.

I would like to uproot this whole tree.

If I am giving you any answer, then many more questions will arise out of it. Your mind will convert that answer into many questions.

I am absolutely absurd. I am not a philosopher—maybe a mad poet, a drunkard. You can love me, you cannot follow me; you can trust me, you cannot imitate me. Through your love and trust, something tremendously valuable will be transferred to you. It has nothing to do with what I say; it has something to do with what I am. It is a transmission beyond the scriptures.

So never in my life have I been cornered. It is impossible—you cannot corner a madman.

The second question:

Osho, kindly explain the relative importance of intellect, intuition, and pratibha in their proper perspective. Pray, specially explain why and how life should be pratibha-oriented and how only such an orientation is adequate for life and life's evolution at its highest and best.

The intellect is the lowest functioning of your being, but because it is the lowest, it is the most efficient; because it is the lowest, it is the most developed. Because it is the lowest, it can be educated, disciplined; because it is the lowest, all the universities, colleges, schools, exist for it. And every man has it more or less.

It is tremendously useful in the outer world. Without intellect, it will be difficult for you to be of any utility. That's why Lao Tzu says to his disciples, 'Become useless.' Unless you are ready to become useless, you will not be ready to leave intellect behind, because intellect gives you utility. You become a doctor—you become useful to society: you become an engineer; you become a professor—this and that. It is through intellect that you become *somebody* and the society can use you—and the society can use you as a means. The more utility you fulfil, the more society values you; hence, the hierarchy—the *brahmin*, the *kshatriya*, the *vaishya*, the *sudra*.

Highest is the scholar, who is pure intellect—the brahmin. Lower than him is the warrior, the kshatriya, because he has to protect the country. Lower than him is the businessman, because he is the whole blood-circulating system of the society—he is the economics, the belly. And the lowest is the sudra, the untouchable, the proletariat, because his work is manual, menial, and not much intellect is needed. The sudra needs the least development of intellect and the brahmin needs the highest development of intellect, but the whole division is because of intellect.

Intellect has its utility, but you are bigger than the intellect, vaster than the intellect. If you become identified with the intellect too much, you will become a doctor or an engineer or a professor, a businessman, a warrior, but you will lose your being. You will not be yourself. You can become so identified with your function that you can forget your being. You can forget that you are a man; you can become so much of an engineer or a judge or a politician that you can forget that you are a man. You are losing much; then you are just a mechanism. The society will use you—while you can be used—then you will be retired from society. Then society waits for you . . . when you are going to die.

Retired people die sooner than they would have died if they had not been retired; they become old sooner; their life becomes less by almost ten years. What happens? They become useless. They can feel that everywhere, wherever they go, they are at the most, tolerated; they are not needed. And there is a great need in man to be needed—the greatest need is to be needed. Once you feel you are superfluous, once you feel you can be discarded into the dustbin, once you feel that you don't function as a utility in the society; you start dying. The retirement day becomes the date of dying also—you start dying fast. You yourself know that you will be a burden now. People will tolerate you, people may even sympathize with you, but nobody is going to take you seriously, nobody is going to love you and respect you. You are discarded.

If you get too identified with the intellect, you are becoming a thing, like a mechanism. A good car, but when its utility is finished, it is thrown onto the rubbish heap. Then you are going to be used and thrown, and your innermost core will remain unfulfilled because you were not meant to be just used. You were meant to flower as a being; that was your destiny.

Higher than intellect is intuition. Intuition gives a little romance to your life, a little poetry. It gives you a few glimpses of the nonutilitarian, of your being a person and not being a thing. When somebody loves you, that love hits your intuition, your moon centre. When somebody looks at you with charmed eyes, magnetized, that exhilarates the moon energy within you. When somebody says that you are beautiful, your being feels enhanced. When somebody says you are useful, you feel hurt. Useful? That doesn't seem to be appreciation, because if you are useful then you are replaceable; then you can be thrown, somebody else can replace you. But if you are beautiful then you are irreplaceable, then you are unique. Then when you will be gone from the world, something will always remain empty, something will always be lacking.

That's why you hanker for love; love is food for intuition. If you are not loved, your intuition will not develop. The only way to develop intuition is to shower love upon you. So if a mother loves the child, the child becomes intuitive; if the mother does not love the child, the child becomes intellectual. If the child lives in an atmosphere of love and care and compassion—if the child is accepted for his own self, not for any utility that he can fulfil—then he grows tremendously inside and his energy starts moving through the moon centre.

The moon centre is almost nonfunctioning because you have not been loved.

Watch: if you tell a woman, 'I love you because you have beautiful eyes,' she will not be happy, because tomorrow she can lose her eyes. Eyes are just accidental . . . or some disease may happen and she may become blind, or the eyes may not remain beautiful. When you say, 'I love you because you have a beautiful face,' the woman is not happy, because the face will not remain beautiful forever. The old age is coming every day, every moment. But if you say, 'I love you,' then she feels happy because this 'you' is something permanent, not accidental, nothing can happen to it. When you say to a woman, 'I love you because . . .' then she never feels happy, because the 'because' brings intellect in. You simply say, you shrug your shoulders and you say, 'I don't know why, but I love you.' The moon centre starts functioning, the woman flowers.

Watch a woman when nobody loves her and watch her the next moment when somebody has said to her, 'I love you.' A tremendous difference, of grace, dignity; a tremendous change—her whole face becomes enlightened with something new—a glow comes to her. What has happened? The moon centre has released its energy.

You must have heard the name of one great Dutch painter, Vincent van Gogh. He was ugly, very ugly, and no woman could ever manage to say to him, 'I love you.' Of course, he remained retarded—the moon centre never functioned. He was repulsive. People would look at him and escape. He used to work in an art dealer's shop, and the man, the owner, watched him day in, day out. He looked so dull, as if much dust had gathered on his being, and he did not take interest in anything. Customers would come, he would show the paintings, but he would not take any interest. Continuously burdened, not interested in anything, indifferent. He would walk like a zombie—had to walk, so he would walk, but no zest, no life, no intensity, no passion.

One day suddenly, the owner could not believe his eyes. He had come, and it seemed he had taken a bath after many months, or many years maybe. He had taken a bath, he had combed his hair, and his step had a dance in it and he was humming a tune. Impossible! And he had good clothes on and he was wearing a perfume. Impossible.

The owner called him, 'Van Gogh, what has happened?' Van Gogh said, 'It has happened—a woman has said she loves me. Though the woman was only a prostitute, but still . . . she has said so only for money, but still, a woman has said she loves me.'

Van Gogh asked the woman, the prostitute, 'Why do you love me?' Because that was always a haunting thing in him—nobody loves him, he knew his ugliness. 'Why do you love me?' It was impossible for him to accept that somebody can love him just for himself, 'Why?' And the prostitute was at a loss because there was nothing to say, because whatsoever she said would look ridiculous. She cannot say, 'Because of your eyes,' she cannot say, 'Because of your face,' she cannot say, 'Because of your body'—everything was somehow wrong. She said, 'Because of your ears. They are so beautiful.' Ears? Have you ever heard? And he was so enchanted that he went back home, cut off one ear, wrapped it in a parcel, went back, and presented the ear to the woman. He said, 'Nobody has ever liked anything in me. This is a poor man's present, but keep it.' The woman was aghast. She could not believe, what type of madman is this?

But he felt very good, he felt tremendously good. He wrote in one of his letters, 'That was the peak of my life. Somebody had liked something in me, and I could share my being.'

Watch, observe. Whenever somebody loves you, and simply loves you, unconditionally loves you, simply says, 'I love you because you are you, I love you because you *are*,' what happens within your energies? The sun has moved toward the moon. Now the sun is not so hot; the moon is cooling it. And the grace of moonlight spreads all over your being.

If the world exists more in tune with love, people will have more intuition and less intellect, and they will become more beautiful. They will not be like things; they will each be more of a person—alive with zest, with passion, intensity. They will have a flame and a celebration.

Intuition is totally different. It functions without any process: it simply jumps to the conclusion. In fact, intuition is an opening towards the reality—a vision comes to it. Logic has to grope in darkness; intuition never gropes, just a vision. It simply sees it.

People who are intuitive become religious naturally. People who are intellectual cannot become religious naturally; at the most, they can be intellectually involved in some sort of a religious philosophy, but not in religion as such. They can be involved in theology, but not in religion. They can talk about the proofs for God, but to talk about God is not to talk about God. To 'talk about' is to miss the target—about and about, they move in a circle. They always go on beating around and around the bush; they never hit the target.

Intellectuals have no natural tendency to become religious. That's the reason you see temples, churches, so full of women; the moon feels naturally in tune with religion. Buddha had three times more women than men as his disciples. The same proportion was with Mahavira: he had 10,000 monks and 30,000 nuns. You would find the same around Jesus—and when he was crucified, all the men followers fled.

When Jesus' body was brought down from the cross, only three women were there. Because those men were watching from the crowd for some miracle: they were trying to convince their sun centre that, 'Yes, this is God's only son,' but nothing happened. They were asking for a proof. They were praying to God and to Jesus, 'Show us a miracle so that we can be convinced.' Once they saw that Jesus died like an ordinary man, *absolutely* ordinary—there were two other men who were dying on crosses just to the side of Jesus, two thieves, and Jesus died just like them, with no difference at all—the men became sceptical. Then this man was bogus, he was not really a son of God. So he was not a god; they escaped.

But this idea never arose to the women. They were not looking for a miracle; they were just looking at Jesus. They were not looking for a miracle, they were just looking at Jesus, and they saw the miracle. They saw the miracle: that Jesus died so ordinarily. That was the miracle. He didn't try to prove anything, because people who try to prove are defensive. He was not defensive. He simply said to God, 'Thy kingdom come, thy will be done.' That was his miracle. And he said to God, 'Forgive these poor people because they don't know what they are doing.'

That was the miracle: he could pray for those who were murdering him, pray for compassion. He told God, 'Put your judgement aside, put your judgeing attitude aside. Listen to me. These people are innocent; they don't know what they are doing. They are ignorant. Please don't be angry with them, don't be annoyed. Forgive them.' That was the miracle.

The women could see it because they were not looking for a miracle. The intellect is always looking for something; the intuition is simply open, not looking for something in particular, just looking—it is a vision. That is the meaning of the word *intuition*.

When Jesus appeared after three days, first he approached the men disciples. He walked with them, he talked with them, but they couldn't recognize him; they had accepted the idea that he was dead—finished. In fact, they must be feeling sorry, 'We wasted so many of our years with this man.' Now they must be looking for some other miracle-monger, some juggler; they must be looking for somebody else. And Jesus walked with them, talked to them, and they did not recognize him. Then he had to approach the women; and when he came close and Mary Magdalen saw him, she ran—she wanted to embrace him. She immediately recognized him, and she did not even ask, 'How has it happened? Three days before, you were crucified.' The intuition never asks how and why, it simply accepts; it is a deep acceptability, total acceptability.

If you live in a loving atmosphere . . . And you have to create the atmosphere around you, nobody is going to create it for you: love people, so that they will love you. Love people, so that love is reflected back, resounded back; love people, so that you are showered by love. Your intuition will start functioning; you will start seeing things that you had never seen before. And the world remains the same, but some new meaning appears in it. The flowers remain the same, but some new mystery is revealed to you. The birds go on singing the same way, but now you can understand their language; suddenly, there is communication, suddenly, there is communion.

Intuition is closer to truth than intellect is because it makes you a person—more of a person—than intellect.

And then there is *pratibha*—that which is beyond both, the supra-intuition. Nothing can be said about it because all that can be said can be said either in sun language or in moon language. Either it can be described in a scientific way or it can be sung in a poetic way, but there is no way to describe pratibha. It is beyond; one has to feel it, one has to live it to know it.

People would come to Gautam Buddha and they would say, 'Tell us something about God.' And he would say, 'Keep quiet, be silent. Remain with me, and it will happen to you.'

It is not a question that can be asked and answered, and it is not a problem that can be solved. It is a mystery to be lived. It's an ecstasy; it's a tremendous experience.

The way of the intellect:

One day Mulla was in the village mill, filling his bag with a little bit of every other person's wheat.

'Why are you doing that, Nasruddin? ' someone asked.

'Because I am a fool,' Mulla replied.

'Why don't you then fill other people's bags with your own wheat, if you are a fool?'

'Then,' Mulla answered, 'I would be more of a fool.'

Intellect is cunning, intellect is calculating, intellect is always trying to exploit others. Intuition is just the opposite; it is not exploitative.

Now let me tell you one thing. People think that someday or the other the world will come to a point where there will be no classes, no economic hierarchy, no poor, no rich. And the people who have given much thought to this dream, this utopia—Marx, Engels, Lenin, and Mao—they are all intellectuals, and intellect can never bring this state of affairs; only in an intuitive world is it possible that classes may disappear. But they are against intuition: Marxists think intellect is all in all; there is nothing beyond it. If that is so, then their utopia is never going to be fulfilled, because intellect as such is exploitative; it is cunning. Intellect is violent, aggressive, destructive.

The sun energy is very violent and hot; it burns, it kills.

If there is ever really going to be a world without classes, a really communist world, where communes exist and there are no classes, then that world has to be completely anti-Marxist. It has to be intuitive. And the builders of that world cannot be politicians; only poets, imaginative people, dreamers.

I would like to say that man cannot be the creator of that world, only woman; the moon can create a world of equality, not the sun.

A Buddha, a Jesus maybe, can be helpful towards that utopia and the fulfilment of it, but Marx? No, absolutely no: he is too calculative, too clever, too intellectual. But the world has been ruled by the sun up to now. That was also natural because the sun is aggressive.

Now the possibility opens that the sun is tired, exhausted, frustrated, and humanity may start looking for another centre to work with. That will be the real rise of women in the world: if the moon rises. But, as I see, in the West there is great excitement amongst women, great movement, revolutionary thinking, radical thought—the lib movement—but they are all falling and becoming intellectuals. They are becoming more like men. If women react to men, they will become more like men themselves; that is the danger.

The woman should remain woman, only then is there a possibility of a different world and a different society—the moon-oriented society. But if the woman herself becomes aggressive, as she is becoming, then she is learning the nonsense of man and the aggression of man and the violence of man. She may succeed, but the sun will succeed in her again.

One has to be very, very alert in radical times. When changes are going to happen in human consciousness, one has to be very alert; just a single wrong step, and the whole thing can go wrong.

Now, the possibility is there that the moon can function and the moon can become dominant, but the woman, if she becomes aggressive, will miss, and again man will win through her and the sun will remain in power.

From intellect to intuition and from intuition to beyond, this is the right direction of evolution: from man to woman and from woman to beyond.

Now one question has been asked; that this is understandable as far as man is concerned, what about women? They are on the moon centre, what do they have to do?

They will have to absorb the sun centre. As man has to absorb the moon centre, the woman has to absorb the sun centre. Otherwise something remains denied in them; then they will not be *whole* women. So a man has to move from the sun centre to the moon, from intellect to intuition; the woman has to learn intellect also, has to learn the logic of life too. She knows the love of life, man knows the logic of life; man has to learn the love of life and woman has to learn the logic of life. Then a balance arises.

Woman will have to absorb the sun centre—and she can absorb very easily because her moon is functioning; the moon just has to open in the direction of the sun. The path is going to be just a little different: for man, the sun energy has to be brought to the moon; for women, they have just to open their moon towards the sun and the energy will start flowing.

But both have to become total. The conscious has to absorb the unconscious and the division has to drop.

Jesus says, 'A man becomes a woman and a woman becomes a man.' When you accept your totality and you don't deny any part of your being, everything becomes balanced. And when woman and man are balanced within you, they negate each other. Suddenly, you are free; those two forces negate each other, and suddenly you are no longer in bondage.

You can remain in bondage only if one is more powerful than the other. If the sun is more powerful than the moon, then you will be in the bondage of your man—the male mind. If the moon is stronger than the sun, then you will remain in the bondage of woman—the female. When both are equal, balancing, they negate each other; suddenly, your energy is free: you are not in any form now, you become formless. That formlessness is pratibha. Then you start rising higher and higher and higher—and there is no end to this growth.

That is the meaning when we say God is infinite: you go on growing and growing—you go on becoming more perfect, more perfect, more perfect . . . . Each moment is perfect and each next coming moment is more perfect than that.

The third question:

Osho, kindly elaborate the phrase 'in the bad company of yogis and sadhus'.

Yogi Chinmaya, let me tell you one anecdote:

There was a young man in a small town whose nose had been cut off because he had done something very wrong. People used to make fun of his cut nose and he was naturally humiliated by these insults. Everyone treated him with contempt. He pondered over the situation and soon found a way to make people honour and respect him.

He went to another village, put on the cloth of a sadhu, obtained other accessories of a sadhu, and sat in 'meditation' under a tree. Men and women gathered around him. At last he opened his eyes and the people asked him who he was, and what he could do for them.

'I can do a lot for you,' he replied. 'I can show you God if only you agree to cut off your nose—I did the same and I can see God very clearly, everywhere. Only God is.' Three people in the crowd agreed to have their noses cut off . . . .

You can always find people more stupid than yourself—
they become your followers.

. . . He took them to a tree some distance away, cut off their
noses, applied some medicine to stop the bleeding, and whispered
in their ears, 'Look, now there is no point in saying to them that
you have not seen God. They will laugh at you and they will
insult you and you will become a laughing stock of the whole
village. So listen, you must now go and tell others that as soon as
your nose was cut off, you began seeing God.'
    They were so filled with shame at their folly that they accepted
the suggestion and went to the crowd and said most
enthusiastically, 'Of course, we can see God. God is everywhere.'
    And so everyone in the town got his nose cut off and achieved
'God-realization.'

You can find many sadhus in India: in some way or the other
their noses have been cut off. When I say, 'in the bad company of
sadhus and yogis', I mean these people. When I say their noses
have been cut off, I mean they have denied some part of their
being. They have not accepted their whole being: their noses
have been cut off. Somebody has denied his sex, somebody has
denied his anger, somebody has denied his greed, somebody
something else. But the denied part takes revenge, and these people
would like to cut off your noses also.
    When I say 'in the bad company of sadhus and yogis', I mean
people who have not understood anything but have tried many
things, and have really crippled themselves in many ways. If you
remain with them, you will become crippled.
    Chinmaya has become crippled. When I look at him, I can
feel where he has become crippled, and once he understands it,
he can drop it immediately, there is no problem. The nose can
grow again. It is not a problem—it is not something that you can
really cut; it can grow again, once he understands. For example,
he has lost the capacity of humour. He cannot laugh; even if he

laughs—he tries hard—you can see his face is false. He is very sincere, but there is no need to be serious. Sincerity is one thing, it is honesty; seriousness is disease. Never mistake seriousness for sincerity. You can become a long face; that is not going to help. In fact, if you become completely humourless, your life will become dry, it will lose juice. Humour is like juice: it gives you a liquidity, a flow.

But in India, sadhus are serious; they have to be serious, they cannot laugh, because if they laugh, people will think they are also ordinary—just like other people they are laughing . . . . How can a sadhu laugh? He has to remain something extraordinary. That's an ego trip.

I tell you to be just ordinary, because to try to be extraordinary is a very ordinary thing—everybody wants that; and just to be ordinary, accept it, is very extraordinary because nobody wants it. I would like you to be just ordinary, so much so that nobody recognizes you as somebody in particular, so much so that you can be lost in the crowd. You will have a total freedom of being; otherwise, you have to continuously hold yourself up—then you are continuously on display—and that becomes a tension, that creates seriousness, that becomes a heavy burden. There is no need to be continuously in the show window. You can relax, you can laugh.

I allow you everything that is human. All that is human is yours: laugh like human beings, cry, weep, like human beings. Be ordinary.

If you remain ordinary, the ego will not arise. The ego arises with the idea of the extraordinary: so whatsoever people are doing, you are not meant to do it. If they walk on their feet, you are meant to stand on your head. Then they will come and worship you; they will say, 'You are so extraordinary.' But you are simply being foolish. Don't be bothered with their praise, because once you become addicted to their praise, you will be caught—then you will remain standing on your head for your whole life. You will lose all beauty of movement, and of course you cannot dance on your head. Have you ever seen any yogi dance? At the most, you can just stand dead, doing *shirshasan*, the headstand.

When I say 'bad company', I mean you have learned ego tricks from people who are deep in their egos. Avoid and escape from anybody who is on any ego trip because the possibility is he will give you some infection or the other.

And people learn to do things by imitation.

I have heard about one:

A very well travelled executive returned from his trip to Italy and called a friend in New York to meet him for lunch.

'Did you do anything exciting over there, while you were in Italy?' the friend asked.

'Oh, you know the old saying,' the executive, the American, shrugged. 'When in Rome, do as the Romans do.'

'Well, exactly what did you do?' the friend persisted.

'What else?' the businessman replied. 'I seduced an American schoolteacher.'

Now to go to Italy from America to seduce an American schoolteacher . . . but that's what Italians are doing, and 'do in Rome as the Romans do.'

When I say 'the bad company', I mean that the mind is imitative. Mind is unconsciously imitative. You will start learning tricks, and once you have learned them, it will be difficult to drop them, and more so if those tricks have a great investment.

If people come and appreciate you, if people start respecting your non-laughing, non-humorous face and they think that you are very, very controlled, disciplined, and they come and touch your feet; it will be very difficult now for you to drop your habit of seriousness, because you will be enjoying it. Now you have invested in your disease.

Drop it. Your life has to be lived from the within, not from the without. Don't be bothered about what people say: empty praise.

Just look to what you are; if you are enjoying, delighting in your being, if you have a dancing soul inside—enough! Then if everybody condemns you, accept that; but never compromise with your inner delight, because ultimately that is going to decide who you are. What people say is irrelevant. Who you are is relevant. Always go in and look at what you are doing to yourself.

If you are happy, then there is no question. If you feel that you are happy with your seriousness, then too there is no question; then you can be happy that way, then it is your choice. But I have never seen a man who is happy and serious. He will be joyous, he will be celebrating, he will be enjoying and sharing, and he will be laughing.

Laughter is so spiritual, nothing like it. Have you seen? When you laugh deeply, all tensions disappear. Have you watched? When you laugh deeply, suddenly, as if you have come to an open sky, the walls disappear around you. If you can laugh, you can always relax.

In Zen monasteries, the monks are taught that the first thing to do in the morning is to laugh, begin the day with laughter. Ridiculous, because for no reason—just getting out of bed, the first thing to be done is to laugh. In the beginning, it looks very difficult because there is nothing to laugh at. But it is a meditation, and, by and by, one gets in tune with it and one comes to know that there is no reason to laugh. Laughter is such a great exercise in itself, why wait for any reason? And it relaxes the whole day.

Let me tell you in terms of sun and moon. The sun person is serious; the moon person is nonserious. The sun person cannot laugh, it is difficult; the moon person can laugh easily, naturally, spontaneously. To a moon person laughter arises at every situation; he remains laughing. He does not wait for any excuse. But the sun person is very closed in; it is very difficult—even if you say a joke to him, he will look and listen to the joke as if you are giving him a mathematical problem.

That's why Germans cannot understand jokes. There was one joke, Priya told Haridas, and Haridas has not got it yet!

One man entered a restaurant and he asked for coffee.

And the waiter said, 'How do you like your coffee?'

The man said, 'I like my coffee just as I like my women—hot.'

The waiter said, 'Black or white?'

It is difficult if you start thinking about it, otherwise it is simple. What can be simpler? But once you start thinking about it, if you are serious, as if you are reading the Vedas, then you miss.

Avoid all serious company; avoid people who are trying to become somebody. Get more and more in tune with people who are simply living their life, not trying to become anybody, who are simply being as they are; move to them, they are the real spiritual people in the world. The religious leaders are not the real spiritual people in the world; they are politicians, they should have been in politics. They have corrupted religion very badly. They have made religion so serious that churches look more like hospitals or cemeteries. The jubilation, the enjoyment, is completely lost; you cannot dance in a church, you cannot laugh in a church. The laughter has gone out of the churches—but remember, the day laughter goes out of a church, God also goes out of it.

Let me tell you one very famous story:

Sam Burns, a Southern Negro, was refused entrance in a 'white' church. The sexton told him to go to his own church and pray to God and he will feel much better.

The next Sunday, he was back again. 'Don't get upset,' he said to the sexton. 'I am not forcing my way in. I just came to tell you that I took your advice and it came out just fine. I prayed to God and he told me, 'Don't feel bad about it, Sam. I have been trying to get into that church for years myself and I have not made it yet!'

Once a church is Christian, a temple is Hindu, a mosque is

Mohammedan, God is not to be found there—things have become serious, politics has entered, laughter has gone out.

Let laughter be your temple, and you will feel in deep contact with the divine.

The fourth question:

Osho, this ego seems to feed on every possible type of situation, and the situations that give it the most strength and nourishment are the supposed spiritual situations. I would like to take sannyas but I can already feel the whole ego thing happening in an intensely strong way. Feeding or starving it, retreating or confronting it, it derives nourishment both ways. What to do?

The question is from Michael Wise. Be wise—listen to me. Give the ego to me, that's what sannyas is. If *you* take sannyas, then the ego can feed itself upon it. I give you sannyas; you simply accept it. You have only to have that much courage, and then ego cannot exist—you have not done anything.

Whenever you come to me, first I try to give you sannyas. But there are very foolish people; they say, 'We will think.' They think they are clever; they start thinking about it: that someday they will come, and they come, and they ask for sannyas and I give them. But in the first place, I was going to give them—that would have been totally different. Then it would have been a gift from me, not a doing on your part. If you do something, then the ego can feed on it. It is just a gift from me; then there is no question of the ego. But you miss the gift and then you come and beg; then the whole beauty is lost. You take sannyas because of *your* decision; then the ego can come in. If you leave it to me, then there is no point . . . then it is my problem, you need not be worried about it.

Give your ego to me and forget all about it and start living, and I will take care of your ego.

So Michael Wise, be wise.

The fifth question:

Osho, how are we supposed to drop the mind when you keep cluttering it with all this interesting stuff at the lectures?

If you don't drop it, I am going to make it more and more heavy so it drops on its own accord—so that you cannot hold it. That's what my lectures are all about. I go on putting more weight, more weight . . . . I am waiting for the last straw so the camel drops down.

It is a competition between me and you—hope that you are not going to win.

The sixth question:

Osho, when I feel enlightened:
A. Do I tell you?
B. Do you tell me?
C. Is my ego asking this question?

No to all three . . . When you become enlightened, the enlightenment says everything, shows everything; there is no need for you to tell me, there is no need for me to tell you. Enlightenment is self-evident; it needs no certificate. It is self-evident, as if in the night suddenly a ray of light enters. There is no need to say anything about it. You will not really be able to say anything; all your thinking will stop. It is so tremendously silent. And it has such absolute certainty that there is no need to ask anybody. So there is not going to be any need from your side or from my side to tell.

And, 'Is my ego asking the question?' No. The ego never asks about enlightenment. It cannot ask about it, because enlightenment is going to be its death.

When you start meditating, loving, laughing, when you start moving into that dimension beyond, naturally the idea arises, 'If it happens, who is going to tell me?' Because up to now, whatsoever has happened, somebody was needed to tell it to you. This is much more so for a moon-oriented person.

When a woman falls in love, she waits for the man to tell her that he loves her. She will not even say it, that 'I love you.' The moon centre is not so certain as the intellectual centre always is. The moon centre is vague, misty. One feels, and yet one cannot say what it is. A woman remains uncertain about her love until the man comes and tells her and makes her certain that, 'Yes, it has happened.' That's why women are not known to propose, and whenever a woman proposes to a man, the man will escape immediately, because this woman is no woman; she is already a man. Propositioning from a woman looks absurd. The moon never proposes; it waits.

So I know why this question has arisen. If you cannot be certain even about your love, when God is going to happen to you, who is going to tell you? You will need somebody to make you assured.

There will be no need because God never happens on the sun centre, people who are foolishly certain; it never happens on the moon centre, people who are deliciously uncertain; it happens beyond both. It happens in pratibha, it happens in a supra-rational state where it is absolutely mysterious and yet absolutely certain.

The whole world is transformed with your enlightenment. Not only you, your whole past world disappears; a totally new experience, a totally new existence.

The last question:

Osho, firstly I did not believe that it was at all possible, but somehow I followed you. Thereafter, I did not think that it would ever be so soon, but somehow I persisted with you. And then, through you, the impossible has become possible, the distant the immediate.
Though I know that I have only taken the first few steps, more and more moments are gathering when it feels like the end of the

journey. It is painful and yet sweet: painful not to see you there anymore, but sweet to feel you everywhere.
Lest I disappear without so much as saying thank you to you, may I please say it now, when you are still there for me?

This is going to be so for each one of you. You have to come with me, 'somehow.' That 'somehow' is important. You cannot be knowingly with me, because you don't know where you are being led. You cannot be consideredly with me, logically, rationally with me, because I am taking you into the unknowable. I am taking you somewhere where you have never been, to a space that has never happened to you. 'Somehow' is the right word— somehow you come with me. In love, in a sort of madness, drunk with me you come with me; then, by and by, things start happening. Of course you had never believed that they would happen so soon.

In the darkness in which you are, you cannot believe that the light can happen to you ever, and when it starts happening, it seems almost that the impossible is happening. You cannot trust your own eyes; you feel as if you are moving in a dream. But by and by, the dream becomes the real and the real becomes the dream.

Exactly this is going to happen to you all, what has happened to him.

Let me repeat it: *'Firstly I did not believe that it was at all possible, but somehow I followed you.'* Those who can follow me, somehow, are the courageous ones. I cannot convince you to come with me, because there is no way to convince you about something you have never known. There is no way to convince you about something of which you have never heard. You have to trust me; you have to come with me somehow.

I cannot argue because the experience that I am going to communicate to you, the experience that I am going to transfer to you, cannot be argued about. It is beyond argument. If you are not convinced, I cannot convince you. If you are convinced, then

I can take you over, then I can possess you.

So only people who are mad enough are ready for me. Those who are very clever, I am not for them; they will have to wander a little longer, stumble in darkness and grope in darkness.

I can give you the gift of the unknown, it is ready, but you have to be ready to receive it. And of course you can only be somehow ready. It is a miracle; to be with me is a miracle; it cannot happen logically, but it happens. That's why people will say to you that you are hypnotized. In a way, they are right. You are not hypnotized, but you are in a sort of drunkenness.

'Thereafter I did not think that it would ever be so soon, but somehow I persisted with you. And then, through you the impossible has become possible, the distant the immediate.

'Though I know that I have only taken the first few steps, more and more moments are gathering when it feels like the end of the journey. It is painful and yet sweet: painful not to see you there anymore . . .'

The moment you can see yourself, you will not see me anymore because then two emptinesses will be facing each other, two mirrors facing each other. They will mirror infinitely, but nothing will be mirrored.

'It is painful and yet sweet: painful not to see you there anymore, but sweet to feel you everywhere.' Yes, the moment you cannot see me here in this chair, you will be able to see me everywhere.

'Lest I disappear without so much as saying thank you to you, may I please say it now, when you are still there for me?'

There is no need. Your whole being has become a thank you toward me. No need to say it . . . I have heard it before, you have said it.

Enough for today.

Seven

Beyond the Error of Experiencing

*Experience is the result of the inability to differentiate
between purush, pure consciousness, and sattva, pure
intelligence,
although they are absolutely distinct.
Performing samyama on the self-interest
brings knowledge of the purush
separated from the knowledge of others.*

*From this follows intuitional hearing,
touching, seeing, tasting, and smelling.*

*These are powers when the mind is turned outward,
but obstacles in the way of samadhi.*

One of the most important sutras of Patanjali—the very key
. . . This last part of Patanjali's yoga sutras is called
'*kaivalya pada.*' Kaivalya means the *summum bonum*—the
ultimate liberation, the total freedom of consciousness, which
knows no limitation, which knows no impurity. The word *kaivalya*
is very beautiful; it means innocent aloneness, it means pure
aloneness.

The word *aloneness* has to be understood. It is not loneliness.
Loneliness is negative: loneliness is when you are hankering for
the other. Loneliness is the feeling of the absence of the other;

aloneness is the realization of oneself. Loneliness is ugly; aloneness is tremendously beautiful. Aloneness is when you are so content that you don't need the other, that the other has completely disappeared from your consciousness—the other makes no shadow on you, the other creates no dream in you, the other does not pull you out.

The other is continuously pulling you off the centre. Sartre's famous saying—Patanjali would have understood it well—is, 'The other is hell.' The other may not be hell, but the hell is created by your desire for the other. The desire for the other is hell.

And to be desireless of the other is to attain to your pristine clarity of being. Then you are, and you are the whole, and there exists nobody except you. This Patanjali calls kaivalya.

And the way, the path, toward kaivalya is: first, the most essential step, *vivek*, discrimination; the second important step is *vairagya*, renunciation; and the third is the realization of kaivalya, aloneness.

Why are you hankering so much for the other? Why this desire, this constant madness for the other? Where have you taken a wrong step? Why are you not satisfied with yourself? Why don't you feel fulfilled? Why do you think that somehow you lack something? From where does this misconception that you are incomplete arise? It arises out of the identity with the body; the body is the other. Once you have taken the first wrong step, then you will go on and on, and then there is no end to it.

By 'vivek' Patanjali means: to discriminate yourself as separate from the body, to realize that you are in the body but you are not the body; to realize that you are in the mind but you are not the mind; to realize that you are always the pure witness—*sakshin, drashta*—the seer. You are never the seen, you are never the object; you are pure subjectivity.

Soren Kierkegaard, one of the most influential existential thinkers in the West, has said, 'God is subjectivity.' He comes very close to Patanjali. What does he mean when he says God is subjectivity? When all objects are known as separate from you, they start disappearing. They exist through your cooperation. If you think you are the body, then the body continues; it needs your help, your energy. If you think you are the mind, the mind functions; it needs your help, your cooperation, your energy.

This is one of the inner mechanisms: that just by your presence, nature becomes alive. Just by your presence, the body functions as alive; just by your presence, the mind starts functioning.

In yoga, they say it is as if the master had gone out, then he comes back home. The servants were chit-chatting and sitting on the steps of the house and smoking, and nobody was worried about the house. The moment the master enters, their chit-chat stops, they are no longer smoking, they have hidden their cigarettes and they have started working. They are trying to show that they are so much involved in their work that you cannot even conceive that just a moment before they were gossiping, sitting on the steps idling, lazy, resting. Just the presence of the master, and everything settles—as if the teacher had gone out of the class and there was much turmoil, almost a chaos, and the teacher comes back and all the children are in their seats and they have started writing, doing their work, and there is complete silence. The very presence . . .

Now, scientists have something parallel to it; they call it the presence of the catalytic agent. There are a few scientific phenomena in which a certain element is needed just to be present. It does not act in any way, it does not enter into any activity, but just the presence of it helps some activity to happen—if it is not present, that activity will not happen. If it is present, it remains in itself, it does not go out; just the very presence is catalytic, it creates some activity in somebody else, somewhere else.

Patanjali says that your innermost being is not active; it is inactive. The innermost being is called in yoga the *purush*. Your pure consciousness is a catalytic agent. It is just there doing nothing; seeing everything, but doing nothing; watching everything, but getting involved in nothing. By the sheer presence of the purush, the *prakriti*—nature, the mind, the body, everything, starts functioning.

But we get identified with the body, we get identified with the mind: we slip out of the witnesser and become a doer. That's the whole disease of man. Vivek is the medicine: how to go back home, how to drop this false idea that you are a doer, and how to attain to the clarity of just being a witness. The methodology is called vivek.

Once you have understood that you are not the doer and you are the watcher, the second thing happens spontaneously: renunciation, sannyas, vairagya. The second is: now whatsoever you were doing before, you cannot do. You were getting involved too much in many things because you were thinking you are the body, because you were thinking you are the mind. Now you know that you are neither the body nor the mind, many activities that you were following and chasing and getting mad about simply drop. That dropping is vairagya; that is sannyas, renunciation.

Your vision, your vivek, your understanding, brings a transformation: that is vairagya. And when vairagya is complete, another peak arises, which is kaivalya—for the first time, you know who you are. But the first step of identification leads you astray; then once you have taken the first step, once you have ignored your separation and you have got caught in the identity, then it goes on and on and on. One step leads to another, then to another, and you are more and more in the mire and in the mess.

Let me tell you one anecdote:

Two young friends were breaking into society and young Cohen had high hopes of marrying an heiress. To give him moral support, he took young Levy along with him to meet the girl's parents. The parents smiled at young Cohen and said, 'We understand you are in the clothing business?'

Cohen nodded nervously and said, 'Yes, in a small way.'

Levy slapped him on the back and said, 'He is so modest, so modest. He has twenty-seven shops and is negotiating for more.'

The parents said, 'We understand you have an apartment?'

Cohen smiled, 'Yes, a modest couple of rooms.'

Young Levy started laughing, 'Modesty, modesty! He has a penthouse in Park Lane.'

The parents continued, 'And you have a car?'

'Yes,' said Cohen. 'Quite a nice one.'

'Quite nice nothing!' interjected Levy. 'He has three Rolls-Royces, and that is only for town use.'

Cohen sneezed. 'Do you have a cold?' asked the anxious parents. 'Yes, just a slight one,' replied Cohen.

'Slight, nothing!' yelled Levy. 'Tuberculosis!'

One step leads to another, and once you have taken a wrong step, your life becomes an exaggeration of that wrong; it is mirrored and reflected in millions of ways. And if you don't correct it there, you can go on correcting all over the world, you will not be able to correct it.

Gurdjieff used to tell his disciples, 'The first thing is, to become non-identified and to remember continuously that you are a witness, just a consciousness, neither an act nor a thought.' If this remembrance becomes a crystallized phenomenon in you, you have attained to vivek, discrimination; then spontaneously follows vairagya. If you don't become discriminating, spontaneously follows *samsara*, the world; if you become identified with the body and the mind, you move out—you go into the world, you are expelled from the Garden of Eden. If you discriminate, and you remember that you are in the body and the body is an abode and you are the owner; and the mind is just a biocomputer, you are the master and the mind is just a slave—then, a turning in. Then you are not moving into the world, because the first step has been removed. Now you are no longer bridged with the world, suddenly you start falling in. This is what vairagya is, renunciation.

And when you go on falling in and in and in, and there comes the last point beyond which there is no go, the summum bonum, it is called kaivalya: you have become alone. You don't need anybody. You don't need the constant effort of filling yourself with something or the other. Now you are in tune with your emptiness, and because of your tuning in with the emptiness, the very emptiness has become a fullness, an infinity, a fulfilment, a fruition of being.

This purush is there in the beginning, this purush is there in the end, and between the two is just a big dream.

The first sutra:

> *Experience is the result of the inability to differentiate*
> *between purush, pure consciousness, and sattva, pure*
> *intelligence,*
> *although they are absolutely distinct.*
> *Performing samyama on the self-interest*
> *brings knowledge of the purush*
> *separated from the knowledge of others.*

Each word has to be understood because each word is tremendously significant.

'*Experience is the result of the inability to differentiate . . .*' All experience is just an error. You say, 'I am miserable,' or you say, 'I am happy,' or you say, 'I am feeling hungry,' or you say, 'I am feeling very good and healthy'—all experience is an error, is a misunderstanding.

When you say, 'I am hungry,' what do you really mean? You should say, 'I am conscious that the body is hungry.' You should not say, 'I am hungry.' You are not hungry; the body is hungry, you are the knower of the fact. The experience is not yours, only the awareness; the experience is of the body, the awareness is yours. When you feel miserable, again, the experience may be of the body or of the mind—which are not two.

Body and mind are one mechanism. The body is the gross mechanism of the same entity; the mind is the subtle mechanism. But both are the same. It is not good to say 'body and mind'; we should say 'bodymind.' The body is nothing but mind in a gross way, and if you watch your body, you will see that the body also functions as a mind. You are fast asleep, and a fly comes and hangs around your face, you remove it with your hand without in any way getting up or waking up. The body functioned, very mindfully. Or something starts crawling on your feet; you throw it away, fast asleep, you will not remember in the morning. The body functions as a mind—very gross, but it functions as a mind.

So bodymind has all the experience; good or bad, happy, unhappy, it makes no difference. You are never the experiencer; you are always the awareness of the experience. So Patanjali says in a very bold statement, *'Experience is the result of the inability to differentiate . . .'* All experience is an error. The error arises because you don't discriminate, you don't know who is who.

It happens many times. In the Amazon, there is a small tribe of primitive people. When the wife is giving birth to a child, the husband also lies down on a cot; the wife starts screaming and yelling, and the husband also starts screaming and yelling. When for the first time it was discovered, it was unbelievable. What is the husband doing, and for what? The wife is passing through pain, but why this husband is doing this? Is he simply acting? And then much research was done upon it and it has been found that the husband is not acting. The pain really starts happening once you get identified. Since millennia, the mind of that tribe has been conditioned that because the wife and husband both are the parents of the child, both should suffer.

Seems perfectly okay . . . the women's lib movement would agree with them. Why only women? And these husbands just go on . . . they don't suffer, they don't carry the child in their womb for nine months . . . and then again when the child is born, the whole responsibility seems to be of the mother. Why this?

But that tribe has lived that way. Psychologists, medical research workers, have observed the man really goes through pain—really. Unbelievable to us because we are not identified that way; the husband is so identified with the wife—the very identification that 'she is going through pain'—he starts having pangs.

You may have watched it sometimes. If you love somebody very much and he is suffering, you start suffering. That's what empathy is; if your loved one is suffering, you start suffering; if your loved one is happy, you start feeling happy; if your loved one is dancing, you feel like dancing. You get in tune with your loved one—you become identified.

Now this seems to be a very absurd case that this society has continued and the husbands really suffer almost as much as the wife, and there is no difference. Now, new light has come upon women's suffering also. One psychoanalyst in France has worked deeply upon it, and he says that women are suffering only because they believe that way; there are tribes in which not even the wife suffers.

In India there are tribes. In primitive societies, the wife will go on working in the field, cutting wood, carrying wood, and suddenly she will give birth to a child, put the child in her bucket, and go home. She will give birth to the child in the field, put the child under a tree and continue her work; the work has to be finished, and by evening she will take the child home. No pain. What has happened? That too is a belief, a conditioning.

And now millions of women are getting ready to give birth to a child without any pain in the Western world, painless childbirth; just the belief system has to be changed, they have to be de-hypnotized—they have to be told that this is just an idea—the pain really does not happen, it is just an idea. And once you have an idea, you create it; once you have an idea, it starts happening—it is your projection.

Patanjali says all experience is an error—error in your vision. You become identified with the object, and the subject starts thinking as if it is the object. You feel hunger, but you are not hungry, the body is hungry. You feel pain, but you are not in pain, the body is in pain; you are only alert.

Next time something happens to you—and every moment

something or the other is happening—just watch. Just try to keep hold of this remembrance that 'I am the witness,' and see how much things change. Once you can realize you are the witness, many things simply disappear . . . start disappearing. And one day comes which is the final day, the day of enlightenment, when all experience falls flat. Suddenly, you are beyond experience: you are not in the body, you are not in the mind; you are beyond both. Suddenly, you start floating like a cloud, above all, beyond all. That state of no-experience is the state of kaivalya.

Now one thing more about it: there are people who think that spirituality is also an experience—they don't know. There are people who come to me, and they say, 'We would like to have some spiritual experience.' They don't know what they are saying. Experience as such is of the world; there is no spiritual experience, there cannot be. To call an experience 'spiritual' is to falsify it. The spiritual is only a realization of pure awareness, purush.

How does it happen? How do we get identified? In yoga terminology, the truth, the ultimate truth, has three attributes to it: *sat chit anand—sat-chit-anand*. Sat means being, the quality of eternity, the quality of permanence, being. Chit: chit means consciousness, awareness—chit is energy, movement, process. And anand: anand is blissfulness. These three have been called the three attributes of the ultimate. This is the yoga trinity; of course, more scientific than the Christian trinity because it does not talk about persons—God, the Holy Ghost, the Son. It talks about *realizations*. When one reaches to the ultimate peak of existence, one realizes three things: that one is and one is going to remain, that is sat; the second, one is and one is conscious—one is not like dead matter, one is and one knows that one is, that is chit; and, one knows that one is and one is tremendously blissful.

Now let me explain it to you. It is not right to call it 'blissful,' because then it will become an experience. So a better way will be to say, 'one is bliss'—not 'blissful.' One is sat, one is chit, one is anand; one is being, one is consciousness, one is bliss.

These are the ultimate realizations of the truth. Patanjali says these three, when they are present in the world, create three qualities in prakriti, in nature. They function as a catalytic agent; they don't do anything. Just their presence creates a tremendous activity in prakriti. That activity is corresponded by three *gunas*, qualities: *sattva, rajas, tamas.*

Sattva corresponds to anand, the quality of bliss. Sattva means pure intelligence; the closer you come to sattva, the more you feel blissful. Sattva is the reflection of anand; if you can conceive of a triangle, then the base is anand and the other two lines are sat, chit. It is reflected into the world of matter, prakriti. Of course, in the reflection, it becomes upside down: sattva and rajas, tamas—the same triangle.

But the ultimate truth is not doing anything—that is the emphasis of Patanjali, because once the ultimate truth is doing something, he becomes a doer and he has already moved into the world. In Patanjali, God is not the creator; he is just a catalytic agent. This is tremendously scientific because if God is the creator then you will have to find the motive, why he creates; then you will have to find some desire in him to create, then he will become just as ordinary as man. No, in Patanjali, God is absolute, pure presence. He does not do anything, but by his presence, things happen—the prakriti, the nature, starts dancing.

There is an old story:

A king had made a palace; the palace was called the Mirror Palace; the floor, the walls, the ceiling, were all covered in millions of mirrors, tiny, tiny mirrors. There was nothing else in the whole palace; it was a mirror palace. Once it happened, the king's dog by mistake was left inside the palace in the night, and the palace was locked from the outside. The dog looked, became frightened; there were millions of dogs everywhere. He was reflected; down, up, all directions—millions of dogs. He was not an ordinary dog, he was the king's dog—very brave—but even then, he was alone. He ran from one room to another, but there was no escape, there was no go. All over. He became more and more frightened, he tried to get out, but there was no way to get out, the door was locked.

Just to frighten the other dogs, he started barking, but the moment he barked, the other dogs also barked, because they were pure reflections. Then he became more frightened. To frighten the other dogs, he started knocking against the walls. The other dogs also jumped into him, bumped into him. In the morning, the dog was found dead.

But the moment the dog died, all the dogs died. The palace was empty. There was only one dog and millions of reflections.

This is the standpoint of Patanjali: that there is only one reality, millions of reflections of it. You are separate from me as a reflection, I am separate from you as a reflection, but if we move toward the real, the separation will be gone; we will be one. One reflection is separate from another reflection. You can destroy one reflection and save another.

That's how one person dies . . . There are many argumentative people in the world who ask, 'Then if there is only one Brahman, one God, one being spread all over, then when one dies, why don't others die also?' This is simple. If there are a thousand and one mirrors in the room, you can destroy one mirror, one reflection will disappear, not others. You destroy another, another reflection will disappear, not others. When one person dies, only one reflection dies. But the one who is being reflected remains undying; it is deathless. Then another child is born—that is, another mirror is born—again another reflection.

This story goes on and on; that's why Hindus have called this world a *maya*: maya means a magic show. Nothing is there really; everything only appears to be there. And this whole magic world depends on one error, and that error is of identity.

'*Experience is the result of the inability to differentiate between purush, (absolute) pure consciousness, and sattva, pure intelligence . . .*' purush is reflected into prakriti as sattva. Your intelligence is just a reflection of the real intelligence; it is not the real intelligence. You are clever, argumentative, groping in the dark, thinking, contemplating, creating philosophies, systems of thought—this is just a reflection. This intelligence is not the real intelligence because the real intelligence need not discover anything: for the real intelligence, everything is already discovered.

Now look at the different paths of philosophy and religion. Philosophy moves in the reflected intelligence, into sattva—it goes on thinking and thinking and thinking and goes on creating bigger palaces of thought. Religion moves into purush—it drops this so-called intelligence; hence the insistence of meditation, to drop thinking.

I have heard:

Once it happened, in the bazaar Mulla Nasruddin saw a crowd gathered around a small bird offering big prices for it. 'No doubt the price of birds and fowls has gone very up,' Mulla thought to himself. He went home, and after some chase, succeeded in catching his old turkey. In the bazaar, they offered only two silver coins for the turkey.

'It is not fair,' Mulla said. 'My turkey is several times as big as that little bird auctioned at so many gold pieces.'

'But that bird was a parakeet—it talks.'

Mulla took a glance at the turkey dozing in his arms. 'Mine meditates,' he said.

Become a turkey—meditate. Thinking is just dreaming logically, it is creating verbal palaces; and sometimes one can get caught so much in the verbal, then one completely forgets the real. The verbal is just a reflection.

Language is one of the reasons we got so caught up in the verbal. For example, in English, it is very difficult to drop the use of the 'I,' it is very prominent in English. The 'I' stands so vertical—almost a phallic symbol. It is phallic; that's why perceptive people like E. E. Cummings started writing 'I' in the lower case. And it is not only vertical, phallic, when you write; when you say, 'I,' it is phallic, like an erection, egoistic. Just watch how many times 'I' has to be used, and the more you use it, the more it is emphasized, the more ego becomes prominent—as if the whole English language hangs around 'I.'

But in Japanese, it is totally different. You can talk for hours without using 'I.' It is possible to write a book without using 'I'; the language has a totally different arrangement, the 'I' can be dropped easily.

No wonder Japan became the most meditative country in the world and achieved to the higher peaks of Zen, *satori*, and *samadhi*. Why did it happen in Japan? Why has it happened in Burma, in Thailand, in Vietnam? In all the countries which have been influenced by Buddhism, the language is different from the countries which have never been influenced by Buddhism, because Buddha said there is no 'I'—*anatta*, *anatma*, no-selfness, there is no 'I.' That emphasis entered the languages.

Buddha says, 'Nothing is permanent.' So when for the first time, the Bible was being translated into the Buddhist languages, it was very difficult to translate it. The problem was very basic—how to put 'God is.' Because in Buddhist countries, 'is' is a dirty word; everything is *becoming*, nothing *is*. If you want to say, 'The tree is,' in Burmese, it will come to mean, 'The tree is becoming.' It will not mean, 'The tree is.' If you want to say, 'The river is,' you cannot say it in Burmese, it will come to mean, 'The river is becoming.' And that's true because the river never *is*, it is always in a process—the river is 'rivering.' It is not a noun; it is a verb. The river is rivering, becoming. Never in any stage can you catch it as 'is.' You cannot take a snap of it; it is a movie, a continuous process. You cannot have a photograph—the photograph will be false because it will be 'is,' and the river never is.

Buddhist languages have a different structure to them; they create a different mind. The mind depends much on language, its whole game is linguistic; beware of it.

Let me tell you one anecdote. It happened in a very esoteric, small Sufi community:

A pedantic grammarian happened to pass by a Sufi gathering and heard the sheikh say, 'Indeed, we are from Him and to Him we will return.'

At this, the grammarian began to tear his clothes and utter strange yawps and cries. People gathered around him, wondering what had happened; he had never been of religious inclination or mystical talent.

Seeing that the Koranic line had brought the grammarian to such ecstasy, the sheikh said again, 'Indeed, we are from Him and to Him we will return.' And again the grammarian tore his clothes, stomped his feet, and groaned and yelled.

When the session was over and the grammarian had not one piece of clothing left on his body, the sheikh took him into a corner, splashed water on his face, and said, 'Tell me, sir, what happened that a paraphrase from the Koran made you behave like that?'

'Why not!' the grammarian said vehemently. 'In all my life, in all my speeches and writings, and in all the writings of scholars, recent and old, the first person plural has been used with *shall*, and not as you say, "To Him we will return!"'

The question was of 'will' and 'shall'—'will' is not right! Looks absurd, looks almost mad, crazy, but this is what is happening. If Buddha comes to you and says, 'There is no God,' you immediately get anxious, worried. What has he said? He has simply said something that goes against your linguistic pattern, that's all. If he says, 'There is no self, no 'I', you become disturbed. What has he done? He has simply taken away a strategy of your ego, nothing else. He has simply shattered your linguistic pattern.

It is happening every day here. When I say something, and I destroy some linguistic pattern in you, you become annoyed, you become angry. If you are a Christian, of course, you have a

Christian house of language. If you are a Hindu, you have a Hindu house of language. I am neither, and I am here to destroy all linguistic patterns. You get angry. You become annoyed. You start thinking, 'What to do?' But what am I doing? What can I take from you? Can Buddha take God from you if you have known God—can he take it from you? Then there is no question. But he can take a linguistic theory; he can take a hypothesis from you.

'*Experience is the result of the inability to differentiate between purush, pure consciousness, and sattva, pure intelligence . . .*' Language belongs to sattva: theories belong to sattva; philosophies belong to sattva. Sattva means your intelligence, your mind. Mind is not you.

Christianity, Hinduism, Jainism, Buddhism, belong to the mind. That's why Buddhist monks say, 'If you meet Buddha on the way, kill him immediately.' Buddhist monks saying that? They say, 'Kill the Buddha if you see him, immediately.' They are saying, 'Kill the mind, don't carry a theory about the Buddha, otherwise you will never become a buddha. If you want to become a buddha, drop all ideas about Buddha—all ideas. Kill Buddha immediately!' They say, 'If you utter the name of Buddha, immediately wash and rinse your mouth, the word is dirty.' Buddhist monks saying that? They are amazing people . . . but really wonderful. And they mean it. And if you can see their point, you will become able to see many more things.

Bodhidharma says, 'Burn all the scriptures, all, including Buddha's.' Not only the Vedas, Dhammapada included. Burn all scriptures. There is a very famous painting of Lin-chi burning all the scriptures, creating a *holi*. And they were very, very deep into reality. What are they doing? They are simply taking away your mind from you. Where is your Veda? It is not in the book; it is in your mind. Where is your Koran? It is in your mind; it is not in the book. It is in your mental tape. Drop all that. Get out of it.

Intelligence, the mind, is part of nature; it is just a reflection. It looks almost like the real, but remember, even 'almost like the real,' then too it is not real. It is as if on the full moon night, you see the moon reflected in the cool, placid lake. No ripple is arising, the reflection is perfect, but still it is a reflection. And if the reflection is so beautiful, just think about the real. Don't get caught in the reflection.

What Buddha says is a reflection, what Patanjali writes is a reflection, what I am saying is a reflection; don't be caught in it. If the reflection is so beautiful, try reality. Move away from the reflection towards the moon.

And the path is going to be just the opposite from the reflection. If you go on looking at the reflection and you become hypnotized by the reflection, you will never be able to see the moon in the sky, because it is diametrically opposite. If you want to see the real moon, you will have to move away from the reflection; you will have to burn scriptures and you will have to kill Buddhas. You will have to move in the very opposite, diametrically opposite, dimension. Then your head moves toward the moon; then you cannot see the reflection. The reflection disappears.

All scriptures at the most can train and discipline your intelligence. No scripture can lead you toward the real, pure purush, the witness, the awareness.

'. . . inability to differentiate between purush, pure consciousness, and sattva, pure intelligence . . .' That is the very cause of getting into ignorance, into the dark night, into the world, into matter, losing contact with your own reality and becoming a victim of your own ideas and projections.

'. . . although they are absolutely distinct.' You can see that; even the greatest idea is different from you—you can watch it arising as an object inside you. Even the greatest idea remains a thing within you and you remain far away from it, a watcher on the hills looking down at the idea. Never get identified with any object.

'Performing samyama on the self-interest brings knowledge of the purush separated from the knowledge of others'—'svartha samyamat purush gyanam.' Patanjali is saying, 'Selfishness brings the absolute knowledge'—svartha—become selfish, that is the very core of religion. Try to see what your real self-interest is, where your real self is. Try to distinguish yourself from others—'parartha'—from the others.

And don't think that the people who are outside you are the others. They are others, but your body is also the other; it will return to the earth one day, it is part of the earth. Your breathing is also the other; it will return to the air. It is just given to you for a time being; you have borrowed it, it will have to be returned. You will not be here, but your breath will be here in the air. You will not be here, but your body will lie down in deep sleep in the earth—dust unto dust. That which you think of as your blood will be flowing in rivers. Everything will go back.

But one thing you have not borrowed from anybody: that's your witnessing, that's your *sakshin bhav*, the awareness.

Intellect will disappear; reasoning will disappear. All these things are like formations of clouds in the sky: they come together, they disappear, but the sky remains. You will remain as a vast space. That vast space is purush; the inner sky is purush.

How to come to know it?—samyama on the self-interest. Bring your concentration, *dharana*; your contemplation, *dhyan*; your ecstasy, *samadhi*; bring all the three to your self-interest—turn in. In the West, people are turning 'on'—then you turn *out*. Turn in. Just bring your consciousness to a focus, to who you are. Differentiate between the objects. Hunger arises; this is an object. Then you are satisfied, you have eaten well, a certain well-being arises; that too is an object. Morning comes; that too is an object. Evening comes; that too is an object. You remain the same—hunger or no hunger, life or death, misery or happiness, you remain the same watcher.

But even in watching a movie you get caught. You know well there is only a white screen and nothing else, and shadows are moving on it . . . But have you watched people sitting in a movie house? A few start crying when something tragic is happening on the screen, their tears start coming. Just see—there is nothing real on the screen, but the tears are very real. The unreal is bringing tears? People reading a story in a book become so excited, or seeing a picture of a nude woman become sexually aroused. Just see—there is nothing, just a few lines, nothing else. Just a little ink spread on the paper. But their sexual arousal is very real.

This is the tendency of the mind; to get caught with the objects, become identified with them. Catch yourself red-handed as many times as you can; again and again, catch yourself red-handed and drop the object. Suddenly, you will feel a coolness, all excitement gone. The moment you realize there is only the screen and nothing else, then 'For what am I getting so much excited, for what?' The whole world is a screen, and all that you are seeing there are your own desires projected; whatsoever you want, you start projecting and believing. This whole world is a fantasy.

And, remember, you don't all live in the same world. Everybody has his own world because his fantasies are different from the others. The truth is one; fantasies are as many as there are minds.

If you are in a fantasy, you cannot meet the other person, you cannot communicate with the other. He is in his fantasy. That is what is happening; when people want to relate, they cannot relate. Somehow, they miss each other; lovers, wives, friends, husbands, miss each other, go on missing. And they are very worried why they cannot communicate; they wanted to say something, but the other understands something else. And they go on saying, 'I never meant this,' but the other goes on hearing something else.

What is happening? The other lives in his fantasy, you live in your own fantasy. He is projecting some film onto the screen; you are projecting some other film onto the same screen. That's why a relationship becomes such an anxiety, anguish. One feels to be alone is to be good and happy, and whenever you move with somebody, you start getting into a mire, into a hell. When Sartre says, he says through his experience, 'The other is hell.' But the other is not creating the hell; just two fantasies clashing, just two worlds of dreams clashing.

Communication is possible only when you have dropped your fantasy world and the other has dropped his fantasy world. Then two beings face each other—and they are not two, because the 'twoness' drops with the world of fantasy. Then they are one.

When a buddha faces somebody who is also a buddha, they are not two. That's why two buddhas have not been known to talk to each other, there are not two persons to talk. They remain quiet; they remain silent. There are stories that when Mahavira and Buddha were alive . . . They were contemporaries, and they moved, wandered, in the same small province of Bihar; it is called Bihar because of these two people—*bihar* means wandering. Because these two persons wandered all over the place, it became known as the province of their wandering. But they never met. Many times they were in the same town—the place is not very big—many times they stayed in the same place, a small village. Once it happened that they stayed in the same *serai*, in the same *dharmashala*, but they never met.

Now a problem arises: Why? And if you ask Buddhists or Jainas why they didn't meet, they feel a little embarrassed. The question seems embarrassing, because that simply shows maybe they were very egoistic? Who should go to whom?—Buddha to Mahavira or Mahavira to Buddha? Nobody can do that. So Jainas and Buddhists avoid the question, they have never answered it. But I know: the reason is there were not two persons to meet. It is not a question of egoism; simply there were not two persons to meet! Two emptinesses staying in the same serai, so what to do? How to bring them together? And even if you bring them together, they will not be two. There will be only one emptiness; when two zeros meet, it becomes one zero.

Performing samyama on the self-interest brings knowledge of the purush separated from the knowledge of others.

Tatah pratibh shravan vedana darsh asvad varta jayante.

From this follows intuitional hearing,
touching, seeing, tasting, and smelling.

Again the word pratibha has to be understood: one who attains to pure attention, to pure awareness, to pure inner clarity, innocence, attains to pratibha. Pratibha is not intuition. Intellect is sun-oriented; intuition is moon-oriented; pratibha is beyond both. Man remains an intellectual, woman intuitional, but the buddha—purush—one who has attained, is neither man nor woman.

If you are an intellectual, you will be aggressive. Intellect is aggressive; the sun energy is aggressive. That's why we have never heard of a woman raping a man—it is impossible. Only a man can rape a woman; the sun energy is aggressive, the moon energy is receptive. Intellect is aggressive; intuition is receptive. If you are receptive, you will become intuitional. You will start seeing things that the intellectual can never see because he is not open. The strangest thing is this: that the intellectual is looking for them but cannot see, and the intuitional is not looking for them but can see.

In fact, all the great discoveries have been done by intellectual people—but in their intuitional moods. The great discoveries are not by intuitional people because they are not looking for them. Even if they come by the side, even if they face them, they forget about them; that's why women have never discovered anything. Not that those things have never happened to them—they happen more to them than to man. Just look; even the science of cooking is developed by men, not by women. All the great cooks are men. At least this should not be so, but all the great hotels, big hotels, famous hotels, will not allow any woman to be a cook there. They have been cooking for millennia, but all the discoveries, innovations, are by men. Not that things don't come their way— they come—but they are simply receptive. They come and they go, but they don't hold them.

Intellectuals are looking constantly, looking everywhere; they are trying to uncover every nook and comer. Psychologists say that the male sex energy is the very cause of all scientific research. You give a toy to a boy, within minutes it is gone—he has opened it, he is looking inside, what is there. You give a toy to a girl, she will protect it for years, she will keep it in the cupboard, lock it, she will decorate it. But the boy will immediately destroy it. He wants to know how it ticks; he wants to know from where the whole functioning is coming, he wants to go deep in; he wants to search.

The whole of science is, in a way, male sexuality—searching and searching, uncovering.

I will tell you one anecdote:

After a rough tour of duty, the Marine regiment was sent back for rest. At the base, they found a contingent of women Marines awaiting assignments to various posts. The Marine colonel warned the women's commander that his men had been in the lines for a long time and might not be too careful about their attitude towards the women.

'Keep them locked up,' he warned, 'if you don't want any trouble.'

'Trouble?' said the woman commander sarcastically. 'There will be no trouble.' She tapped her forehead significantly, 'My girls have it up there.'

'Madam!' exclaimed the colonel, 'it makes no difference where they have it, my boys will find it. Keep them locked up!'

The whole of human sexuality is divided into the aggressive and the passive. That's why woman is stronger than man and yet has been always oppressed. She is stronger than man, remember, in many ways. She lives longer than man, an average of five years more; if a man is going to live up to seventy-five, the woman is going to live up to eighty. Lives a more healthy life than man; is less ill, recovers better and sooner whenever she is ill—but still she has been oppressed. Is more resistant, more flexible, more alive, gives birth to children and still survives; goes on sharing her life giving life to others and still survives, and survives beautifully. Is more strong—may not be more muscular, but to be muscular is not the only criterion of being strong. But still she has been oppressed because she is passive, receptive. The functioning of her energy is not aggressive—more inviting and less aggressive.

Intellect happens easily to men because intellect, again, is in the same direction as aggression, argument. Women are more intuitive; they live by hunches, they suddenly jump to conclusions—that's why it is very difficult to argue with a woman—she has already arrived at the conclusion, argument is not needed. You are simply wasting your time. She knows all the time what is the end result. She is just waiting to declare it. You go on arguing this way and that, it is futile; she is conclusive.

Intuition is conclusive; that's why women are more telepathic. Women are more visionary, and many intuitional things happen to them. All the great mediums are women; hypnosis, telepathy, clairvoyance, clairaudience, all belong to the world of women. Just let me tell you one thing about the past history:

Witchcraft was a woman's craft. That's why it is called *witch*craft. The whole world of witches was intuitional. Priests were against it; their whole world was intellectual. Remember, all the witches, almost all the witches, were women; and all the priests, almost all the priests, were men. First, the priests tried to burn the witches. Thousands of women were burned in Europe in the Middle Ages because the priests could not understand the world of intuition; they could not believe in it—it looked dangerous, strange. They wanted to wipe it out completely.

And they wiped it out completely. They tried to destroy one of the most beautiful instruments of receptivity, of a higher knowledge, of higher realms of being, of superior possibilities, they destroyed completely; wherever they could find a mediumistic woman, they killed her. And they created such fear that even women lost that capacity, just because of the fear.

Now again the same continues to be the case. Psychoanalysts are against witchcraft—they are all men. Now the psychoanalysts have taken the place of the priests—they are all men. Freudians,

Adlerians, they are all men. Now they are against the woman. And do you know? More or less all their patients are women. This is something. And when the witches existed, more or less all their patients were men. I am surprised, but it looks as it should be. When the witches existed, their patients were all men: the intellect seeking the help of the intuition, the man seeking the help of the woman. Now just the reverse has happened: all the psychoanalysts are men and all their patients are women. Now intuition has been so crippled and killed that it has to seek the help of intellect.

The higher is seeking the help of the lower. It is a very miserable state of affairs. It should not be so.

The whole history of science proves this in many ways. When intuition was used as the method, then alchemy existed. When intellect came into power, alchemy disappeared; chemistry was born. Alchemy is intuitional; chemistry is intellectual. Alchemy was moon; chemistry is sun. When moon was predominant, intuition was predominant; there was astrology. Now there is astronomy. Astrology has disappeared. Astrology is moon; astronomy is sun. And the world has become very poor because of that.

Woman has to flower in her moonhood as man has to flower in his sunhood, but pratibha is beyond both. Intellect is psychological, intuition parapsychological, pratibha para-parapsychological.

'From this follows intuitional hearing, touching, seeing, tasting, and smelling.' Remember this: that it can happen on two levels. If you are a moon person, a feminine person—maybe man or woman, that doesn't make any difference—if you function from the moon centre, you will be able to hear many things which others cannot hear and you will be able to see many things which others cannot see. You will become perceptive of the hidden. The hidden dimension will be not so hidden for you; the secret will become a little open for you.

That's what is being studied by parapsychology. Now it is gaining momentum; a few of the world's universities have opened parapsychological departments. Much research work is being done, even in Russia. Because man has failed in a way; the sun centre has failed. We have lived through that sun centre for thousands of years; it brings only violence, war, misery. Now the other centre has to be tackled.

Even in Russia, which is dominated by the sun centre, by the communists, who don't believe in any possibility of the beyond, even they are trying. And they have done much work, and they have discovered much. Of course, they interpret it in terms of intellect—they don't call it 'extrasensory,' they don't call it parapsychological. They say, 'This is also sensory, only refined.' Eyes can become more refined and they can see things that ordinarily cannot be seen. For example, eyes can see your inner body just as an X-ray can see it. If the X-ray can see it, then the eye can also see it; one just needs to train the eyes.

And in a way they are right. Intuition is not beyond the senses; it is a refinement of senses. Pratibha is beyond the senses; it is non-sensory, it is immediate, the senses are dropped. This is the yoga standpoint, that within you, you are all knowing—all knowingness is your very nature. In fact, you think that you see through the eyes; yoga says you are not seeing through the eyes, you are being blinded by the eyes. Let me explain it to you.

You are standing in a room and you are looking outside through a small hole. Of course, in a room you will feel that small hole gives you at least a certain knowledge about the world outside. You may become focused on it, you may think without this hole it will be impossible to see. Yoga says you are getting into a very, very erroneous attitude; this hole allows you to see, but this hole is not the cause of seeing: seeing is your quality. You are seeing through the hole, the hole is not seeing. You are the seer. You are looking through the eyes into the world. You are looking at me; your eyes are just the holes in the body, but you are the seer inside. If you can get out of the body, the same will happen as will happen if you can open the door and can come out into the open sky.

Because of the hole being lost, you will not become blind. In fact, then you will understand that the hole was blinding you; it was giving you a very limited vision. Now, open under the sky, you can see the whole in a total, instantaneous vision—altogether. Now your vision is not linear and your vision is not limited, because there is no window to it. You have come under the sky: you can see all around.

The same is the standpoint of yoga, and true. The body is giving only small holes to you: from the ears you can hear, from the eyes you can see, from the tongue you can taste, from the nose you can smell. Small holes, and you are hiding behind. Yoga says come out, get out, go beyond. Get out of these holes, and you will become all-knowing, omniscient, omnipotent, omnipresent. This is pratibha.

'*From this follows . . .*' the hearing that is of the beyond, the hearing that is not through the intellect nor through the intuition, but through pratibha; and touching and seeing and tasting and smelling . . .

Remember it that one who has achieved, lives life in its totality for the first time. The Upanishads say, '*Ten tyakten bhunjithah*'— 'Those who have renounced, only they have indulged.' Very paradoxical: 'Those who have renounced, only they have known and experienced and enjoyed, indulged.' Your limitation in the body is making you impoverished. Getting up beyond the body, you will become richer. One who has attained is not poorer; he becomes tremendously rich, he becomes a god.

So yoga is not against the world; in fact, you are against the world. And yoga is not against bliss; you are against bliss. And yoga wants you to drop the world so all limitations can be dropped and you can become unlimited in your being, in your experiencing.

> *These are powers when the mind is turned outward,*
> *but obstacles in the way of samadhi.*

But Patanjali is always aware to tell you again and again—

he goes on hammering the point to hit it home—that even these powers, of immediate hearing, listening, tasting, smelling, touching: remember, they are powers if you are going outward, but if you want to go in, they become hindrances. All powers become hindrances when one is going in.

The person who is going out, is going through the moon and to the sun and to the world. And the person who is going in, his energy is moving from the sun to the moon and from the moon to the beyond. Their target and goals are totally different, diametrically opposite.

It happens, when sometimes you start feeling the first glimpse of pratibha, of the beyond, and you become so powerful—you are filled with power, you *are* power—and in that moment, you can fall again. Power corrupts; you can fall. You can get into the head so much, you can get into the ego so much, that you would like to have a ride on it, the power. You would like to do miracles or other foolish things.

All miracle-mongers are in a way foolish—whatsoever they say. They may say that they are doing these miracles to help people. They are not helping anybody; they are simply harming themselves, and harming others also. Because in doing such things, they are falling below the beyond. And then their whole thing becomes just trickery. There are tricks of the parapsychic, of the intuitional, of the moon world, with which, once you know them, you can play around. They are tricks, still, and the ego can again use those tricks.

I have heard one very beautiful story:

A Catholic priest, an Anglican minister, and a rabbi were fishing in a small boat in the middle of a quiet lake. From dawn till lunchtime, they sat there, not moving, not speaking. Then the Catholic priest said, 'Well, time for lunch. I will see you two in the pub.'

At which he got up, cocked a leg over the side of the boat and walked across the water to the pub at the lakeside.

The minister then said, 'I think I will have some lunch too.'

Saying which, he also cocked a leg over the side of the boat, walked across the water in the same direction as the Catholic priest.

The rabbi was amazed and dumbfounded at this display of miraculous Christian solidarity. However, feeling that his faith and traditions were at stake, he offered a swift prayer to Jehovah and stepped over the side of the boat.

Splash! Down he went to the bottom. He swam to the surface, pulled himself over the side of the boat and tried again, uttering still more fervent prayers. Splash! Again he plummeted like a stone.

The Catholic priest, having reached the lakeside, was watching this involuntary diving display, and as the Anglican minister also reached the shore, he said, 'We should have told the poor chap where the stepping stones are.'

Everywhere there are stepping stones. All your Satya Sai Babas . . . Don't be amazed too much at what they are doing; look for the stepping stones—there are. And these people are not spiritual at all.

Patanjali says, *These are powers when the mind is turned outward, but obstacles in the way of samadhi.*' If you want to attain to the ultimate, you have to lose all. You have to lose all! This is the way of the real seeker: whatsoever he gains, he goes and sacrifices it to God. He says, 'You have given it to me, but what am I going to do with it? I put it again back at your feet.' He goes on sacrificing whatsoever he attains, and he remains always empty of attainment. That is spirituality: to remain always empty of attainment, and whatsoever comes by the way, one goes on sacrificing it.

Let me tell you another story:

A group of ministers were discussing how they allocated their congregations' offerings.

The Dissenter proclaimed, 'Everything my people put into the plate goes on God's work—I don't keep one penny for myself!'

The Anglican, while applauding his zeal, admitted, 'I keep the copper in the collection plate, and the silver goes to God.'

The Catholic priest present admitted that, 'I keep the silver and the copper goes to God—mind you, there is a lot of copper in a poor parish.'

So far the rabbi had kept silent, but when pressed, said, 'Well, I put all the collection money in a blanket and I toss it all up in the air. What God wants he keeps, and what he does not want, I keep.'

Don't be cunning—don't be the rabbi, because in the end, only you will be at a loss, not God. Whatsoever comes on your way of inner growth . . . and much comes, every moment is a new discovery on the inner path, every moment something suddenly falls in your hands—you had not even imagined, you had never asked for it. Millions are the gifts of the path, but only the one who goes on offering those gifts back to God reaches to the end. Otherwise, if you start clinging to the gifts, then and there your progress stops. Then and there your growth stops. Then and there you make an abode and start living there.

'Te samadhav upasarga vyutthane siddhayah.' If you want samadhi, the ultimate peace, the ultimate silence, the ultimate truth, then never get attached to any attainment whatsoever: worldly, other worldly, psychological, parapsychological, intellectual, intuitive, whatsoever. Never get attached to any attainment; go on offering it to God, go on offering it to God— and more will be coming! Go on offering it to God.

When you have offered *all*, God comes. When you have offered all, given him back, he comes as the last gift. God is the last gift.

Enough for today.

Eight

Always Remember to Laugh Twice!

The first question:

Osho, not to be identified with mind and body—still I don't know how to do it. I tell myself: you are not the mind, don't listen to your fear, love yourself, be content, etc., etc.
Please explain again how not to get identified or, at least, why I still don't understand you.

It is not a question of telling yourself that you are not the mind, you are not the body, because the one who is telling it is the mind. That way, you are never going to get out of the mind. All telling is done by the mind itself, so you will be emphasizing the mind more and more. The mind is very subtle; you have to be very, very alert about it. Don't use it. If you use it, you strengthen it. You cannot use your mind to destroy your mind. You have to understand that this mind cannot be used for its own suicide.

When you say, 'I am not the body,' it is the mind saying so. When you say, 'I am not the mind,' it is again the mind saying so. Look into the fact; don't try to say anything. Language, verbalization, is not needed; just a deep look. Just look inside, don't say anything. But I know your trouble. From the very beginning we are taught not to see but to say. The moment you see a roseflower you say, 'How beautiful!' Finished; the roseflower is gone—you killed it. Now something has come between you and the rose. 'How beautiful it is!' These words will now function as a wall.

And one word leads to another, one thought to another. And they move in association, they never move alone; you will never find a single thought alone. They live in a herd; they are herd animals. So when once you have said, 'How beautiful is the rose!' you are on the track, the train has started moving. Now the word *beautiful* will remind you of some woman you once loved. The rose is forgotten, the beautiful is forgotten, now the idea, a fantasy, imagination, memory, of a woman. And then the woman will lead to many other things. The woman you loved had a beautiful dog . . . here you go! And now there is no end to it.

Just see the mechanism of the mind, how it functions, and don't use the mechanism. Resist that temptation. It is a great temptation because you are trained for it, you work almost like a robot; it is automatic.

Now the new revolution that is coming into the world of education has a few proposals. One proposal is that small children should not be taught language first. First, they should be allowed time to crystallize their vision, to crystallize their experiencing. For example, there is an elephant, and you say to the child, 'The elephant is the biggest animal.' You think you are not saying anything nonsensical, you think it is absolutely reasonable and the child has to be told the fact; but no facts need to be told. It has to be experienced; the moment you say, 'The elephant is the biggest animal,' you are bringing something which is not part of the elephant.. Why do you say the animal is the biggest animal? Comparison has entered, which is not part of the fact.

An elephant is simply an elephant, neither big nor small. Of course, if you put it by the side of a horse, it is big, or by the side of an ant it is very big; but you are bringing the ant in the moment you say the elephant is the biggest animal. You are bringing something which is not part of the fact, you are falsifying the fact; comparison has come in.

Just let the child see. Don't say anything. Let him feel. When you take the child to the garden, don't say that the trees are green. Let the child feel, let the child absorb. Simple things, 'The grass is green'—don't say it.

This is my observation, that many times when the grass is not green, you go on seeing it as green—and there are a thousand and one shades of green. Don't say that the trees are green, because then the child will see just green—any tree and he will see green. Green is not one colour; there are a thousand and one shades of green.

Let the child feel, let the child absorb the uniqueness of each tree, in fact of each leaf. Let him soak; let him become like a sponge who soaks reality, the facticity of it, the existential. And once he is well grounded and his experience is well rooted—then tell him the words, then they will not disturb him, then they will not destroy his vision, clarity. Then he will be able to use language without being distracted by it. Right now, your language goes on distracting you.

So what is to be done? Start seeing things without naming them, without labelling them, without saying 'good,' 'bad,' without dividing them. Just see and allow the fact to be there in your presence without any judgement, condemnation, appreciation, whatsoever. Let it be there in its total nudeness. You simply be present to it. Learn more and more how not to use language. Unlearn the conditioning, the constant chattering inside.

This you cannot do suddenly; you will have to do it by and by, slowly. Only then, at the very end of it, can you simply watch your mind. No need to say, 'I am not this mind.' If you are not, then what is the point of saying it? You are not. If you are the mind, then what is the point of repeating that you are not the mind? Just by repeating it, it is not going to become a realization.

Watch; don't say anything. The mind is there like a constant traffic noise. Watch it. Sit by the side and see. See this is mind. No need to create any antagonism. Just watch, and in watching, one day, suddenly the consciousness takes a shift, changes, a *radical* change—from the object, suddenly, it starts focusing on the subject, if you are a watcher. In that moment, you know that you are not the mind. It is not a question of saying; it is not a theory. In that moment, you know—not because Patanjali says so, not because your reason, intellect, says so. For no reason at all, simply it is so. The facticity explodes on you; the truth reveals itself to you.

Then suddenly you are so far away from the mind, you will laugh how you could believe in the first place that you were the mind, how you could believe that you were the body. It will look simply ridiculous. You will laugh at the whole stupidity of it.

'Not to be identified with mind and body—still I don't know how to do it.' Who is asking this question, 'How to do it?' See it immediately; who is asking this question, 'How to do it?' It is the mind who wants to manipulate, it is the mind who wants to dominate. Now the mind wants to use even Patanjali. Now the mind says, 'Perfectly true. I have understood that you are not the mind'—and once you realize that you are not the mind, you will become a super-mind. The greed arises in the mind, the mind says, 'Good. I have to become a super-mind.'

The greed for the ultimate, for bliss, the greed to be in eternity, to be a god, has arisen in the mind. The mind says, 'Now I cannot rest unless I have achieved this ultimate, what it is.' The mind asks, 'How to do it?'

Remember, the mind always asks how to do a thing. The 'how' is a mind question. Because how means the technique. The how means 'Show me the way so I can dominate, manipulate. Give me the technique.' The mind is the technician. 'Just give me the technique and I will be able to do it.'

There is no technique of awareness. You have to be aware to be aware. There is no technique. What is the technique of love? You have to love to know what love is. What is the technique of swimming? You have to swim. Of course, in the beginning, your swimming is a little haphazard. By and by, you learn . . . but you learn by swimming, there is no other way. If somebody asks you,

'What is the technique of bicycling?'—and you do bicycle, you ride on the cycle—but if somebody asks, you will have to shrug. You will say, 'Difficult to say.' What is the technique? How do you balance yourself on two wheels? You must be doing something. You are doing something, but not as a technique; rather as a knack. A technique is that which can be taught, and a knack is that which has to be known. A technique is that which can be transformed into a teaching, and a knack is something that you can learn but you cannot be taught. So learn by and by.

And start from less complicated things. Don't suddenly jump to the very complicated. This is the last, the most complicated thing: to become aware of the mind, to see the mind and see that you are not the mind. To see so deeply that you are no longer the body and no longer the mind, that is the last thing. Don't jump. Start with small things.

You are feeling hungry. Just see the fact. Where is the hunger— in you, or somewhere outside you? Close your eyes, grope in your inner darkness; try to feel and touch and figure out where the hunger is.

You have a headache. Before you take an aspirin, do a little meditation; it may be that the aspirin is not needed then. Just close your eyes and feel where the headache is exactly, pinpoint it, focus on it. And you will be amazed, that it is not such a big thing as you were imagining before, and it is not spread all over the head. It has a locus, and the closer you come to the locus, you become distant from it. The more diffused the headache, the more you are identified with it. The more clear, focused, defined, demarked, localized, the more distant you are.

Then there comes a point where it is just like a needle point, absolutely focused; then you will come to have a few glimpses; sometimes the needle point will disappear, there will be no headache. You will be surprised, 'Where has it gone?' Again it will come. Again focus; again it will disappear. At the perfect focusing, the headache disappears, because at the perfect focusing you are so far away from your head that you cannot feel the headache. Try it. Start with small things; don't jump to the last thing so immediately.

Patanjali also has travelled a long way to come to these sutras of *vivek*, discrimination, awareness. He has been talking about so many things as preparatory, as basic requisites. Very necessary: unless you have fulfilled all that, it will be difficult for you to non-identify yourself with the mind and body.

So never ask *how* about it; it has nothing to do with how. It is a simple understanding. If you understand me, in that very understanding, you will be able to see the point. I don't say you will be able to understand it, I say you will be able to see it. Because the moment we say, 'understand,' intellect comes in, the mind starts functioning. 'Seeing it' is something which has nothing to do with the mind.

Sometimes, you are walking on a lonely path and the sun is setting and the darkness is descending, and suddenly you see a snake crossing the path. What do you do? You brood about it? You think about it, what to do, how to do it, whom to ask? You simply jump out of the way. That jumping is a seeing; it has nothing to do with mentation. It has nothing to do with thinking. You will think later on, but right now it is just a seeing. The very fact that the snake is there, the moment you become aware of the snake, you jump out of the way. It has to be so because the mind takes time and the snake won't take time. You have to jump without asking the mind. The mind is a process; snakes are faster than your mind. The snake will not wait, will not give you time to think what to do. Suddenly, the mind is put aside and you function out of the no-mind, you function out of your being. In deep danger, it always happens.

That is the reason why people are so attracted to danger. Moving in a speedy car, going one hundred miles per hour or even more, what is the thrill? The thrill is of no-mind. When you are driving a car one hundred miles per hour, there is no time to think; you have to act out of no-mind. If something happens and you start thinking about it, you are lost. You have to act immediately; not a single moment has to be wasted. So the greater the speed of the car, the more and more the mind is put aside, and you feel a deep thrill—a great sensation of being alive—as if you have been dead up to now and suddenly you have dropped all deadness and life has arisen in you.

Danger has a deep, hypnotic attraction, but the attraction is of no-mind. If you can do it just sitting by the side of a tree or a river or just in your room, there is no need to take such risks. It can be done anywhere. You have just to put the mind aside—wherever you can put the mind aside—and just see things without the mind interfering.

I have heard:

An anthropologist in Java came across a little-known tribe with a strange funeral rite. When a man died, they buried him for sixty days and then dug him up. He was placed in a dark room on a cool slab, and twenty of the tribe's most beautiful maidens danced erotic dances entirely in the nude around the corpse for three hours.

'Why do you do this?' the anthropologist asked the chief of the tribe who replied, 'If he does not get up, we are sure he is dead!'

That may be the attraction of forbidden things; if sex is forbidden, it becomes attractive. Because all that is allowed becomes part of the mind. Try to understand this.

All that is allowed becomes part of the mind; it is already programmed. You are expected to love your wife or your husband; it is part of the mind. But the moment you start becoming interested in somebody else's wife, it is not part of the mind; it is not programmed. It gives you a certain freedom; a certain freedom to move off the social track, where everything is convenient, where everything is comfortable—but everything is also dead. You become deeply interested in somebody else's woman. He may be fed up with that woman, he may be just trying to find some other way to become alive again—he may even get interested in your wife.

The question is not of a particular woman or man; the question is of the forbidden, the not allowed, the immoral, the repressed—that it is not part of your accepted mind, it has not been fed into your mind.

Unless man is completely capable of becoming a no-mind, these attractions continue.

And this is the absurdity of the whole thing: that these attractions were created by the people who think themselves moral, puritan, religious. The more they reject something, the more attractive it becomes, more inviting; because it gives you a chance to get out of the rut, it gives you a chance to escape to somewhere which is not social. Otherwise, the society goes on and on, crowding you everywhere. Even when you are loving your wife, the society stands there watching.

Even in your privacy, the society is there, as much as anywhere else, because the society is in your mind, in the programme, that it has given to your mind. From there it goes on functioning. It is a very cunning device.

Once in a while, everybody feels just to do something which is not allowed, just to say yes to something for which one has always been forced to say no—just to go against oneself, because that 'oneself' is nothing but the programme that the society has given to you.

The more strict a society, the more possibility of rebels; the more free a society, the less possibility for rebels. I will call a society revolutionary where rebels disappear, because they are no longer needed. I will call a society free when nothing is rejected, so there is no morbid attraction in it. If the society is against drugs, drugs will attract you, because they give you an opportunity to put the mind aside—you are burdened with it too much.

Remember, this can be done without being suicidal. The thrill that comes to you when you are doing something that the society does not allow is coming from a state of no-mind, but at a very great cost. Just look at small children hiding somewhere behind a wall, smoking. Watch their faces—so glad. They will be coughing and tears will be coming to them because taking smoke in and throwing it out is just foolish. I don't say it is a sin; once you say it is a sin, it becomes attractive. I simply say it is stupid; it is unintelligent. But watch a small child puffing a cigarette . . . his face. Maybe, he is in deep trouble, his whole breathing system is feeling troubled, nauseous, tears are coming, and he is feeling tense—but still glad he can do something which is not allowed. He can do something that is not part of his mind, which is not expected. He feels free.

This can be attained very easily through meditation. There is no need to move on such suicidal paths. If you can learn how to put the mind aside . . .

When you were born, you had no mind; you were born without any mind. That's why you cannot remember a few years of your life, just the first years, three, four, five years. You don't remember. Why? You were there, why don't you remember? The mind was not yet crystallized. You go backwards, you can remember something that happened near the age of four, and then suddenly there is a blank, then you cannot go deeper. What happened? You were there, very alive, in fact more alive than you will ever be again, because scientists say that at the age of four a child has learned, known, seen, 75 per cent of all the knowledge that is going to be there in his whole life. Seventy-five per cent at the age of four! You have lived 75 per cent of your life already, but no memory? . . . Because the mind was not yet crystallized, the language was to be learned, things were to be categorized, labelled. Unless you can label a thing, you cannot remember it. How to remember it? You cannot file it in your mind somewhere; you don't have a name for it. So first the name has to be learned; then you can remember.

A child comes without mind. Why am I insisting on this? To tell you that your being can exist without the mind; there is no necessity for the mind to be there. It is just a structure that is useful in the society, but don't get too fixated with the structure. Remain loose so you can slip out of it. It is difficult, but if you start doing it, by and by, you will be able to.

When you come home from the office, on the way, try to drop the office completely. Remember again and again that you are going home, no need to carry the office there. Try not to remember the office. If you catch yourself red-handed remembering something of the office again, drop it immediately. Get out of it, slip out of it. Make it a point that at home, you will be at home. And in the office, forget all about the home, the wife, the children, and everything. By and by, learn to use the mind and not to be used by it.

You go to sleep and the mind continues; you again and again say, 'Stop!' but it doesn't listen because you have never trained it to listen to you. Otherwise, the moment you say, 'Stop!' it has to stop. It is a mechanism. The mechanism cannot say, 'No!' You put the fan on, it has to function; you put it off, it has to stop. When you stop a fan, the fan cannot say, 'No! I would like to continue a little longer.'

It is a biocomputer, your mind. It is a very subtle mechanism, very useful; a very good slave but a very bad master.

So just be more alert, try to see things more. Live a few moments every day, or a few hours if you can manage, without the mind. Sometimes swimming in the river, when you put your clothes on the bank, then and there put the mind also. In fact, make a gesture of also putting the mind there, and go into the river alert, radiant with alertness, remembering continuously. But I am not saying verbalizing, I am not saying that you go on saying to yourself, 'No, I am not the mind,' because then this is the mind; just nonverbal, tacit understanding.

Sitting in your garden, lying down on the lawn, forget it, there is no need. Playing with your children, forget it, there is no need. Loving your wife, forget it, there is no need. Eating your food, what is the point of carrying the mind? Or taking a shower, what is the point of taking it in the bathroom?

Just by and by, slowly . . . and don't try to overdo, because then you will be a failure. If you try to overdo, it will be difficult and you will say, 'It is impossible.' No, try it in bits.

Let me tell you one anecdote:

Cohen had three daughters and was desperately looking around for sons-in-law. One such young man came on the horizon and Cohen grabbed him. The three daughters were paraded in front of him after a lavish meal. There was Rachel, the eldest, who was decidedly plain—in fact she was downright ugly. The second daughter, Esther, was not really bad looking but was decidedly plump—in fact she was disgustingly fat. The third, Sonia, was a gorgeous, lovely beauty by any standards.

Cohen pulled the young man aside and said, 'Well, what do you think of them? I have got dowries for them—do not worry: five hundred pounds for Rachel, two hundred-fifty pounds for Esther, and three thousand pounds for Sonia.'

The young man was dumbfounded: 'But why, why have you got so much more dowry for the most beautiful one?'

Cohen explained, 'Well, it is like this. She is just a teeny-weeny, itsy-bitsy little bit pregnant.'

So start getting a little bit pregnant every day—with awareness. Don't just become pregnant in a wholesale way; a little bit, by and by. Don't try to overdo, because that too is a trick of the mind. Whenever you see a point, the mind tries to overdo it. Of course you fail. When you fail, the mind says, 'See, I was all the time saying to you this is impossible.' Make very small targets. Move one foot at a time, inch by inch even. There is no hurry. Life is eternal.

But this is a trick of the mind; the mind says, 'Now you have seen the point, do it immediately—become non-identified with the mind.' And of course the mind laughs at your foolishness. For lives together, you have been training the mind, training yourself, getting identified; then in the sudden flash of a moment, you want to get out of it. It is not so easy; bit-by-bit, inch-by-inch, slowly, feeling your way, move. And don't ask too much, otherwise, you will lose all confidence in yourself. And once that is lost, the mind becomes a permanent master.

People try to do this all the time. For thirty years, a person has been smoking, and then suddenly one day, in a crazy moment, he decides not to smoke at all. For one hour, two hours, he carries on, but a great desire arises, a tremendous desire arises. His whole being seems to be upset, in a chaos. Then, by and by, he feels this is too much. All his work stops; he cannot work in the factory; he cannot work in the office. He is almost always clouded by the urge to smoke. It seems too disturbing, at such a great cost. Then again in another crazy moment he takes the cigarette out of the pocket, starts smoking, and feels relaxed; but he has done a very dangerous experiment.

In those three hours when he didn't smoke, he has learned one thing about himself: that he is impotent, that he cannot do anything, that he cannot follow a decision, that he has no will, that he is powerless. Once this settles, and this settles in everyone by and by . . . You try once with smoking, another time with dieting, and another time with something else, and again and again, you fail. The failure becomes a permanent thing in you. By and by, you start becoming driftwood; you say, 'I cannot do anything.' And if you feel you cannot do, then who can do?

But the whole foolishness arises because the mind tricked you; it always told you to immediately do something for which a great training and discipline is needed, and then it made you feel impotent. If you are impotent, the mind becomes very potent. This is always in proportion: if you are potent, the mind becomes impotent. If you are potent, then the mind cannot be potent; if you are impotent, the mind becomes potent. It lives on your energy, it lives on your failure; it lives on your defeated self, defeated will.

So never overdo.

I have heard about one Chinese mystic, Mencius, a great disciple of Confucius. A man came to him who was an opium taker, and the man said, 'It is very, very impossible. I have tried every way, every method. Everything fails finally. I am a complete failure. Can you help me?'

Mencius tried to understand his whole story, listened to it, came to understand what had happened: he has been overdoing. He gave him a piece of chalk and told him, 'Weigh your opium against this chalk, and whenever you weigh, write "one", next time write "two", again write "three", and go on writing on the wall how many times you have taken opium. And I will come after one month.'

The man tried. Each time he took opium, he had to weigh it against the chalk, and the chalk was disappearing by and by, very slowly, because each time he had to write 'one,' then with the same chalk 'two,' 'three' . . . It started disappearing. It was almost invisible in the beginning; each time the quantity was reduced, but in a very subtle way. After one month when Mencius went to see the man, the man laughed; he said, 'You tricked me! It is working. It is so invisible—that I cannot feel the change, but the change is happening. Half the chalk has disappeared—and with half the chalk, half the opium has disappeared.'

Mencius said to him, 'If you want to reach the goal, never run. Go slowly.'

One of the most famous sentences of Mencius is: 'If you want to reach, never run.' If you really want to reach, there is no need even to walk. If you really want to reach, you are already there. Go so slowly! If the world had listened to Mencius, Confucius, Lao Tzu, and Chuang Tzu, there would be a totally different world. If you asked them how to manage our Olympics, they would say, 'Give the prize to the one who gets defeated fast. Give the first prize to one who is the slowest walker, not for the fastest runner. Let there be a competition, but the prize goes to one who is the slowest.'

If you move slowly in life, you will attain much, and with grace and grandeur and dignity. Don't be violent; life cannot be changed by any violence. Be artful. Buddha has a special word for it; he calls it *upaya*, 'Be skilful.' It is a complex phenomenon; watch every step and move very cautiously. You are moving in a very, very dangerous place, as if moving between two peaks on a tightrope, like a tightrope walker. Balance each moment and don't try to run, otherwise failure is certain.

'*Not to be identified with mind and body—still I don't know how to do it. I tell myself: you are not the mind, don't listen to your fear, love yourself, be content . . .*' Stop all this nonsense. Don't say anything to the mind, because the sayer is the mind. You rather be silent and listen; in silence, there is no-mind. In small gaps, when there is no word, there is no-mind. Mind is absolutely linguistic—it is language. So start slipping into the gaps. Sometimes just see, as if you are an idiot, not thinking, just seeing. Sometimes go and watch people who are known as idiots. They are simply sitting there—looking but not looking at anything. Relaxed, perfectly relaxed, their face has a beauty. No tension, nothing to do, completely at ease, at home. Just watch them.

If you can sit for one hour like an idiot every day, you will attain.

Lao Tzu has said, 'Everybody seems to be so clever except me. I look like an idiot.' One of the most famous novelists, Fyodor Dostoevski, has written in his diary that when he was young, he had an epileptic fit, and after the fit, for the first time, he could understand what reality is. Immediately after the fit, everything became absolutely silent. Thoughts stopped. Others were trying to find medicine and the doctor, and he was so tremendously glad. The epileptic fit had given him a glimpse into no-mind.

You may be surprised to know that many epileptics have become mystics and many mystics used to have epileptic fits—Ramakrishna even. Ramakrishna would go into a fit. In India, we don't call it a fit; we call it *samadhi*. Indians are clever people; when one is going to name a thing, why not name it beautifully?

If we call it *no-mind*, it looks perfectly good; if I say, 'Be an idiot,' you feel disturbed, uneasy. If I say, 'Become a no-mind,' everything is okay. But it is exactly the same state.

The idiot is below mind, the meditator is above mind, but both are without any mind. I am not saying that the idiot is exactly the same, but something is similar. The idiot is not aware that he has a no-mind, and the no-mind man is aware that he has a no-mind. A great difference, but a similarity also. There is a certain similarity between mad people and the realized ones. In Sufism, they are called 'the mad ones'; the realized ones are known as the mad people. They are mad in a way: they have dropped out of the mind.

By and by, learn it slowly. Even if you can have a few seconds of this superb idiocy, when you are not thinking anything, when you don't know who you are, when you don't know why you are, when you don't know anything at all and you are deep in a non-knowledge state, in deep ignorance, in the deep silence of ignorance; in that silence the vision will start coming to you, that you are not the body, you are not the mind. Not that you will verbalize it! It will be a fact, just as the sun is shining there. You need not say that there is the sun and the shine. As the birds are singing—there is no need to say that they are singing. You can just listen and be aware and know that they are singing, without saying it.

Exactly the same way, prepare yourself slowly, and one day you will realize you are neither the body nor the mind—nor even the self, the soul. You are a tremendous emptiness, a nothingness— a no-thingness. You are, but without any boundary, with no limitation, with no demarcation, with no definition. In that utter silence, one comes to the perfection, to the very peak of life, of existence.

The second question:

Osho, each time I feel one with myself and in communion with you, my mind creates an enormous ego trip about how well I am progressing. Soon I am back in the mud. Please, will you encourage me?

. . . Again? Again you will be in the mud! You ask for encouragement? I cannot encourage you. I am going to discourage you totally, so you are never again in the mud. Who is asking for encouragement? The same ego . . .

You go on changing your question, but it remains in a subtle way the same—as if you have decided not to see the fact. Now you have seen the fact; still you want to falsify it.

'Each time I feel one with myself and in communion with you, my mind creates an enormous ego trip about how well I am progressing. Soon I am back in the mud.' Whenever the ego arises, sooner or later, you will be in the mud. You cannot avoid the mud if you cannot avoid the ego.

See: scientists say that even to say, 'Tomorrow again in the morning the sun will rise,' is just an assumption. It may not be so; there is no certainty about it. It has been so up to now, but what is the certainty that again tomorrow the sun is going to rise in the morning? There is no absolute certainty about it. It is just an inference based on the past experience that every day it has been so, so it is going to be so. But it cannot be made a scientific assertion. It may be so; it may not be so.

But as far as you are concerned, the moment you have taken birth, your death is absolutely certain—more certain than the sunrise tomorrow. Why? Even scientists cannot say, 'Maybe you will die or maybe you won't die.' No, you will die. It is certain! Because in the very birth, the death has already happened; birth is already death, one side of the same coin. So if you are born, you are going to die.

Scientists say that if you want to make a guarded statement, you can say this much: that if every circumstance remains the same, then the sun will rise again tomorrow. With this condition: that if everything remains the same. But the same is not applicable to death; whether everything remains the same or not, a man who is born is going to die. Death seems to be the only certainty in life—the only. Everything else seems to be just a perhaps, a maybe.

The same is true about the ego and the mud. Once the ego has arisen, you will be in the mud; because the ego and the mud are two aspects of the same coin. You cannot avoid falling in the mud once you have risen with the wave of the ego. You can avoid rising with the wave of the ego—that you can avoid; then mud is also avoided. So beware at the very beginning.

'Please, will you encourage me?' you ask me. If I encourage, you will again be flying high, you will again start thinking you are doing well. No, I am here to discourage you. I am here to destroy you, to annihilate you, so that the whole ego trip disappears. Otherwise again and again you will be asking the same question, from one corner, from another corner.

And my answer remains the same. You seem to ask different questions; you are not asking different questions. And I may be appearing to answer you different answers—that too is not true. You ask the same question, you formulate it in a different way; I answer the same answer, I have to formulate it in a different way because of you.

Let me tell you one anecdote:

A visitor to Ulster found himself approached by a menacing gang of toughs.

'Are ye Catholic or Protestant?' asked the leader, swinging his cosh significantly.

The visitor, unable to ascertain which answer was the desired one, resorted to subterfuge. 'Actually, I am a Jew,' he said.

His subterfuge was of little avail.

'A Catholic Jew or a Protestant Jew?' was the next question.

You cannot avoid. The question has to be faced; and the question has to be answered not by me but you, because it is your question.

If you can see that the moment the idea arises that 'I am going perfectly well, doing well,' the ego arises; then when the idea next arises that you are doing well, have a good laugh, a belly laugh. Laugh immediately; don't waste a single moment. Laughter is tremendously helpful in destroying the ego. Laugh at yourself. See the point of it: again? Have a good laugh, and suddenly you will see you have not been on the right track, and there will be no mud. The mud is created by the ego; it is a by-product.

Go on watching. It is arduous, but once you get the knack of it, it becomes very simple.

And never ask for encouragement from me. Just ask for understanding. Ask for awareness, but not for encouragement. The language of encouragement is the language of the ego. You want encouragement; somebody to clap, appreciate and say that you are doing perfectly well. You want the whole world to garland you, to say that you are great. But why does this need arise? This need arises because deep down you are not certain, deep down you are not certain whether you are really doing well. If you are really doing well, no encouragement is needed. If you are really doing well, you don't hanker for people to clap and to appreciate and garland you; there is no need. The need arises because of an inner ambiguity, an inner confusion, an inner vagueness, an inner uncertainty.

And, remember, you can gather a crowd to appreciate you, but that is not going to help you. That will be able to deceive you; you may be able to deceive yourself, but that is not going to help you. That's what politics is. The whole of politics is nothing but seeking encouragement from others. You become a president of a country—you feel very good, very high—but in the first place, that you wanted the encouragement of the people, you wanted their applause, shows that deep down you feel very inferior, that you don't value your being. You wanted it to be auctioned in the market to know.

I have heard, once Mulla Nasruddin went to the marketplace

with his donkey. He wanted to sell it because he was fed up with it. It was the worst donkey possible. He will not go where the Mulla would like him to go; he will go only where he wants to go. And he will kick and he will create much fuss—anywhere. And wherever there will be a crowd, he will create trouble for Mulla. So, fed up one day, he went to the market. Many customers asked, and he told the whole story, the true story, of what type of donkey this is. So nobody was ready to purchase it. Who will purchase such a donkey? And it was evening time, and the whole day many people had come and he will tell the whole story truthfully . . . and people will laugh.

Then one man came, and he said, 'You are a fool. You will never be able to sell this donkey; this is no way. You give me a little commission and I will auction it. Just see how it is done.'

So Mulla said, 'Okay,' because he was also tired.

The man stood on a chair, shouted loudly, 'The greatest donkey there has ever been, the most beautiful animal, the most loving animal, obedient—almost religious!'

The crowd gathered and they started bidding, and the price started getting higher and higher; and even Mulla got excited. He said, 'Wait! I don't want to sell such a beautiful animal! I cannot sell. I never knew these qualities about him. You take your commission; I don't want him sold.'

This is what politics is. You don't know your value, you go in the marketplace, you allow yourself to be auctioned, and when people come and they start valuing you—you advertise—when they start valuing you, you feel good. You start feeling that you have a certain value, otherwise why are so many people mad after you?

A man who has felt his being, is not in need of any encouragement. Try to feel yourself. All encouragement, all inspiration, is dangerous—it puffs you up. The ego enjoys it very much, but ego is your illness, your disease. You don't need encouragement; you need understanding, you need clarity to see.

And I am not here creating soldiers, to encourage you and

inspire you and tell you go and fight for the country or for the religion. I am not creating soldiers; I am not creating an army. I am trying to create individuals. I am trying to help you to become so uniquely in tune with yourself that you know where you are, who you are, what you are doing . . . and you enjoy it, because that is the only thing you are meant for. You feel your destiny and you are glad.

I am not here to make you Hindus, Christians, Mohammedans—they need encouragement, they need armies, they need slogans, they need politics, they need some type of mania, obsession, crusade, murder . . . . They need some type of violence so they can become convinced that they are doing great things.

No, I am not here to teach you to do great things. I am here to tell you just one thing, a very simple thing, ordinary: to know who you are. Because I know you are already great. And when I say you are already great, don't get any encouragement from it, because everybody is as great as you are—not a bit less, not a bit more. As I see the world, every individual is unique, incomparably unique. There is no need to compete with anybody; there is no need to prove anything. You are already proved! You are there; the existence has accepted you, given you birth. God has already made an abode in you. What more do you need?

The third question:

Osho, in regard to the Zen monks who laugh as a meditation every morning—don't you think they are taking their laughter a little too seriously?

No, because they laugh again—a second laugh—for the first, that 'How foolish we are! Why are we laughing?'

If you laugh only once, it can be serious. So always remember to laugh twice. First just laugh, and then laugh at the laughter. Then you will not get serious.

And Zen people are, in a way, not what you mean by religious people. They are not; Zen is not a religion, it is a vision. It has no scripture. It has nothing to abide with. It has nowhere to go, it has no goal. Zen is not a means or a method towards some goal and some end. It is the end.

It is very difficult to understand Zen because if you want to understand it, you will have to drop all that you have carried up to now—being a Christian, a Hindu, a Mohammedan, a Jaina. You will have to drop all that nonsense; it is rot. To understand Zen is very, very difficult not because of its intrinsic quality but because of your conditioned mind. If you look as a Christian or as a Hindu, you will not be able to see what Zen is. Zen is very pure; eyes filled with doctrines miss it. Zen is so pure that even a single word arises in your mind and you miss it. Zen is an indication.

Just the other night I was reading: a great Zen Master, Chao-chou, was asked, 'What is the essential religion?' He waited in silence, as if he had not heard the disciple. The disciple repeated again, 'What is the essential religion, sir?' The master continued to look where he was looking; he would not even turn his face towards the disciple. The disciple asked again, 'Have you heard me or not? Where are you?'

The master said, 'Look at the cypress tree in the courtyard.'

Finished; this is his answer: 'Look at the cypress tree in the courtyard.'

It is exactly the same as when Buddha inaugurated the world of Zen with a flower. He looked at the flower, and thousands who had gathered to listen to him could not understand what was happening. Then one monk, Mahakashyapa, smiled, laughed. Buddha called him, gave him the flower and said, 'Whatsoever can be said, I have told you, and whatsoever cannot be said, I give to Mahakashyapa.' He did well by giving a flower because Mahakashyapa flowered in that moment of smile; his being flowered.

What was Buddha saying? Looking at the flower, he was

saying, 'Be herenow. Look at the flower.' They were expecting something else, they were thinking about something else, they were imagining something else. When Chao-chou said, 'Look at the cypress tree in the courtyard,' he said, 'Drop all nonsense about religion and what is essential and nonessential—be herenow. Look. In that look which is herenow is revealed all that is essential religion.'

Zen is totally different. It is something tremendously unique. You cannot understand it if you are caught in dogmas, in creeds.

Let me tell you one anecdote:

A young Catholic girl of fifteen was asked by the Mother Superior what she wanted to be in life.

'A prostitute,' replied the girl.

'A what?' shrieked the aged nun.

'A prostitute,' repeated the girl calmly. 'Oh, the saints be praised,' said the pious old lady. 'I thought you said a Protestant!'

This type of mind will not be able to understand what Zen is; it will be completely beyond its grasp, divided in creeds and cults . . .

Zen people are not serious, but they are very sincere. And these two things are totally different; never misunderstand them, never be confused between them. A sincere man is not serious; he is sincere. If he laughs, he means it. If he loves, he means it. If he is angry, he is angry and he will not pretend otherwise. He is authentic, true. Whatsoever he is, he reveals himself to you. He is vulnerable. He never hides behind masks; he is sincere, true. Sometimes he will be sad—then he will be sad. And sometimes he will feel like crying, then he will cry and he will not hide and he will not try to be something else that he is not. He remains himself. He never deviates from his being and he never allows anybody to distract him.

But a serious person is somebody else, who is not true, who is not authentic but is posing that he is authentic, that he is true. A serious man is an impostor; he is just trying to show that he is authentic, very authentic. He cannot laugh, because he is afraid if he laughs, in the laughter maybe his true face will come to be seen by others. Because many times your laughter shows many things that you have been hiding.

If you laugh, your laughter can show who you are because in a moment of laughter you relax; otherwise you cannot laugh. A laugh is a relaxing. You can remain tight, but then you cannot laugh; if you laugh, the tightness goes. You can remain sombre, long-faced, and you can persist in that, but if you laugh suddenly you will see that the whole body is relaxed, and in that relaxed moment something may bubble up, may surface, which you have been hiding for long and you don't want others to see. That's why serious people don't laugh. Sincere people laugh—only sincere people laugh; their laughter is childlike, innocent.

Serious people will not cry, will not weep, because that will again show their weakness—and they want to prove they are strong, very strong. But a sincere person allows himself to be seen as he is. He invites you into his innermost core of being.

Zen people are sincere but not serious: sometimes so sincere that they look almost profane. You cannot conceive. So sincere that they look almost irreligious, but they are not irreligious. Because sincerity is the only religion there is.

My whole effort is in the same dimension: to help you to become sincere—but not serious. I want you to laugh; I want you to weep. I want you to be sad sometimes, to be happy. But whatsoever you are, you are. Whatsoever you are inside, that's your outside also. You are of one piece; then you will be alive, flowing, moving, growing, reaching to your destiny, revealing, flowering, unfolding.

The last question:

Osho, I feel addicted to you. You are my last vice, my last addiction, my last drug. I want to leave for a while to travel and yet I cannot get away. Every morning like clockwork I show up for the lecture. I feel hypnotized by you . . . . Anything to do?

Let me tell you an anecdote. And the last words of the anecdote are my answer to your question, so listen well.

A jazz musician who had never entered a church in his life found himself passing a little country church just as a service was about to begin. Out of curiosity, he decided to go in and see what it was all about.

After the service, he approached the rector and said, 'Say, Rev, you just about knocked me out with the good words—like I really dug it the most, man. Jeez, baby, I really blew my mind— it was wild, ya dig?'

The rector was flattered, but said, 'Well, thank you—most gratifying, I am sure. However, I wish you would not use these common expressions at the portals of the holy edifice.'

But the musician went on, 'And I will tell you something else, Rev. When the cat came around with the bread plate, I was so high with the whole scene that I came across with a fiver!'

'Crazy, baby, crazy!' said the rector.

Enough for today.

Nine

To Know What Is

*Loosening the cause of bondage and knowing the channels
allows the mind to enter another's body.*

*By mastering the current udana,
the yogi is able to levitate and pass without contact
over water, mire, thorns, etc.*

*By mastering the current samana,
the yogi is able to cause his gastric fire to blaze.*

*By performing samyama
on the relationship between the ether and the ear,
superphysical hearing becomes available.*

*By performing samyama
on the relationship between the body and the ether
and at the same time identifying himself
with light things, like cotton down,
the yogi is able to pass through space.*

A hundred years ago, one of the greatest thinkers of the world, Friedrich Nietzsche, declared that God is dead. He was declaring something that was becoming clearer to everybody. He simply declared the feeling of all the thinkers of the world, particularly the science-oriented people. Science was winning every day against religion, superstition; and science was conquering so much that it was almost certain that in the future God cannot exist, religion cannot exist. It was felt all over the world that God had become part of history and that God would exist in the museums, in the libraries, in the books, but not in human consciousness. It was felt as if matter had won the last, final war with God.

When Nietzsche declared, 'God is dead,' he meant that now life will not in any way be a destiny; it has become accidental, because God is nothing but the coordinating principle of life. God is the organic unity of life. God is that energy which has glued everything together. God is that law which has made a cosmos out of a chaos. Once God is not there, the coordinating principle is not there, the world again becomes a chaos, just an accident. With God, disappears all order. With God, disappears all principle. With God, disappears all possibility to understand life. And with God, man also disappears.

Nietzsche himself declared that God is dead and man is free now, but in fact once God is dead, man is not there. Then man is just matter, nothing more, is explainable, is a mystery no more, has depth no more, has infinity no more, and has meaning no more, significance no more, is just an accident—has appeared accidentally, will disappear accidentally.

But Nietzsche proved wrong. It appears that it was something like the age of scientific youth; the nineteenth century was the age of science's coming of age. And as every youth is too full of confidence, too optimistic, in fact foolishly optimistic, the same was the case with science. In Tibet, they have a saying that every young man thinks old people to be fools, but every old man *knows* that all young people are fools. Young people only *think*, but old people *know*. Science was the youngest growth in human consciousness, and science was much too confident; it even declared God is dead and religion is no longer relevant, it is 'out of context'. Religion was part of humanity's childhood, they declared. Freud wrote a book, *The Future of an Illusion*—about religion, that it is just an illusion and there is no future really.

But God survived, and a miracle has happened within these hundred years. If Nietzsche comes back, he will not be able to believe what has happened; the more the scientific mind penetrated into matter, the more it came to know that matter does not exist. God survived, matter died. Matter has almost disappeared from scientific vocabulary. It exists in ordinary language, but it is just because of old habit; otherwise there is no matter now. The deeper the scientific penetration became, the deeper they came to understand that it is energy not matter. Matter was a misunderstanding; energy is moving so fast, with such tremendous speed, that it gives an illusion of something solid. The solidity is just an illusion.

God is not illusory. The solidity of the world is illusory. The solidity of these walls is illusory; they appear solid because the energy particles, electrons, are moving at such a speed that you cannot see the movement.

Have you sometimes watched the fan going very fast? Then you cannot see the wings, the blades. And if the electric fan is really moving with such speed as electrons, you can sit upon it and you will not fall down, and you will not feel the movement. You can hit it with a bullet and the bullet will not pass between the gaps, because the speed of the bullet will not be as much as the speed of the blades.

This is what is happening. Matter has disappeared, has no more validity.

But what science has discovered is not really a discovery; it is a rediscovery. Yoga has been talking about it for 5,000 years at least. Yoga calls that energy *prana*. This word *prana* is very significant, very meaningful; pregnant with meaning. It is made out of two Sanskrit roots. One is *pra*: pra means the basic unit of energy, the most fundamental unit of energy. And *na* means energy. Prana means: the most fundamental unit is energy. Matter is just the surface. Prana is the real thing there is—and it is not a thing at all. It is more like a no-thing, or you can call it almost nothing. Nothing means no-thing. Nothing does not mean nothing: nothing simply means that it is not a thing. It is not solid, it is not static, it is not visible, it is not tangible. It is there, but you cannot touch it. It is there, but you cannot see it. It is there, beyond and beneath every phenomenon. But it is the most fundamental unit; you cannot go beyond it.

Prana is the basic unit of the whole of life. Rocks, trees, birds, man, God, everything is a manifestation of prana, on different levels, on different understandings, on different integrations. The same prana moves and manifests as millions, as many, but the basic unit is one.

Unless you come to know prana within yourself, you will not be able to know what God is. And if you cannot know it within yourself, you cannot know it without, because within you it is so close. That's why Patanjali could know it 5,000 years before Albert Einstein and company. Five thousand years is a long time for science to come to understand it, but they were trying from the outside. Patanjali dived deep into his own being; it was a subjective experience. And science has been trying to know it objectively. If you want to know something objectively, you have taken a very long route. That's why so much delay. If you go within, you have found the shortest route to know what is.

Ordinarily, you don't know who you are, where you are. What are you doing here? People come to me and they say, 'What are we doing here? Why are we, for what?' I can understand their confusion, but wherever you are and whatsoever you are doing, the problem will remain the same—unless you understand the source from where you come, unless you understand the basic structure of your being, unless you come to know your prana, your energy.

I have heard it happened:

Mulla Nasruddin visited a field and filled his bag full of melons. He was about to leave when the owner showed up.

'I was passing by,' Mulla began to explain, 'when suddenly a strong wind blew me over the fence and into the field.'

'What about the melons?' the owner asked.

'The wind was so strong, sir, that I clutched at anything I could get my hands on. And that's how the melons came loose.'

'But who put them into your bag?'

'To tell the truth,' Mulla replied, 'I was wondering about that myself.'

This is the situation. How are you here? Why are you here? Who has put you into the bag? Everybody is wondering.

Philosophy, they say, comes out of wonder; but don't go on simply continuously wondering and wondering. Otherwise, wondering becomes a sort of wandering. Then you never reach. Rather than simply wondering, try to do something. You are here, that much is certain. You are alert that you are here, that much is also certain. Now these two ingredients are enough for yoga experimentation. You are: the being is there. You are aware that you are: the consciousness is there. These two are enough to make a lab out of your being for yoga experimentation.

Yoga does not need sophisticated, complicated things for its work. It is the simplest. Two things: you and your awareness that you are—enough. These two you have; everybody has them. Nobody is lacking in these two things. You have a certain feel that you are, and of course you are aware of that certain feel. These two things are enough. That's why yogis had no laboratories, no sophisticated instrumentation—and they never needed any grant from Rockefeller or Ford. They needed only just a little bread, water, and they would come and beg in the town and would disappear for days. After a week or two, they would come again and beg again and they would disappear again.

They did the greatest experiment: the experiment in human reality. And only with two small things, but those small things are not small. Once you know them, they are the biggest phenomenon ever.

So the first thing about today's sutras is the discovery of prana. That became the very foundation of the temple of yoga. You are breathing. Yoga says you are not only breathing air; you are also breathing prana. In fact, air is just a vehicle for prana, just a medium. You are not alive by breath; breath is just like a horse, and you have not looked at the rider yet. The rider is prana.

Now many psychoanalysts have come across this mysterious thing—the rider who is coming on the breath, going on the breath, continuously moving in and out. But as yet in the West it is not a recognized scientific fact. It should be because now science says matter is no longer there and everything is energy. The stone, the rock, is energy; you are energy. So there must be many energy games happening within you, tides and ebbs of energy.

Freud stumbled upon this fact. I say, 'stumbled upon it' because his eyes were not open; he was blindfolded. He was not a yogi. He was again caught in the scientific attitude of making everything objective; he called it 'libido.' If you ask the yogis, they will say libido is prana, ill. When prana is not vital, when somehow the energy of prana has become dammed up, blocked; that's what Freud has come to know. And that's explainable because he was working only with ill people, neurotics, mad people, mentals. And working on ill, mentally disturbed people, he came to know that their bodies are carrying some blocked energy and unless that energy is released, they will not be healthy again. Yogis say libido is prana gone wrong; it is just a diseased prana. But still Freud stumbled upon something that later on could become very, very significant.

And one of his disciples, Wilhelm Reich, went deeper into it, but he was caught by the American government because he could not prove very scientifically, that is very objectively, what he was saying. He died in jail as a madman, certified as mad. He was one of the greatest men ever born in the West. But again he was working blindfolded. He was not yet working as a yogi has to work. The scientific attitude was his undoing.

Reich tried to make contact with this energy the yogis call prana, and he called it orgone. Orgone is better than libido, because libido gives a feeling as if all is sexual energy. Orgone is a better word, more inclusive, more comprehensive, bigger than libido, and gives a possibility for the energy to move beyond sex or to touch higher realms of being which are not sexual. But he got into trouble because he felt it so much and he observed it so much that he started to accumulate the prana energy, the orgone, in boxes; he made orgone boxes. Nothing is wrong in them; yogis have been working on that for centuries. That's why yogis try to live in almost boxlike caves, with only one small door.

Now those caves look very unhygienic—how did they live there for years? No air goes in because there is no cross ventilation. So dark, dingy, and yogis have lived so perfectly and so healthily that it is almost a miracle. What were they doing there and how were they living there? According to the modern scientific ideology, they should have died, or at the most they should have lived as very ill people, depressed, but yogis have never been depressed. They are one of the most vital people to come across, very alive. What were they doing? What was happening? They were creating orgone, and for orgone to stay in a particular place, cross ventilation is not needed; in fact cross ventilation will not allow the orgone to accumulate because once the air comes there, the orgone energy is a rider—it jumps on the air and moves out. No air passage is needed; then layers upon layers of orgone go on accumulating, and one can thrive on it and live on it.

Wilhelm Reich created small orgone boxes, and he helped many ill people. He would tell them just to lie down in the orgone box, and he would close the box and tell them to rest; and within an hour, the person is out, feeling very, very vital, alive, tingling all over with energy. And many people have reported that their diseases disappeared after a few experimentations with the orgone.

The orgone box was so effective that, without knowing the laws of the country and without bothering about them, Wilhelm Reich started to produce them on a mass basis and he started selling them. Then he was caught by the Food and Drug Administration and he was asked to prove it. Now it is difficult to prove because the energy is not tangible; you cannot show it to anybody. It is an experience; and a very inner experience.

You don't ask Albert Einstein to show electrons, but you can believe in him because you can go and see Nagasaki and Hiroshima. You can see the effect; you cannot see the cause. Nobody has yet seen the atom, but the atom is, because it can produce effects.

Buddha has defined truth as that which can produce effects. Buddha's very definition of truth is very beautiful. Never again and never before has there been such a beautiful definition of truth: that which can produce effects. If it can produce effects, it is true.

Nobody has seen the atom, but we have to believe it because of Nagasaki and Hiroshima. But nobody listened to Wilhelm Reich and his patients. There were many who were ready to certify, 'We have been cured,' but this is how—once some attitude becomes generally accepted—people become blind. They said, 'All these people are hypnotized. In the first place, they must not have been ill, or they have imagined themselves cured, or it is nothing but suggestibility.' Now you cannot go and tell the people who have died in Hiroshima, 'You have imagined that you are dead'; they have simply disappeared.

Just see the thing: death is more believable than life.

And the whole modern world is more death-oriented than life-oriented. If you kill a person, you will be reported by all the newspapers; you will become a headline. But if you revive a person, nobody will ever come to know about it. If you murder, your name becomes a famous name, but if you give life to people, nobody is going to believe in you; they will say you are a charlatan or a deceiver.

That has always been so. Nobody believed Jesus; they killed him. Nobody believed Socrates; they killed him. They have killed even a very innocent man like Aesop, the famous storyteller. He never did anything, he never created a religion or a philosophy, and he was not saying anything against anybody. He was just creating a few beautiful parables. But those parables offended people because he was saying such great truths in those parables, and in such a simple way, that he was murdered.

You go on killing people who have been affirmative, life enhancing. You ask for proofs.

If somebody comes to me and asks what I am doing here, it will be difficult. If you certify, they will say you have gone mad. This is something. If somebody is against me, they will believe him; if somebody is for me, they will not believe him. If somebody is against—howsoever foolish—they will not argue with him; they will say, 'Right.' And if somebody is with me and for me—howsoever intelligent—they will laugh; knowingly they will say, 'I know, you are hypnotized.' Ask Dr Phadnis; people say that he is hypnotized.

This is a vicious circle of argumentation. If I convince you, you are hypnotized; if I cannot convince you, I am wrong. So either way I am wrong. If somebody is convinced . . .

It happened; Swabhav is here. A few years before, he came with his two brothers; all three had come to argue with me. And Swabhav was the most argumentative of the three; but he is a sincere man, and simple. He became by and by convinced. He had come as a leader with the other two brothers; then he became convinced. Then the other two became against him. Now they say he is hypnotized. They have stopped coming; they won't listen to me. Now they are afraid: if Swabhav can be hypnotized, they can also be hypnotized. They avoid, and they have created a protective defense mechanism around themselves. If I can convince another brother—because I know one can be convinced still—then the remaining one will become more defensive; and then he will say, 'Two brothers gone.' And the remaining one is also very good-hearted; there is a possibility for him also. Then the whole family will think all three have gone mad.

This is how things go. If you cannot convince, you are wrong;

if you can convince, then too you are wrong.

Many people, very intelligent people, Ph.Ds, professors, psychoanalysts certified, but the court wouldn't listen. They said they were all conspirators in the same game. 'Show us where orgone energy is! Open the box and let us see where it is. It is an ordinary box, there is nothing. And you are selling it, deceiving people, cheating.'

Wilhelm Reich died in a prison. It seems humanity is not going to learn anything from history; it goes on repeating the same, again and again.

Why are you so much against love, because orgone energy is love energy? Why are you so much against life and why are you so much in favour of death? Something has not evolved in you. You are so unalive that you cannot believe that life has more and higher possibilities. And if somebody reaches to a higher peak, you cannot believe that is possible. You have to deny; it becomes almost an offence to you.

If I say I am God, it becomes an offence. I am simply saying that you can also become gods, never settle for less. But you feel offended. And you are living only 2 per cent of your possibilities; 98 per cent of your possibilities are being wasted. As if you were given a hundred days to live, and you lived only two days and died. Even your great thinkers, painters, musicians, geniuses, they live only 15 per cent of their potentiality.

If you can blaze to your utmost, you become a god.

The situation is such that I would like to tell you one anecdote to explain it:

Cohen bumped into Levy Isaacs who was looking terribly dejected.

'What is the matter?' he asked.

'I am bankrupt,' said a quiet Isaacs. 'My business failed.'

'Oh, well,' said Cohen, 'what about the property in your wife's name?'

'There is no property in my wife's name.'

'Well, then, what about the property in your children's names?'

'There is no property in my children's names?'

Cohen put his hand on Levy's shoulder, 'Levy, you are very mistaken. You are not bankrupt—you are ruined.'

This is the situation where you are: not only bankrupt, ruined. If you don't become alive, if you don't revitalize your prana and energy, you are ruined—and you will live with the false idea that you lived. And you are supported by the whole mass of people around you because they are almost as dead as you are, so you think this is the rule. This is not the rule.

The effort towards religion starts only when you catch hold of this—this sutra, this thread—that whatsoever you are doing is almost nothing. You are wasting a great opportunity. Unless you start feeling God within you, never settle for anything. It is okay if you stop for a night's rest, okay, but by the morning, start going. Remember it as a criterion that your fulfilment is your godhood.

When your prana flowers, you are God. Right now, your prana is just crawling on the earth—not even standing and walking.

I have heard about one beggar who knocked at a big house. The lady of the house opened the door. The man immediately did a *shashtang*; he bowed down with his whole body on the earth. He crawled at her feet; a very strong man, healthy, perfectly healthy and young. The lady said, 'What are you doing? Why are you wasting your energy and crawling at people's feet? Why don't you work? Why do you go on asking, begging, crawling?'

The man looked up and said, 'Lady, I am a very scientific man. I am moving alphabetically.'

The lady said, 'What do you mean, alphabetically?'

He said, 'Asking—A. Begging—B. Crawling—C. Work is very, very far away . . . .'

Alphabetically! Don't be so alphabetical.

If you are using your prana only for sex purposes, you are crawling. Unless the energy moves to the *sahasrar*, unless the prana comes to the crown of your head, to your very peak, you will not be able to fly in the sky; you will remain imprisoned and you will remain miserable. Happiness is when you are flying. Happiness is when the sky is vast, unlimited. Happiness is when you have learned the pinnacle, the crescendo of your being, when you have touched the highest peak.

Now the sutras:

Loosening the cause of bondage and knowing the channels allows the mind to enter another's body.

'*Bandh karan shaithilyat*'—'*Loosening the cause of bondage . . .*' What is the cause of bondage? Identification; if you are identified with the body, you cannot move beyond it. Wherever your identification is, there is your imprisonment. If you think you are the body, your very thinking will not allow you to do something that can be done only when you know that you are not the body. If you think you are the mind, then the mind is your only world; you cannot go beyond it.

You have learned a particular language, and you go on interpreting all the experiences through that language. Even if you come across a man who has gone beyond body identity, you will reduce his experiences also to your experiences; you will interpret. If you come across a buddha, you will not see his buddhahood; you will see only his body. Because you can see only that which you are, you cannot see anything more. You are your confinement.

Remember not to get identified with lower things.

There are people who are simply living to eat. They don't eat to live; they live to eat. And they go on eating and stuffing. They become just food, nothing else. They are like a refrigerator—stuffed, nothing else in them. And they go on doing it continuously;

and they never think for a single moment, 'What are you doing? Is this the whole of life? Then you are vegetating.'

Mulla Nasruddin fell ill. The wife said, 'Should I call the doctor?'

He said, 'No. Call the vet.'

She said, 'What do you mean? Have you gone mad, or the fever has gone too high? Why the vet, why the veterinary doctor?'

He said, 'I live like a vegetable, I work like a mule, I think like a donkey, and I sleep with a cow. You call the vet; I am not a man. Only the vet can understand me.'

Just watch, observe what you are doing with yourself. Vegetating? Just stuffing with food? Or just hankering for more and more sex indulgence, just chasing women or men . . . ?

One very lovely woman asked me, 'Osho, should I remain alone, or should I chase men?' She has passed her prime, her age. Now it is time to be alone and be happy; now it is almost foolish to chase. So I told her, 'Now there is no need.' But in the West, there is a problem; even old women have to pretend that they are young. And they go on chasing because that's their only life. If sex disappears, they think life disappears, because then for what to live? That was their whole meaning.

The woman understood. It is very easy when you are near me to understand something, but when you go away, the problems come back, because that understanding was because of me. I had almost possessed you; in that lightening you can see many things very easily. Next day, she wrote a letter, 'Osho, you are right. I should not chase, but what about casual affairs?' Here you go again.

Don't crawl; stand up. Upanishads say: '*Uttishtha jagrat prapya varanni bodhayat*'—Stand up; become aware, because to become aware is the only way to stand up, to rise and soar high.

The cause of bondage is identification. The sutra says, '*Loosening the cause of bondage . . .*' If you can loosen it a little, relax it a little, if you can uproot yourself from your body and mind, you will attain to a very great experience; and that experience is: you can enter into another's body.

But why is this a great experience? Once you can enter into another's body, the body identification drops forever. Then you know that you have entered in many bodies before; you have entered millions of bodies, remained, loved, suffered, and thought that you were this body or that. When you are not too identified with the body and the bondage is loose, you can try it.

You can enter into a dead man's body. Buddha used to send his disciples to the cemetery. Sufis have worked very much on this method; they will live in the cemeteries where dead people are, and when a fresh body is buried, they will try to enter into the buried body. Once you can enter into another's body, suddenly, your vision becomes absolutely clear that the body is just a house that you are in. If you have lived in your own house, confined for ever and ever, by and by, you become identified with the house, you start thinking as if 'I am the house'; but if you can go and visit a friend's house, suddenly, you see that you are not the house; the house is left behind, you are in another house. Then the vision becomes clear.

And this loosening of identification can be of much help also. You can help somebody very deeply if you can loosen your bondage. This is one of the methods of *shaktipat*; whenever a master wants to help you, to cleanse you, your energy channel, your passage, if it is blocked, he simply possesses you. He simply descends in you, and his energy—of a higher quality, purer, unbounded—moves in your energy channels. They become open. Then your own energy can move in them easily. This is the whole art of shaktipat. If a disciple is really surrendered, the master can possess him immediately.

And once you are possessed by the energy of the master, once his prana surrounds you, enters in you, much is done very easily which you cannot do in years. It will take years for you because you will be working, working . . . hard is the work, blocks are very, very rocky, you have accumulated them in many, many lives, and your energy is very tiny, just a trickling, a few drops of energy. They are lost again and again in the desert. They are lost again and again against the rock. But if a master can enter in you like a waterfall, many things are simply washed away. And when the master has gone out of you, suddenly you start to be a totally different person—cleaner, younger, vital . . . and all energy passages open. Just knock a little and you move.

When a master enters the body of a disciple, he leaves behind him for a few moments such a great opportunity that if the disciple wants to use it, he can attain—so easily, so simply that there will be almost no effort.

There are certain schools, those schools are called the schools of *siddhas*; they don't allow their disciples to work on any technique. The siddha guru simply tells them to sit by his side and wait. They believe in *satsang*, and it is a tremendously powerful method, but for it a great devotion is needed. A single doubt and it cannot happen; a little resistance and it cannot happen. One has to be completely open. One has to be completely a moon, only then can the master possess you.

'*Loosening the cause of bondage and knowing the channels allows the mind to enter another's body.*' Two things are needed: first, loosening of the bondage; and another, the awareness, the knowledge of the channels from where to leave the body and how to reenter it—how to enter another's body. Because if you don't know from where to leave your body, you may not be able to reenter again; so just loosening of the bondage won't help, you will have to be very, very aware of the inside world of your body.

Ordinarily, we know only the outside, just the skin part. That's why people go on powdering, deodorizing their skin. And that's their whole body. They don't know what a great mechanism is hidden inside. You are not aware; just the skin part, just the surface, which is nothing but the outer shell. As if you go to see the Taj Mahal and you just go round and round and see the outer walls and come back. You look into the mirror, the mirror simply reflects your skin, the outer shell, and you get identified with it. You think, 'I am this man.' You are not. You are very, very great—but you never look from within.

Get disidentified with the body, then close your eyes and try to feel the body from within. Try to touch the body from within, how it feels from within. Get centred and from there look around—and mysteries upon mysteries open their secrets to you. That's how yogis came to know about the channels, the centres, the *nadis*, the energy fields, the working of the energy fields— from where you can get out of the body and how you can reenter and how you can enter into another's body.

A great knowledge, the whole topography of the inner body is needed. One has to know it, otherwise you will miss it; many times it has happened.

That's why Patanjali simply gives the sutra and does not go into detail because if the detail is described, there are foolish people who will try. No detail is given. You cannot do anything just by reading this sutra. In fact, all the practical details have not been opened to you; Patanjali keeps them secret. They are only for those who are working with a master. They cannot be said publicly, because curious people are there and they will try, and sometimes they can get out of the body, but then they will not be able to get in. Sometimes, they can get into another's body and may not be able to get out. Then they will create trouble for themselves and for others.

So details are not being given; details have always been handed over in personal intimacy. These sutras simply give you the framework.

> *By mastering the current udana,*
> *the yogi is able to levitate and pass without contact*
> *over water, mire, thorns, etc.*

When for the first time the Eskimos were discovered, the discoverers were simply amazed to know that they have almost one dozen words for snow—one dozen. They could not believe for what one dozen words are needed. *Snow* is enough. Or you can have one more word, *ice*, but that will do. But Eskimos have almost one dozen, and even more words, for snow. They live in snow; they have seen all the moods of snow. They have known snow in different ways. A man living in a tropical country simply cannot imagine why one dozen words are needed for it.

Yogis say that prana has five different shapes, workings, energy fields in you. You will say simply 'breathing' is enough; we know only two things—exhalation, inhalation—that's all. But yogis live in the world of prana and they have come to know subtle differences, so they have made five divisions. Those divisions have to be understood. They are very significant. First is prana, second is *apana*, third is *samana*, fourth is *udana*, fifth is *vyana*. These are the five prana manifestations in you, and each has a different work to do inside.

Prana, the first, is respiration. Apana, the second, is a help to excretion; it helps to cleanse the body of all excreta. The bowel movement comes from apana, and if you know how to work on it, you can cleanse your bowels as nobody else can. Yogis have the cleanest bowels. And that is very, very meaningful because once the bowel is totally clean, once your intestines are perfectly clean; your whole being feels light, as if you can fly. The burden disappears.

Ordinarily, your intestines carry much rotten excreta—your whole life's, layers upon layers. Inside the inner walls of the intestine, excreta goes on accumulating dry and hard. It creates many poisons; it makes you heavy. It makes you more available to gravitation. Much emphasis is given in yoga to cleanse the whole stomach so that no toxins remain in it, because they go on circulating in your blood, they go on circulating in your brain, and they create a particular energy field around you which is heavy, dark, black.

When the intestines are perfectly clean and clear, the aura arises around your head; and people who have perceptive eyes can see it very easily. And you feel as if you are like a feather.

The second, apana, is excretion. The third, samana, is digestion and providing body heat. If you know the function of the third and if you become aware where it is, your digestion will become absolutely perfect. Ordinarily, you eat much but you don't digest it. You go on eating and you never feel satisfied; you go on stuffing the body without digesting it. If one knows how to use samana, a small quantity of food will give him more energy than a big quantity of food ever gives to you. That's why yogis can fast for many days without any harm to their body. Once in a while, they will take a little quantity of food, and they will digest it totally. Your food is not totally digested. That's why your excreta can become food for some other animal and he can digest it; much food value is still left in it.

The third provides the body heat also. In Tibet, they have developed the whole system of body heat, creating body heat, on samana; they breathe in a certain way, in a certain rhythm, so that the samana vibe functions efficiently within their body. They create much heat; they can create so much heat that snow is falling and a Tibetan lama will stand naked—perspiring—under the open sky. All over is snow; and you will feel freezing, you will not be able to come out of the house, and he is standing in the falling snow—perspiring.

This is one of the examinations; when in Tibet, somebody becomes a physician, first he has to go through an examination in which he has to create his body heat. If he cannot create that, he is not given a certificate to practice medicine. It is very difficult. No other medicine in the whole world asks so much of the physician. It is not just a viva voce; it is not just that you cram something and vomit it in the examination papers. You have to show that really you have become master of your body heat because for the whole life you will be working on the heat energy of your patients; if you are not a master, how can you work upon others? So for the whole night, the examinee has to stand outside in falling snow. Nine times in the whole night, the examiner will come and touch your body to see whether you are still perspiring. If you can create that much body heat, you are a master of samana. Now you can become a healer; your very touch will become a healing miracle.

In Tibet, they teach that when you touch the hand or the pulse of your patient, you have to breathe in a certain way; only then will you know his system of breathing. And once you know his system of breathing, you have known everything about him and you know what is to be done. Ordinarily, doctors try to watch symptoms in the patient, not moving themselves into a particular space of perceptivity, but in Tibet—and their whole method is based on Patanjali's yoga—first the doctor has to move in a certain space from where he can feel, see, where the problem of the patient is, where the patient's prana is entangled, where the prana of the patient is blocked, where to hit.

The same is true about acupuncture; that developed out of Taoist yoga. Seeing inside the functioning of energy, prana, they became aware that there are 700 points in the body which are energy points, and just by pressing those points, the whole energy field of the body can be changed and transformed. When you have a headache, the acupuncturist may not touch your head; there is no need. He will touch somewhere else because the energy in the body exists in a polarity, negative and positive. If you have a headache, then somewhere else—at the opposite pole—he will find a point and he will just push his needle a little. Even that is not needed. Even acupressure—just a little pressure with his thumb—and suddenly the headache is gone. And it is miraculous; how does it happen? He has changed your energy field. By pushing it somewhere, he has changed the whole field; you now have another energy field, a different energy field.

Acupuncture is becoming more and more scientific in the West, particularly in Russia, because a man has developed a new sort of photography; Kirlian photography. And through that photography those 700 points can be seen through photographs— and exactly those 700 points were known by Taoist yogis, without any medium, without any photography, without any camera. They came to know it from the within.

The fourth is udana, speech and communication; when you speak, the fourth type of prana is used. And the same type of prana can be trained; if that prana can be trained, you become a hypnotic speaker, or you can become a hypnotic singer. Your voice can have a hypnotic quality. Just listening to it, people can be magnetized.

And the same is used for communication. People who are in a difficulty of how to communicate—and many people, millions of people, are in that difficulty—how to communicate, how to relate to others, how to love, how to be friendly, how to be open, how not to be closed . . . they all have some difficulty of udana. They don't know how to use the prana energy that makes you flowing, and your energy becomes open and you can easily reach the other and there is no block.

And the fifth is vyana, coordination and integration. The fifth keeps you integrated; when the fifth leaves the body, you die. Then the body starts disintegrating, deteriorating. If the fifth is there, even if all your breathing stops, you will remain alive. That's what yogis are doing. When yogis exhibit that they can stop their heart, they stop four—the first four pranas—they keep on the fifth. But the fifth is so subtle that there exists no instrument yet, which can detect it. So for ten minutes you can observe in every possible way and you will see that the yogi is completely dead and your doctors will certify that he is dead . . . and he will come back. The fifth is the most subtle, the very thread which keeps you as an organic unity.

If you can know the fifth, you will be able to know God, not before that. Because the function of the fifth within you is the same as God's function in the totality; God is vyana, he is keeping the whole together—the stars, millions of stars, the infinity of space, all together. If you know your body, your body is a small microcosm, representative of the whole macrocosm. In Sanskrit, they call the body *pind*, microcosm; and the whole *brahmand*, the macrocosm. And your whole body is a miniature; it has everything that the whole has, nothing is lacking. If you can understand your totality, you will have understood the totality of all.

Our understanding remains at the level where we stand. If somebody says that there is no God, he is simply saying that he has not come to know something integrative in his own being, that's all. Don't fight with him; don't argue with him, because argument cannot give him an experience of vyana. Proofs cannot give him an experience of vyana. Yogis never argue; they say, 'Come, experiment with us—hypothetically. There is no need to believe what we say. Just try; just to try to see what it is. Once you come to feel your vyana, suddenly God appears. Then God is spread all over.'

Let me tell you one anecdote:

The lodger was asked by his landlady to solve a problem for her. She said to him, 'I have got these two parrots in a cage; one is a boy parrot and the other is a girl parrot, but I don't know which is which. Can you help me?'

The lodger said, 'Well, missus, I don't know anything about parrots, but I tell you what; you put a black cloth over their cage, leave them for half an hour, then take the black cloth off and see which of the birds is a bit ruffed up—that will be the male.'

So she did just that: she put a black cloth over the cage, left it for half an hour then took it off. Sure enough one of the parrots was a bit ruffed up.

'There you are,' he said, 'that is the male.'

'Oh, yes,' she said, 'but how am I going to tell in future?'

So he said, 'Tie a bit of ribbon around his neck now, then you will know.'

And this the landlady did.

That afternoon the vicar came to tea. The parrot took one look at his dog collar and said, 'Blimey, they caught you at it as well, did they!'

Whatsoever is our experience becomes the interpretation for the whole. We are confined to our experience; we live through it, we see through it. So when a man says there is no God, feel compassion for him; don't feel angry. He is simply saying that he has not come across anything in him that can correspond to God, which can give an indication. He has not found even a ray of light within his being. How can he believe that there exists the source, the sun, the source of life and light? No, he cannot believe. He is completely blind, utterly blind; not even a ray of light has passed through his eyes. Feel compassion for him; help him. Don't argue, because argument is not going to help him.

Nobody can convince anybody about God. It has nothing to do with conviction; it is a conversion.

'By mastering the current udana, the yogi is able to levitate and pass without contact over water, mire, thorns, etc.' If you have become tuned and you have mastered the prana known as udana, you can levitate because it is udana that connects you with gravitation.

You see so many birds, such big birds, flying. It as yet remains a mystery for scientists how they fly with such weight. Those birds by nature know something about udana; it is spontaneous for them. They breathe in a certain way. If you can also breathe in that way, you will feel suddenly you are cut from gravitation. With gravitation, you have a certain connection from within your being. This can be disconnected.

And it happens to many people without knowing. Sometimes meditating, sitting, suddenly you feel that you are levitating. Open your eyes; you will find yourself sitting on the ground. Close your eyes; again you feel you are levitating. Your physical body may not be levitating, but deep inside, something has become disconnected and you feel a gap between you and gravitation. That's why you feel that you are levitating. This can go deeper and deeper, and one day it is possible you can levitate.

There is a woman in Bolivia who has been observed by all scientific technology, methods. She levitates. She can go for a few seconds four feet above the ground—just by meditating. She sits and meditates, and she starts rising up.

> *By mastering the current samana,*
> *the yogi is able to cause his gastric fire to blaze.*

Then you can digest very easily, and totally. And not only that, when your gastric fire is blazed, your whole body will have a certain radiance around it, a certain quality of fire, aliveness.

And this fire helps the yogi to purify his whole being because this fire burns all that is rotten and rubbish in you; all that should not be there. It destroys all impurities and toxins within your body.

And this fire, if it can be burned really totally, can burn your mind also. Thoughts can burn in it; desires can burn in it.

And Patanjali says that once you have found this fire, by breathing in a certain way and bringing a certain prana energy and accumulating it inside, you can burn the whole desire to live—you can burn the very seed of desire. Then there is no more birth for you. This he calls *nirbeej samadhi*, seedless samadhi, when even the seed has been burnt.

> *By performing samyama*
> *on the relationship between the ether and the ear,*
> *superphysical hearing becomes available.*

The word in Sanskrit for ether is *akash*. It is more comprehensive than ether; akash means the whole space, the whole emptiness that surrounds everything. Akash means the nothingness out of which everything comes and goes back to, the primordial nothingness which was in the beginning and which will be again in the end. Everything comes out of it and disappears into it. This nothingness is not just nothing; it is not negative, it is absolutely potential and positive, but formless.

'*By performing samyama on the relationship*' between this

akash—this formlessness that surrounds you—and your ear . . .
This is a yoga discovery: that your ear is in tune with akash.
That's why you can hear sounds; sounds are created in akash, in
ether, and your ear corresponds to akash within your body. Your
eyes correspond to the sun; your ears correspond to the akash, to
the ether. If you can bring your samadhi to the akash and your
ear and their relationship, you will be able to hear whatsoever
you want to hear.

This is something very miraculous, but not a miracle; it has
as scientific laws behind it as television or radio. Just a certain
tuning is needed. If your ears are in a certain tuning with the
akash, you start hearing that which was not ordinarily available.
You can hear others' thoughts. Not only that, you can hear
thoughts which were uttered thousands of years before. You can
hear Buddha again. You can hear Krishna again giving his
message to Arjuna. You can hear Jesus again giving his Sermon
on the Mount. Because whatsoever is created remains in the akash;
it never goes away; in a subtle way it is preserved.

In Theosophy they call these records *akashic records*.
Everything is there, recorded, taped, once you can find the key;
and that key exists in bringing samyama to the relationship of
the ether with your ear.

> *By performing samyama*
> *on the relationship between the body and the ether*
> *and at the same time identifying himself*
> *with light things, like cotton down,*
> *the yogi is able to pass through space.*

And if you bring samyama to your body and the akash and
their relationship . . . the akash is formless, *nirakar*, the infinities
around you; your body is just a wave in the ocean of akash.
Before it arose, it was unmanifest in the akash; after you will die,
it will again disappear into akash. Right now the wave is joined
with the akash; it is not disjointed. Just bring your awareness to

the wave and the relationship of the wave with the ocean and you will be able to disappear or appear, according to your will.

A yogi can manifest himself in many places simultaneously; he can meet one of his disciples in Calcutta and another in Mumbai and another in California. Once you know how to be in tune with the ocean, you become infinitely powerful.

But remember that these things are not to be desired. If you desire them, they will become bondages. These things should not become objects for your greed. And when they happen on their own, you should go on offering them to God. Tell him, 'What will I do with them?' Whatsoever you attain, go on renouncing it, giving it back to God. More will be coming; give that too. More will be coming still; give that too. And a point comes when you have renounced all; God himself comes to you.

God comes at the moment of absolute, utter sacrifice.

So please, don't start becoming greedy about these things. And I have not given you any details, so even if you become greedy, you cannot do anything. Those details are given in privacy. Those details are given in a person-to-person-relationship. And there is no need for you to come to me for those details; whenever you are ready, they will be given to you wherever you are. Your readiness is all. If you are ready, they will be given to you, and they will be given only in proportion to your readiness so that you cannot harm yourself, you cannot harm others; otherwise man is a very dangerous animal.

Remember that danger always.

Enough for today.

Ten

Nowhere to Go

The first question:

Osho, I feel lost—there is no way back to my old life—the bridges are broken. And I don't see a way in front of me.

There is none. The way is just an illusion of the mind. The mind goes on dreaming about the way to reach its goals, its desires. The way is a shadow of the desiring mind. First you desire something. Of course desire can only be in the future and the future is not there yet. How to bridge that which is not, with that which is? Then you create a way. It is imagination. It is illusion. But with the way, you become joined with that which is not, and then you start travelling. You are playing a game with yourself.

There is nowhere to go, so the way is not needed. You are already there. It is not something to be achieved; it has already been delivered to you. And deep down, religion is not a path but just a realization, a revelation—the realization that you are already there. Your hankering, your desire does not allow you to see the facticity of your being.

So good, old bridges are broken and there seems to be no path, no way ahead. That's what I want to do to you. I want to take all the paths away. Pathless, not knowing where to go, you will go in. If all your paths—all the possibilities to escape from yourself—are taken away, what will you do? You will be yourself.

Just think. Just meditate upon it a little; it is desire, it is competition with others that creates the whole thing, the whole illusion. You are always competing. Somebody else is ahead of you. You would like to put him back; you would like to overtake him. You run fast. You do everything that you can do—just/unjust, right/wrong. You forget everything; you simply want to undo him, to prove him a failure. This way you are not going to achieve your innermost reality. This way you will achieve a little more decoration of the ego. You have defeated one, you have defeated thousands, you have defeated millions—and you are moving and moving and moving. More and more ego will be accumulated. You will become more burdened. You will be more lost; you will be lost in a forest.

Competition is one of the most irreligious things in the world, but that's what everybody is doing. Somebody has a big house; you immediately start desiring a bigger one. Somebody has a beautiful car; immediately you desire to have another, a bigger one. Somebody has a beautiful wife, or somebody has a beautiful face or a beautiful voice; immediately the desire arises.

The desire arises with the idea that you have to compete with others and that you have to prove something against others; that you have to struggle, that you have to achieve something. Not knowing what it is, but you go on moving in a dark valley, thinking that somewhere there must be a goal.

You can go on and on for lives together. That's what you have been doing up to now. You will never reach anywhere. You will be always running and never reaching because the goal is within you, but to see that, you have to drop all competition, all ambition.

And remember, it is very easy to change your competitiveness into a new competitiveness, to drop the old and to have something new again in the same way, the same ambition. You are ambitious in the world, then you drop it; then you become ambitious in the name of religion, spirituality; then again you compete. Then again the same ego enters in.

I have heard one anecdote. Listen to it very alertly.

Two brothers died at the same time and arrived at the Pearly Gates together, where they were interviewed by St. Peter.

He said to the first brother, 'Have you been good during your life on earth?'

And he replied, 'Oh yes, Your Saintliness, I have been honest, sober, and industrious, and I have never messed around with women.'

'Good lad,' said St. Peter, and gave him a beautiful gleaming white Rolls Royce. 'There is your reward for being a good boy.'

Then he said to the other brother, 'And what about you?'

He sighed, 'Well, I have always been very different from my brother. I have been crooked, drunk, idle—and a devil with the women.'

'Ah well,' said St. Peter, 'boys will be boys, and at least you have owned up to it. You can have this, then.' And he gave him the keys to a Mini-Minor.

The two brothers were about to get in their cars when the one who had been naughty started roaring with laughter. The other one said, 'What's so funny then?'

He said, 'I have just seen the vicar riding a bike!'

Your whole enjoyment is always just comparative. Comparison gives you a feeling of where you are—behind the man who has a Rolls Royce but in front of the man who has a bike. It gives you the exact location where you are.

You can pinpoint yourself on the map, but this is not the right way to know where you are, because you are nowhere on the map. The map is illusory; you are somewhere beyond the map. Nobody is in front of you and nobody is at the back. You are alone—tremendously alone. You are unique, you are alone, you are one; and there is nobody else there to be compared with.

That's why people become very much afraid of going within because then they are moving into their aloneness, where all paths disappear, all possibilities of location where you are, disappear. All maps—imaginary, political, cultural, social—all disappear.

Suddenly, you are in the wilderness of your being and you don't know where you are. This is exactly what has happened: *'I feel lost—there is no way back to my old life—the bridges are broken. And I don't see a way in front of me.'*

This is what I call the beginning of meditation, the beginning of the entry within your being. Don't get scared, otherwise you will again become a victim of your dreams. Enter into it boldly, courageously, daringly. If you understand me, it is not difficult; just a tacit understanding is needed.

Of course you will never be able now to know where you are. You will be able to know *who* you are, but you will never be able to know *where* you are because 'where' is always in relation with others. 'Who' is your nature; 'where' is relative.

And now hence onward there will be no bridges with the past; and of course there is no possibility now for any bridges for the future. The past is gone; the future does not exist. The past is just memory and the future is nothing but hope. The past is just a reference and the future is just a dream. Both are gone. You will be living in the present . . . and the present is so vast that you will be lost as a drop of water becomes lost in the ocean.

Be ready for it. Be ready to dissolve, be ready to be annihilated.

The mind will hanker for the past; the identity, the clarity— where you are, who you are. But all those are games, language games.

I have heard one anecdote:

An Englishman touring the States remarked to a man in the West, 'You have a remarkable country here. Lovely women, big cities, but you have no aristocracy.'

'No what?' asked the American.

'No aristocracy.'

'What is that?' asked the American.

'Oh, you know,' he said. 'People who never do anything, whose parents never did anything, and whose grandparents never did anything—whose families have always been people of leisure.'

'Oh, yeah!' said the American. 'We have them here, but we call them hoboes!'

But when you call somebody an aristocrat, it looks very grand. When you call somebody a hobo, suddenly you fall from the peak of Everest into the deepest valley possible. But aristocrats have been hoboes, and hoboes think of themselves as aristocrats.

I have heard that two hoboes were talking to each other, leisurely sitting on a full moon night. The first said, 'What do you want to become in your life?'

The other said, 'I would like to become a prime minister.'

The first said, 'What? Don't you have any ambition in your life?'

A hobo thinking of becoming a prime minister . . . Hoboes have their values.

If you look at your past references, what are they? Language games. Somebody says that he is a *brahmin*. Because the society accepts that there are four classes in India; the brahmin is the highest caste and the *sudra* is the lowest caste. Now this type of caste system does not exist anywhere in the world; it exists only in India. Of course, it is imaginary. You cannot sort out who is a brahmin if he does not say so. The blood will not show, the bones will not show—no examination, no X-ray will show who is a brahmin and who is a sudra. But in India the game has been played so long, it has become so deep rooted in the mind, the moment somebody says he is a brahmin, look at his eyes, look at his nose—the ego radiates. When somebody says that he is a sudra, look at him. The very word humiliates; the very word makes him feel guilty. Both are human beings, but just a labelling that a society has accepted destroys their humanity.

When you say you are rich, what do you mean? You have a certain account in the bank. But that too is a game; money is a game. Because the society has agreed upon something to believe in, the game continues.

I have heard about one miser who had a great treasure of gold hidden somewhere in his garden. Every day he would go and remove a little earth and look at his bricks of gold, hide them again, would come back very happy and glad and smiling, all smiles. By and by, one neighbour started suspecting, because every day—it was almost a religious ritual—every day, exactly in the morning, he would come—it was just like a prayer—remove a little soil, look at his bricks of gold shining in the morning sun, and immediately something would flower in him and he would be so happy the whole day.

One night, the neighbour removed all the bricks of gold. Instead of gold bricks, he put ordinary bricks there and covered the earth. The next morning, the miser came. He started crying and weeping and shouting that he had been robbed. The neighbour was standing in his garden; he said, 'Why, for what are you crying?' He said, 'I have been robbed! My twenty gold bricks have been stolen!' The neighbour said, 'Don't be worried, because you were never going to use them. You can do the same with these ordinary bricks. Come every day in the morning, remove the earth, look at them, be happy and go back. Because you were never going to use them in the first place, so whether of gold or of mud, what difference does it make?'

You may have money; that does not make any difference. You may not have; that too does not make any difference. You may have great recognition, degrees, awards from the society, appraisal, certificates; that does not mean anything—it is a game. Once you look into this game through and through and you realize that in this game you will never be able to find yourself, who you are . . . The society goes on befooling you and giving you some illusory ideas of who you are, and you go on trusting and believing in them. Your whole life is wasted.

So when for the first time meditation starts really working in you and starts destroying you, destructuring you—your name disappears, your caste disappears, your religion disappears, your nationality disappears—by and by, you are simply nude and naked in your pure aloneness. It is scaring in the beginning because you cannot find any place to put your feet and you cannot find any place to continue, to remain in the ego. No help, all props withdrawn, your structure starts falling.

Stand by the side, have a good laugh, and let it fall. Have a good laugh that now there is no way to move back.

In fact, there is never a way to move back; people only believe so. Nobody can go back; in time there is no possibility to go back. You cannot become a child again. You cannot go back into the womb of your mother. But the illusion, the idea that it is possible will haunt you and will not allow you to grow.

I see many men who go on seeking their mother in their love affairs, which is foolish. Out of a hundred, almost ninety-nine men are searching for their mother. The mother has been lost in the past; now they cannot enter the womb of the mother again. Have you watched yourself? Lying in the lap of your beloved, a fantasy arises in you—as if you have found your mother.

Why are men so interested in women's breasts? The interest is basically the search for the mother because the child knew the mother through the breasts and he still hankers for the mother. So a woman who has beautiful, round, big breasts becomes more attractive to men. A flat-chested woman simply becomes unattractive. Why? What is wrong? Nothing is wrong with the woman; something is wrong with the mind. You are seeking the mother, and she cannot help your imagination. She does not fit with your illusion. How can she be your mother, she has no breasts; breasts are the basic necessity.

If you go to Indian temples in Khajuraho or in Puri and you will see such big breasts that it seems almost impossible. How were these women walking? The weight seems too much. But that simply shows the search, the search to go back, to find the mother again. Then your love life will be a disturbance because the woman who loves you is not in search of a child. She is in search of a friend, of a beloved, of a lover. She does not want to become your mother. She wants to become your friend, your companion, your consort. And you are asking her to be your mother, to take care of you as your mother used to take care. And you go on expecting the mother and she goes on frustrating it; the conflict arises.

Nobody can go back. That which is past is past. Past is past and cannot be reclaimed. This understanding makes you a grown up; then you don't hanker for it.

And, remember, if you hanker for the past, you hanker for the future. Your future is nothing but your modified, renovated past. What you desire in the future is nothing but all that was happy in the past, minus all that was not happy. Your future is nothing but your repainted past—closer to the heart's desire, the painful accidents dropped and the pleasant exaggerated. Once you drop the past, you drop the future also, because it is nothing else but the repainted past, and then suddenly you are herenow.

Then I can tell you, 'Look at the cypress in the courtyard.' Or I can take a flower in my hand and just let you see it. And if you can see it just here and now, a mysterious phenomenon starts happening within you: a flower within you starts opening. Something spreads over your being—something existential. It is not a dream; it has no hallucinatory quality in it. It has no ideas, no thoughts, no pictures, nothing; just a tremendously austere emptiness—beautiful, but totally empty.

Don't get afraid. That's how one comes to meet the present and how one comes to meet oneself.

The second question:

Osho, why did Patanjali write and you choose to speak on the yoga sutras when neither of you was prepared to share with us the essential keys of this sadhana?

The essential keys can be shared but cannot be talked about. Patanjali wrote these sutras so that he could share the essential keys with you, but those essential keys cannot be reduced to sutras. The sutras are just introductory, just a preface to the real thing. Let me tell you, the yoga sutras of Patanjali are just a preface to the real transmission he wants to do; it is just introductory. It just gives you an idea that something is possible. It makes you hopeful; it simply gives you a promise, a glimpse. Then you have to do much to come close to Patanjali.

In deep intimacy, the keys will be delivered to you.

And that's why I have chosen to speak on these yoga sutras. It is just to allure you, to seduce you, so that you can come close to me. It is just to help some great thirst in you which you are carrying for lives together; but finding no way to satisfy it, finding no way to quench it, you have forgotten about it. You have dropped it out of your consciousness. You have pushed it into the darkness of the unconscious because it is trouble. If you have a certain thirst and you cannot satisfy it, to allow it to remain in the conscious will be very, very burdensome, very troublesome. It will continuously go on knocking. It will not allow you to do other things, so you have pushed it into the unconscious.

These discourses on the yoga sutras of Patanjali are just to bring that neglected thirst into the focus of your consciousness. This is not the real work; this is just introductory. The real work starts when you have recognized the thirst, accepted it, and you are ready to change, to mutate, to become new—when you are ready to dare to go on this immense journey, the journey into the unknown and the unknowable. It is just to create a thirst, a hunger.

The yoga sutras are just an appetizer. The real thing cannot be written, cannot be said; but something can be written and said which can bring you nearer, closer to the real thing. I am ready to deliver the keys, but you have to be brought to a certain level of consciousness, a certain level of understanding. Only then can those keys start being understood by you.

I have heard:

Two beggars, really down and out, were each lying on the grass.

The sun was shining above, beside them a rippling brook. It was quiet, restful, and peaceful.

'You know,' mused the first beggar, 'right now I would not change places with a man who had a million pounds.'

'How about five million?' asked his companion.

'Not even for five million.'

'Well,' went on his friend, 'how about ten million?'

The first beggar sat up and said, 'That's different. Now you are talking *real* money.'

It is just to give you a glimpse. It is not giving you the real money but just to give you a glimpse of the real money so again the long-denied desire, thirst, discontent arises, again repossesses you, you become aflame; and then you can come close to me.

The third question:

Osho, for years I am most of the time witnessing and I feel it like a disease. So is it that there are two kinds of witnessing and mine is wrong? Tell me.

It must be wrong; otherwise it cannot be felt like a disease. Self-consciousness is not consciousness of the self, and there is the problem. Consciousness of the self is totally different. It is not self-consciousness at all; in fact self-consciousness is a barrier for consciousness of the self. You can try to watch, observe with a very self-conscious mind: that is not awareness; that is not witnessing, because that will make you tense.

That's what happens to people. You go on talking. I have never come across a person who is not a good talker; all people talk well. Talking is so human, so natural. But tell somebody to stand on a stage and talk to people. Even to a small gathering of four hundred, one thousand, people, let somebody stand; and he starts trembling and the fear arises and he feels as if the throat is choking, and suddenly words don't come easily, the flow stops.

What happens? He has always been a good talker, almost to the extent of being a bore, and suddenly . . . suddenly he cannot speak a word.

He has become self-conscious. So many people watching, observing . . . Now he feels as if his prestige is at stake. If he says something wrong or something goes wrong, what will people think of him? He had never thought about it that way, but now with so many people facing him—and these may be the same people with all of whom he has been talking individually—but now standing on a stage looking at people, and so many people looking at him together—all their eyes like arrows penetrating him—he becomes ego-conscious. His ego is at stake; that creates the tension. Remember, witnessing is not an ego-consciousness. Ego has to be dropped. And you are not to make it a strain. It has to be relaxed; it has to be in a deep let-go.

Let me tell you one anecdote:

A priest was unburdening himself to a rabbi. 'Oh, rabbi, things are very bad. The doctor tells me I am very sick and that I must have a very serious operation.'

'It could be worse,' said the rabbi.

'My congregation is deserting me for another parish because my sermons are so bad and I don't make house calls,' continued the priest.

'It could be worse,' said the rabbi.

'My housekeeper has given in her notice, my organist has resigned, and I can't get any boys to serve on the altar,' continued the priest, close to tears.

'It could be worse,' said the rabbi.

'The parish treasurer has decamped with the funds, and the bishop is due to make a visitation; one of the Children of Mary is pregnant, the roof leaks, and my car has been stolen,' moaned the priest.

'It could be worse,' said the rabbi.

'How could it be worse?' asked the priest, finally stung by the rabbi's lack of compassion.

'It could happen to me,' said the rabbi.

If you are continuously thinking in terms of the ego, then even your witnessing will become a disease, then your meditation will become a disease, then your religion will become a disease. With the ego, everything becomes a disease. The ego is the great inconvenience in your being. It is like a thorn in the flesh; it goes on hurting. It is like a wound.

So what to do? The first thing is, when you are trying to watch, the first thing that Patanjali says is: concentrate on the object and don't concentrate on the subject. Start from the object— *dharana*, concentration. Look at the tree, and let the tree be there. You forget yourself completely; you are not needed. Your being there will be a continuous disturbance in the experience of the greenery, of the tree, of the rose. You just let the rose be there. You become completely oblivious of yourself, you focus on the rose. Let the rose be there: no subject, just the object. This is the first step of *samyama*.

Then the second step: drop the rose; drop the emphasis on the rose. Now emphasize the consciousness of the rose—but still no subject is needed, just the consciousness that you are watching, that there is watching.

And only then can the third step be taken, which will bring you close to what Gurdjieff calls self-remembering, or Krishnamurti calls awareness, or the Upanishads call witnessing. But first the two steps have to be fulfilled; then the third comes easily. Don't start doing the third immediately; first the object, then the consciousness, then the subject.

Once the object is dropped and the emphasis on the consciousness is no longer a strain, the subject is there but there is no subjectivity in it. You are there but there is no 'I' in it, just being. You *are*, but there is no feeling that 'I am.' That confinement of 'I' has disappeared; only 'amness' exists. That amness is divine. Drop the 'I' and just be that amness.

And if you have been working too long on witnessing, then for a few months—at least for three months—drop it completely, don't do anything about it. Otherwise, the old pattern may continue and may pollute the new awareness. For three months give a gap, and for three months, you meditate with cathartic methods—Dynamic, Kundalini, Nataraj—that type in which the whole emphasis is on doing something . . . and that something is more important. Just dancing, and the dance becomes important, not the dancer. The dancer has to lose himself completely in dancing. So, for three months, drop witnessing and be absorbed in some meditation. This is totally different; being absorbed in something is completely forgetting yourself. Dancing will be very good, singing will be very good—forget yourself completely in it. Don't keep yourself apart and divided.

If you can dance in such a way that only the dance remains and the dancer disappears, one day suddenly you will see the dancing has also disappeared. And then there is an awareness that is not of the mind and not of the ego. In fact, that awareness cannot be practised; something else has to be done as a preparation, and that awareness comes to you. You have just to become available for it.

The fourth question:

Osho, 'these things can only be transmitted in the close personal relationship between disciple and master.' Well, what have we here? I have that relationship with you, and these things are not transmitted.

You cannot decide whether you have that relationship with me or not. Only I can decide. Your greed may tell you that you have that relationship; your desire to achieve it may tell you that you are ready, but your saying that you are ready does not make you ready. Unless I see, it cannot be transmitted.

And if you look down, you will also see that you are not

ready. Just being here is not enough. Just becoming a sannyasin is not enough—necessary, but not enough. Something more, something of a greater sacrifice is needed, in which you dissolve. When you are not, the keys can be delivered, not before it. If you are there watching and waiting, that very watching and waiting will become a barrier.

Let me tell you one anecdote:

Three novices joined a Trappist monastery. After a year, they were seated at breakfast and the Abbot turned to a novice:

'Brother Paul, you have been with us a whole year and you have kept your vow of silence. If you wish, you may now speak. Do you have anything to say?'

'Yes, Abbot, I don't like the breakfast food.'

'Very well, perhaps we shall do something about it.'

Nothing was done, and another year passed, a year of silence. Once again they were seated about the breakfast table and the Abbot turned to another young monk:

'Brother Peter, I commend you for having kept your peace for two years. If you wish, you may now speak. Do you have anything to say?'

'Yes, Abbot, I don't see anything wrong with the breakfast food.'

A third year passed, a year of silence. Again the Abbot turned to the third novice:

'Brother Stephen, I commend you highly for your vow of silence which you have kept for three whole years. If you wish, you may now speak. Do you have anything to say?'

'Yes, Abbot, I do. I can't stand this constant bickering.'

All those three years have been lost on the breakfast food, and deep down in the mind it has continued to be a problem. All three have answered differently, but all are concerned with it. Their differences of answers are just on the surface; deep down they have all been obsessed with it.

You can be ready only when all such obsessions disappear. It is very easy to be silent. But the inner chattering continues; then it is not a silence, it is just outwardly an exhibition of silence. In fact, people when they take a vow of silence, chatter more in their minds than ordinarily because ordinarily they chatter with others and much of the stream is let out. When they keep silent, there is no door for the stream to go out—all valves are closed, so the stream goes on, round and round and round inside. It becomes a whirlwind, a whirlpool, and they go on chattering and chattering.

These three years, all three novices have been chattering and chattering and chattering. On the surface, everything looks perfectly calm and quiet, but it is not so in the depth.

So whenever you are ready . . . and you cannot decide; it cannot be left for you to decide. Those who have become ready, to them the keys have been already delivered; and those who will be becoming ready, the keys will be always ready to be delivered to them. In fact, not a single moment is lost; the moment you are ready, *immediately*, *instantly*, the key is delivered. The key is not something material, that I have to give it to you and to call you. It is something—a transmission . . . Once you are in tune with me, so much so that you are not even bothered about the keys, you have left the whole thing to me; that's what surrender is. You say, 'Whenever, if ever, you feel right, I am ready. If you feel it is not right, then I am ready to wait forever. Even if it doesn't happen, it doesn't matter.' Only then, in that total acceptance, you become really open to me, otherwise you are trying to use me. You cannot use me.

I am available, but you cannot use me. You can simply become vulnerable to me—and you will be satisfied beyond all satisfactions. But for that, infinite patience, emptiness is needed.

Another question of the same type:

Osho, in one of your previous lectures you have accepted that

*you are fully ready on your side to push sadhakas toward the
unknown peak of the soul. You have further said, 'I am waiting
for persons of such types who are ready to do any kind of
experiments for ascending to the unknown peak of the soul.' The
time since I have heard this statement I have been preparing
myself to face this challenge of yours. In my personal interviews
with you when I accepted that I am fully ready on my side, you
admitted that you were not ready at that time. Why this duality
in your statements? Please clear my doubts.*

There is no duality—just etiquette. You are not ready, but I didn't
want to hurt you, so I said that I am not ready.

The very tenseness and eagerness and greed is creating a
disturbance. If you are ready and I say to you, 'Wait,' you will
listen to me. This question is from Anand Samarth. Just a few
days before, he was there to ask me, and I again and again said,
'Wait'; and he would say, 'Now I cannot wait anymore. You
have said before, "Whenever anybody is ready, I am ready to
transmit to him." Now I am ready; then why do you say to me,
"Wait"?' And I again said to him, 'Wait,' but he would not listen.
You are not even ready to listen to me. What type of surrender is
this? You are completely deaf, and still you think you are ready.
Your greed is there; that I understand. Your ego is there; that I
understand. You are in a hurry; that I understand. And you are
trying to get things very cheap; that I understand. But you are not
ready.

Let me tell you one anecdote:

Two nuns were driving through the country when their car ran
out of petrol. They walked on a couple of miles and eventually
came to a farmhouse, where they explained their problem.

'You can siphon some petrol out of my tractor,' said the
farmer, 'but I have not got anything to put it in.'

However, after some thought, he produced an old chamber
pot which appeared to be the only available utensil. So, with the

pot filled with petrol, the nuns walked back to their car and began pouring it in.

A rabbi passed by in his car, saw this extraordinary sight, stopped and said, 'I don't agree with your religion, sisters, but I admire your faith!'

I also don't agree with your readiness, but I admire your faith. I admire that the thirst has arisen. Good. But thirst in itself is not enough readiness. It is the beginning, but not the end. Let it flower in silence, let it flower in patience, let it flower in a deep let-go. Don't be in a hurry. Move slowly; almost try to float with me. And don't try to go ahead of me—that will not be possible.

The sixth question:

Osho, peace is here with you but how do I get this monkey mind to become unattached to the old so as to move with the new?—Michael Stupid

Good, very good. It is better than Michael 'Wise.' You are becoming wise; to accept one's stupidity is a great step towards wisdom.

But don't just try to be clever. You cannot deceive me, because the next question is again from Michael Wise.

Let me read the next question:

Osho, peace is here with you. If someone were to ask Lao Tzu if he should take sannyas, would he answer:
'What, and divide the world? The flowers know no uniform; and the sunrise is not beautiful?'
Or:
'If someone is crazy enough to take your mind, give it to him.'
Or:
'The flower has already answered; there is no need for me.'
— Michael Wise (Stupid)

Again, Michael Wise; now 'Stupid' is in brackets. Already you have fallen from your wisdom.

And you are not Lao Tzu. If you were, you would not be here in the first place. For what would you be here?

And I tell you one thing: if I say so to Lao Tzu, he will take sannyas. But I am not going to say it to him. What is the point? Why disturb the old man?

The eighth question:

Osho, you are not my guru, but you are my mentor. You and I think alike; feel alike. Whatever you say, I seem to have known before; you are helping me to remember. I have been hearing you for many years and I am in total empathy with you. If such is the case, what is my exact relationship with you?

I think you must be my guru.

The ninth question:

Osho, you have often mentioned in your lectures, 'Don't think that you have come on your own. I have cast the net and have selected you.' I know it is true, but how do you manage to know that the person is ready to receive what you compassionately want to share?
I had been pining for self-realization from the very young age of fifteen and was in search of a master, which took me to Swami Sivanand of divine life society, Sant Lilashah, and Sadhu Vaswani, from whom I picked up a few jewels, but the Kohinoor of self-realization was not there. I heard Radhaswami, Chinmayanand, Dongre Maharaj, and Swami Akhandanand, but self-realization was not there.
I had even heard you in Mumbai four or five years back a few times, did some meditations with your sannyasins on Juhu beach, and appreciated them, but was not fully drawn to you, until it

*happened last year. I had come as a critic, but a few meditations
and two or three lectures convinced and converted me. It happened,
I surrendered.*
*I am fully convinced that I am in the safe hands of the master,
who is every moment guiding properly.*
*I am experiencing ecstasy, or rather joy, but not the final stage of
enlightenment. I am living the moment, not caring for the past or
the future.*
Am I on the right track? Kindly enlighten.

You are on the right track, but even that track has to be dropped
because in the world of the ultimate, all tracks are wrong; track
as such is wrong. No way leads to it. All ways help you go
astray. The very idea to reach God is wrong. God has already
reached you; you have just to start living it. So the whole effort is
in a way futile.

You are here with me. Now allow me to take all tracks away
from you. Allow me to take not only the jewels, but the Kohinoor
also. Allow me to empty you. Don't try to fill yourself with me,
because then I will become the barrier. Beware of me. No need to
cling to me. All clinging is dangerous. You have to attain to a
state of mind that is of no clinging. Be with me, but don't cling to
me. Listen to me, but don't make knowledge out of it. Listen to
my gossips, but don't make gospels out of them. Enjoy being
with me, but don't depend on it. Don't make it a dependence,
otherwise I am not your friend. I am already an enemy then.

So what have you to do? You have been to Sant Lilashah, to
Swami Sivanand, to Swami Akhandanand. You have left all of
them behind you. You have to leave me also behind. If I cannot
help you in that, then I am going to be a barrier on your path.

So love me, be close to me, feel my presence, but don't depend
on it.

And why do you ask whether you are on the right track or
not? The mind would like to cling. So if everything is certain and
the track is right, you would say, 'Now, okay. So I can blindfold

my eyes. Now there is no need to go anywhere.' There is no need to go anywhere—not because you have to cling to me—there is no need to go anywhere because you are already there where you want to go. Let me help you to know yourself.

It is delicate, subtle, very subtle, because what I say, if it appeals to you, there is a possibility you will make a philosophy out of it. What I say, if it convinces you—as the questioner says, 'I became convinced' . . . I am not arguing with you, and I am not giving any arguments. I am completely absurd, irrational. I am trying to drop argumentation from your mind so that you can be left behind, pure, unpolluted, uncontaminated by words, theories, dogmas, scriptures; so that you can attain to your pure, crystal-like quality of consciousness, just an emptiness, a great space.

What I am trying is to give you the goal and not the path. My effort is to deliver to you the whole, the all. I am not giving you means; I am giving you the end, the very end. That's where the mind feels boggled. The mind wants to know about the means so it can reach to the end. The mind wants to know the method. The mind wants to know the path. The mind wants to be convinced and converted. I want to destroy it, not to convince it. So if you are really convinced with me, drop the mind. If you have seen and heard me, and if you have loved me, then don't allow the relationship with me to be a relationship of ideology. Let it be just pure love, with no ideology. You simply love me and let me love you, for no reason whatsoever. Let this love be unconditioned.

If you love me because what I say appears to you to be true, then this love is not going to last very long; or even if it lasts, it is not going to give you that love which is God. It will remain a conviction, an argument in the mind. And I am a dangerous man in that way because today I will say something and you are convinced, and tomorrow I will say just the opposite, and then what will you do? Then you will be confused.

You can remain with me only if you are not trying to convince your mind; then I can never confuse you because you never cling to any idea. I will go on saying a thousand and one things, this way and that. These are all devices to destroy the mind.

And this difference you have to understand: if you go to some master, he has a certain discipline, a certain scripture, a certain ideology. There are even masters whose ideology is no ideology, but they have a very, very strict ideology of no ideology—that is their scripture. I don't have any ideology, not even the ideology of no ideology.

If you try to understand me through the mind, I will mess you up; you will become more and more confused. Just listen to me. Let it be just an excuse to be with me, and forget all about it, what I say. Don't gather it; don't accumulate it. Mind is accumulation. If you don't accumulate, the mind drops by and by. And listening to me from various standpoints, diametrically opposite to each other, by and by, you will be able to see that all standpoints are just games.

And no standpoint can lead you to the truth. When you drop all standpoints, suddenly, you find that the truth is there. You were too worried about the standpoints; that's why you couldn't see it. Truth is that which is. Buddha called it *tathata*; it means 'suchness': it is already there—such is the case.

So when you have come somehow, don't miss this opportunity, this door.

And you have asked, '*How do you manage it—how do you manage to know that the person is ready to receive what you compassionately want to share?*' These things are not managed; they happen. If you are thirsty, you will seek a source of water. And if there is a source of water, the source of water will send messages for you—through the wind, the coolness. If there is a stream, it sends messages through the winds, all around; and some thirsty traveller, tired, comes across a cool breeze; he knows, now, this is the direction.

Neither does the stream know about the traveller, whether he is there or not, nor is the traveller exactly certain whether the river is there or not, but it happens: the message is received, in a very vague way, and the traveller starts finding from where this cool breeze is coming. Sometimes he stumbles, goes wrong, but then there is no cool breeze; then he again tries. Through trial and error he finds that if he moves in a certain direction, the breeze becomes cooler and cooler. And the stream has sent the message unaddressed. It is not for anybody in particular; any tired traveller who is thirsty . . .

Things are happening that way. It is not that I am managing. That will be almost maddening. How can I manage? It is not the law of cause and effect; it is the law of synchronicity. I am here; certain cool breezes are spreading all over the world. Wherever somebody is thirsty, he will start feeling a certain desire to move towards me. That's how you all have come.

And when you come here, it is up to you, to drink or not to drink. Your mind may create troubles for you because if you want to drink, you will have to lean down, to surrender and submit. You will have to fold your hands, cup your hands and go down to the river; only then does the river become available to you. Otherwise, you can stand on the bank. Many of you who come new, stand for months on the bank—thirsty, feverishly thirsty—but the ego says, 'Don't. Don't submit. Don't sacrifice yourself.' Then the river goes on flowing by your side and you remain thirsty. It is up to you.

There is no management about it. Many people think it is as if I send some astral message to you, then you come. No, the message is going, but it is unaddressed. It is not for anybody in particular—it cannot be—but whosoever is ready anywhere in the world will come by and by. He will start moving in this direction. He may not even be aware where he is moving. He may be just coming to India, not to me. Then from Mumbai airport, his direction may change; he will start moving towards Pune. Or he may be just coming to see some friend of his who is in Pune, and he may not be coming to see me. Things happen in a mysterious way, not in a mathematical way.

But don't be bothered about these things. Whether managing

or happening, you need not be concerned. You are here. Don't miss the opportunity.

And I am ready to give you the very goal. Don't ask for the way. And I am ready to reveal the truth to you. Don't ask for the argument.

The last question:

Osho, I wish to bring to your notice that there are now three crooks running the affairs of your place, and masquerading under the guise of beautiful and simple women. In case this question incurs your displeasure, I wish to use the nom de plume—Nemo.

Nothing offends me; nothing incurs my displeasure. And remember, even God has to take the help of the devil to run the affairs of the world. Without the devil, even he cannot run the affairs. So I had to choose devils, Beelzebubs. And then I thought, why not with style?—let them be women. Why not with taste? Devils they are going to be. I decided for women—more are wanted.

And there is no need to be anonymous, no need. You can just say who you are; there is no need to hide the name.

Let me tell you one anecdote:

A priest and a rabbi were discussing the finances of their respective parishes.

'We do very well out of envelope collection,' said the priest.

'Envelope collections—what are they?' asked the rabbi.

'We hand out little envelopes to each household, and each member of that family puts in a few pence each day; then on Sunday, they put the envelope into the collection plate. The envelopes are not marked or numbered in any way, so it is completely anonymous.'

'A lovely idea!' exclaimed the rabbi. 'I will try that myself.'

A week later, the priest bumped into the rabbi and asked him how the envelope scheme was progressing.

'Fair, fair,' said the rabbi. 'I have collected six hundred pounds—anonymous cheques.'

'Anonymous cheques?' queried the priest.

'Yes—unsigned!'

Jews are Jews. Don't be a Jew with me; you can sign.

And remember again, more devils are needed. If you find any, particularly in the beautiful guise, masquerading as women, bring them—fetch them immediately. I need more.

In the Western mind, there is a division between God and the devil, not in the Eastern mind. The polarity is one. So if you look at the lives of Eastern gods, you will be puzzled; they are both—godly and devilish. They are more whole, more holy. The Western God seems to be almost dead, because all the life has gone to the devil. The Western God seems to be a very uptight gentleman. You can call him almost an English gentleman—very uptight, needs psychoanalysis. And the devil of course is much too alive. That too is dangerous.

All divisions are dangerous. Let them meet and mingle. This place makes no difference between the devil and the divine. I absorb all. So whosoever you are, I am ready to absorb you. And I use all sorts of energies; and if the devilish energy can be used in a divine way, it becomes tremendously fruitful. I don't deny anything, so you cannot find any other place on the whole of the surface of the earth like this. And this is just a beginning. When more devils come, you will see.

Enough for today.

Osho Meditation Resort

An Invitation To Experience

Every year Osho Meditation Resort welcomes thousands of people from over 100 countries that come to enjoy a holiday in an atmosphere of meditation and celebration. The forty-acre resort is located about 100 miles south-east of Mumbai (Bombay), in Pune, India, in a tree-lined residential area set against a backdrop of bamboo groves and wild jasmine, peacocks and waterfalls.

The basic approach of the resort is that of Zorba the Buddha: living in awareness, with a capacity to celebrate everything in life. Many visitors come to just be, to allow themselves the luxury of doing nothing. Others choose to participate in a wide variety of courses and sessions that support moving towards a more joyous and less stressful life by combining methods of self-understanding with awareness techniques. These courses are offered through Osho Multiversity and take place in a pyramid complex next to the famous Osho Teerth zen gardens.

You can choose to practise various meditation methods, both active and passive, from a daily schedule that begins at six o'clock in the morning. Each evening there is a meditation event that moves from dance to silent sitting, using Osho's recorded talks as an opportunity to experience inner silence without effort.

Facilities at the resort include tennis courts, a gym, sauna, jacuzzi, a large 'nature-shaped' swimming pool, classes in zen archery, t'ai chi, chi gong, yoga and a multitude of bodywork sessions.

The kitchen serves international gourmet vegetarian meals, made with organically grown produce. The nightlife is alive with outdoor eating areas that fill with friends, music and dancing.

Make online bookings for accommodation inside the resort at the new Osho Guesthouse through the website below or drop us an email at guesthouse@osho.com.

Take an online tour of the meditation resort, and access travel and programme information at: www.osho.com

(i)   For detailed information to participate contact:

Osho Meditation Resort
17 Koregaon Park, Pune-411001, MS, India
Ph: 020 4019999 Fax: 020 4019990
Email: resortinfo@osho.net Website: www.osho.com

(ii) Further Information
Many of Osho's books have been translated and published in a variety of languages worldwide.

For information about Osho, his meditations, and the address of an Osho meditation/information centre near you, contact:

Osho Commune International
17 Koregaon Park, Pune-411001, MS, India
Ph: 020 4019999 Fax: 020 4019990
Email: visitor@osho.net Website: www.osho.com

For information about Osho's books and tapes contact:

Sadhana Foundation
17 Koregaon Park, Pune-411001, MS, India
Ph: 020 4019999 Fax: 020 4019990
Email: distrib@osho.net Website: www.osho.com

www.osho.com
A comprehensive website in different languages featuring Osho's meditations, books and tapes, an online tour of Osho Commune International, a list of Osho Information Centres worldwide, and a selection of Osho's talks.